2/16

The Cambridge Introduction to

Scenography

Scenography – the manipulation and orchestration of the performance environment – is an increasingly popular and key area in performance studies. This book introduces the reader to the purpose, identity and scope of scenography and its theories and concepts. Settings and structures, light, projected images, sound, costumes and props are considered in relation to performing bodies, text, space and the role of the audience. Concentrating on scenographic developments in the twentieth century, the *Introduction* examines how these continue to evolve in the twenty-first century. Scenographic principles are clearly explained through practical examples and their theoretical context. Although acknowledging the many different ways in which design shapes the creation of scenography, the book is not exclusively concerned with the role of the theatre designer. In order to map out the wider territory and potential of scenography, the theories of pioneering scenographers are discussed alongside the work of directors, writers and visual artists.

JOSLIN MCKINNEY is Lecturer in Scenography at the University of Leeds.

PHILIP BUTTERWORTH was formerly Reader in Medieval Theatre and Dean for Research at the University of Leeds.

The Cambridge Introduction to
Scenography

JOSLIN McKINNEY
PHILIP BUTTERWORTH

CAMBRIDGE
UNIVERSITY PRESS

CAMBRIDGE UNIVERSITY PRESS
Cambridge, New York, Melbourne, Madrid, Cape Town, Singapore, São Paulo,
Delhi, Dubai, Tokyo

Cambridge University Press
The Edinburgh Building, Cambridge CB2 8RU, UK

Published in the United States of America by Cambridge University Press, New York

www.cambridge.org
Information on this title: www.cambridge.org/9780521612326

First published 2009

Printed in the United Kingdom at the University Press, Cambridge

A catalogue record for this publication is available from the British Library

ISBN 978-0-521-84765-0 Hardback
ISBN 978-0-521-61232-6 Paperback

For
Rob and Robbie

Contents

Illustrations

Boxed quotations

Preface

The aim of this book is to introduce the reader to the purpose, identity and scope of scenography and the theories and concepts which provide a critical framework within which it may be discussed. The work concentrates on scenographic developments in the twentieth century and considers how these continue to evolve in the twenty-first century. Scenographic principles are explained through practical examples and their theoretical context.

Although there are many instances which illuminate different ways in which design shapes the creation of scenography, the book is not exclusively concerned with the role of the theatre designer. In order to map out the wider territory and potential of scenography the work discusses the practice and theory of pioneering scenographers together with the work of directors, writers and visual artists.

Scenography is located as an emergent academic discipline through provision of a conceptual framework for consideration as performance practice and modes of communication with audiences.

The book is intended to be of principal value to university students, both undergraduate and postgraduate, who study theatre and performance. It provides conceptual tools to analyse and discuss scenographic aspects of these disciplines.

In *Part 1, Elements*, Chapter 1 discusses definitions of the term scenography and its relation to other aspects of the theatrical event. It identifies key elements in scenography. Chapter 2 extends understanding of these elements by discussing the practice and principles of key scenographic innovators in the twentieth century.

Part 2, Processes of Scenography, examines issues and concerns of scenography from three perspectives: text, space and technology. These concerns are identified as key drivers in the development of scenographic thinking. Chapter 3 examines the relationship between image and text. How does scenography arise in response to the theatrical text? How does scenography provide contemporary perspectives on classic texts? Chapter 4 asks: What are the basic characteristics of performance space? How can scenography best make use of spatial features?

How do scenographers use space and time to develop their work? How does space shape audience experience? Chapter 5 deals with such questions as: How does scenographic practice make use of stage technology? How is the incorporation of technology part of the dramaturgical impetus and intention? What is the scenographic relationship between technological interventions and the performer?

In *Part 3, Realisation and Reception,* Chapter 6 considers ways of analysing scenography. It demonstrates approaches that have been developed for the production of theatre and suggests other perspectives that are helpful in identifying and discussing particular characteristics of the scenographic. Chapter 7 discusses ways in which audiences experience the scenographic dimension of performance. Chapter 8 concludes the work by examining the potential for scenographic images to reach audiences in ways that are significant and resonant. It draws on new research to reflect upon the extent to which audiences can be said to be collaborators in the realisation and perception of scenography.

Acknowledgements

We are grateful to staff and students at the University of Leeds, especially Professor Christopher Baugh, Scott Palmer, Fiona Mathers and Dr Helen Iball. Conversations about scenography with students on the Performance Design programme have proved invaluable.

We have also been inspired by discussions with members of the scenography working group of the Theatre and Performance Research Association (TaPRA), the scenography working group of the International Federation for Theatre Research (IFTR) and the Education and the History and Theory Commissions of the Organisation Internationale des Scénographes, Techniciens et Architectes de Théâtre (OISTAT). Additionally we would like to record our gratitude for enlightened exchanges with Dr Dorita Hannah.

We would also like to thank Victoria Cooper and Rebecca Jones for their guidance and patience.

Part 1

Elements

Chapter 1

What is scenography?

The origins of the term 'scenography' are associated with both scene painting and architectural perspective drawing.[1] In the twentieth century the term has gradually gained currency by drawing attention to the way stage space can be used as a dynamic and 'kinaesthetic contribution' to the experience of performance.[2] This suggests a difference in intention from the static and pictorial scene design of previous centuries. Architect and scenographer João Mendes Ribeiro says that scenography is concerned primarily with the 'inhabitability of the space'; that is, the creation of spaces with which performing bodies can interact: 'The scenographic concept, as currently understood by the majority of artists, is a far cry from the pictorial two-dimensional scenography and focuses much more on the three-dimensional (architectural) nature of the space or the scenic object and its close relationship with the performers.'[3] Contemporary use of the term has also been influenced by the work of theatre designers such as Josef Svoboda. His concern with the actualisation of a play rather than the decoration of the stage underlines the need to consider scenography as a component of performance: 'True scenography is what happens when the curtain opens and can't be judged in any other way.'[4]

> 1 My great fear is that of becoming a mere 'décorateur.' What irritates me most are such terms as 'Bühnenbildner' or 'décorateur' because they imply two-dimensional pictures or superficial decoration, which is exactly what I don't want. Theatre is mainly in the performance; lovely sketches and renderings don't mean a thing, however impressive they may be; you can draw anything you like on a piece of paper, but what's important is the actualization. True scenography is what happens when the curtain opens and can't be judged in any other way.
> Josef Svoboda in Jarka Burian, *The Scenography of Josef Svoboda*, p. 15

Pamela Howard's *What Is Scenography?* (2002) reflects a continuing debate about use of the term. In this work she used her extensive experience as a designer to articulate a practice of scenography defined thus: 'Scenography is the seamless synthesis of space, text, research, art, actors, directors and spectators that contributes to an original creation.'[5] For Howard, scenographic aspects are central to both compositional and production processes of per-formance and also to audience experience: 'The scenographer visually liberates the text and the story behind it, by creating a world in which the eyes see what the ears do not hear. Resonances of the text are visualised through fragments and memories that reverberate in the spectator's subconscious, suggesting rather than illustrating the words.'[6] The assertion is that scenography extends and enriches audience experience of performance through images which operate in conjunction with, but in different ways from, other aspects of the stage.

In this book, scenography is defined as the manipulation and orchestration of the performance environment. The means by which this is pursued are typically through architectonic structures, light, projected images, sound, costume and performance objects or props. These elements are considered in relation to the performing bodies, the text, the space in which the performance takes place and the placement of the audience. Scenography is not simply concerned with creating and presenting images to an audience; it is concerned with audience reception and engagement. It is a sensory as well as an intellectual experience; emotional as well as rational. Operation of images opens up the range of possible responses from the audience; it extends the means and outcomes of theatrical experience through communication to an audience.

Scenography, mise-en-scène, theatre design and visual dramaturgy

Scenography has affinities with other terms which describe the visual, concep-tual and organisational aspects of performance; in particular mise-en-scène, theatre design and visual dramaturgy.

'Mise-en-scène' refers to the process of realising a theatrical text on stage and the particular aesthetic and conceptual frames that have been adopted as part of that process. The mise-en-scène is a means of staging the text through 'the physical arrangements which articulate and set a frame to the activity within them'.[7] Scenographic concerns, clearly, form a major part of the mise-en-scène. But they are not limited to this. The mise-en-scène does not refer to the performance itself. It is 'a *synthetic* system of options and organizing principles' which will be apparent in the performance, but it describes 'an abstract theoretical concept' rather than what actually happens at the point of performance.[8] Scenography, as shown, is defined in its realisation and performance rather than its intentions.

Pavis points out that a traditional approach to the mise-en-scène is one where performance is discovered in the text:

These philological positions all have in common a normative and derivative vision of mise-en-scène according to which mise-en-scène should not be arbitrary, but should serve the text and justify itself as a correct reading of the dramatic text. It is presupposed that text and stage are bound together, that they have been conceived in terms of each other: the text with a view to a future mise-en-scène, or at least a given acting style; the stage envisaging what the text suggests as to how it should be performed in space.[9]

This is the approach that has dominated the general practice of theatre design and one which can be found reflected in most handbooks on the subject.[10] Individual designers, such as those referred to in this book, have resisted this rather simplistic approach. They have sought to investigate the potential of scenography as an expressive and affective agent of performance. Svoboda explored how to harness new materials and technologies in order to find ways that make the play work in a given time and place[11] and, in doing so, went far beyond what playwrights might have envisaged for their texts. For Svoboda it was the theatre itself, and what happened on stage as much as the text, that inspired scenography. This condition defines the essential difference between scenography and theatre design: 'Scenography must draw inspiration from the play, its author, all of theatre. The scenographer must be in command of the theatre, its master. The average designer is simply not that concerned with theatre.'[12] In a similar way Bertolt Brecht identified the difference between an approach to design where the aim was to 'evoke an atmosphere, give some kind of expression, [and] illustrate a location'[13] without much thought given to the performance itself. He and Caspar Neher worked together and let the designs evolve through rehearsal. Here, design ideas were dialogical interventions in the rehearsal process which led to the development of presentations, situations and characters, which influenced audience and reception. It is this second approach that is scenographic in its orientation; it is one where the space of the performance and the bodies of the performers can interact. Ribeiro says that the 'inhabitable spaces' which scenography creates are 'determined by the circumstances and purposes of the action in question and by the movement of the bodies within the space, in order to create a formally coherent and *dramatically* functional system'.[14] The scenography is part of the performance.

The concept and practice of scenography does not promote existing hierarchies of roles and functions in the creation of theatre, dance or performance. Scenography and its production sit uneasily within the existing functions of writer, director, choreographer, designer and performer because each, or any combination, of these roles is capable of producing scenography in ways that will not accept restriction implicitly imposed by such singular identities.

Creation of theatre design by its designer does not necessarily accept adoption of the above scenographic criteria or principles in its execution. Even though there is potential for much overlapping of territory and content between scenography and theatre design, the different identities are essentially defined by a different purpose and by the nature of its realisation. In any case, existing structures within professional theatre contexts are changing. New technology is having the effect of expanding and blurring the roles in production teams. In the light of this, it is perhaps more productive to focus on the intentions and outcomes of scenography rather than the functions of particular roles and jobs.[15]

Contemporary, experimental forms of theatre are often seen to utilise scenography rather than theatre design. Hans-Thies Lehmann has examined 'postdramatic' theatre and new forms of theatrical performance, evolved since the 1960s, which do not focus on the dramatic text. Here, visual dramaturgy replaces dramaturgy which is determined by a theatrical text. Traditionally, dramaturgy refers to the process of realising literary text as a performance. Visual dramaturgy differs both in form and in the manner of its operation: 'Visual dramaturgy here does not mean an exclusively visually organized dramaturgy but rather one that is not subordinated to the text and can therefore freely develop its own logic.'[16] The logic of visual dramaturgy develops through 'sequences and correspondences, nodal and condensation points of perception'[17] rather than linear narrative structures. Scenography is often the central component of visual dramaturgy.

Elements of scenography

The particular materials and resources which scenography draws upon overlap with those used in theatre design. Broadly, these include the scenic environment, objects, costumes, light and sound. However, because scenography focuses more specifically on performance, other elements become equally important. Consideration of space and time are central to scenography. Regard for the performer within the scene underlines the essential three-dimensional nature of scenography and the way this evolves over the duration of performance. Even where scenography is not conceived as kinetic in a physical sense, from an audience perspective, scenography is capable of evolving in its impact and meaning as the performance unfolds.

Performers, too, may from time to time be implicated in the scenography. In performance terms, it is sometimes hard to distinguish clearly between what is achieved through the performer's body and movement of the performer's costume. Does the performer animate the costume? Does the costume determine bodily gestures? In similar ways, settings, costume and lighting can be seen to drift between categories. Non-naturalistic costume can behave like an environment for the performer; it takes up space and receives light.[18] Light can also be made to appear solid and can define and sculpt space as effectively as more resistant materials.

The multi-sensory aspect of scenography is important. Dorita Hannah, theatre architect, designer and academic, defines scenography as 'The dynamic role design plays upon the stage, orchestrating the visual and sensory environment of performance'.[19] Although the visual aspect of scenography tends to dominate, it can also work with sound. There are also various ways in which aspects of space may be apprehended, such as the 'kinaesthetic' (sense of movement through muscular effort) and the 'proxemic' (pertaining to distances between people) and the 'haptic' (understanding through sense of touch). Scenographies may also include smell and taste as part of the audience experience.

The audience is a vital component in the completion of scenography. Svoboda and others stress that scenography happens with audiences as witnesses. Vsevolod Meyerhold felt his productions were 'unfinished' when they reached the stage and required an audience to make the 'crucial revision'.[20] These comments suggest that scenography defines an active role for the audience. In some work, especially that which takes place outside a theatre building, scenography is used to shape a particular spatial relationship, a certain kind of encounter between audience and performance.

Scenography as an object of study

Although practitioners themselves have offered definitions and principles of scenography, it is only recently that scholarly study of scenography has begun to gain ground. Perhaps this is not too surprising given the ephemeral nature of the traces left by scenography. Models or drawings developed as part of the production process may remain, but what endures after production can only provide a partial impression of what actually happened. Photographs of productions may appear to provide accurate records, but in actuality they are selective and inadequate. Photographers make their own aesthetic judgements in framing and selecting static images that represent performance. Video recordings of performances are similarly problematic. Choices made regarding the number and location of cameras and the nature of editing mediate the original scenography and re-present it through another medium in ways different from those in which it might have been experienced by observers who were actually present during performance. Video recordings do not replicate 'the perceptual discourse of the spectator's eye'[21] because the camera determines the limits of what the viewer can see. In the theatre, spectators are free to look wherever they choose. According to Peggy Phelan, once performance is recorded, documented or represented it 'becomes something other than performance'.[22] In recordings, the multi-sensory experience of live scenography is altered. The auditory and visual are prioritised while spatial dimensions involving depth, scale and proportion, so crucial to the reception of scenography, are adapted. Factors such as vital reference points for appreciation of the spatial, dimensions and dynamics of the performance venue, and the sensing body of the spectator are all downplayed, if not lost, as the live event is edited for the screen.[23]

Despite the above caveats, retrospective exhibitions of scenography (and their associated publications) have provided a valuable way of preserving and examining scenography.[24] Nonetheless, until recently, it has been perceived that within the study of theatre and performance, scenography has been marginalised.[25] This, however, has begun to change. Arnold Aronson has drawn on past and contemporary American work to analyse scenography as the physical and 'spatiovisual aspect' of the theatrical event in order to restore it to its 'proper place' as an element that is integral to performance.[26] At the same time, Christopher Baugh's examination of how theatre technology has influenced development of scenography in the twentieth century shows how this has affected development of theatre as a whole.[27]

This book aims to contribute to an understanding of scenography by examining practices and theories of the twentieth and twenty-first centuries. The work begins by considering some of the practitioners, designers, directors and artists who have helped to shape notions of scenography. Some, like Antonin Artaud, are essentially theorists or visionaries, who left very little behind by way of practice, but who nonetheless have inspired others. Some, like Josef Svoboda and Robert Wilson, are practitioners who have helped define notions of scenography through their work. Between them key concerns can be identified that have influenced the development of scenography. Many of these considerations continue to raise pertinent issues for contemporary theory and practice.

Chapter 2

Twentieth-century pioneers of scenography

The previous chapter attempts to determine the nature of scenography and define its territory. In this chapter, emphasis is given to the means by which such definitions have been achieved. What were the influences and who created or promoted them to determine the concept and practice of scenography? It will not be too surprising to know that influences have come from people who represent a number of disparate sources which occupy some common and related ground. Between them they span a range of perspectives and include: artists, designers, directors, writers and performers. These individuals were and are pioneers in their thinking and vision of and for the theatre. Few of them have referred to their thinking in terms of scenography. It is the accumulative contributions of their work that enable such a concept as scenography to be recognised as relevant to the production of theatre today. Each of these pioneers concentrates on points of focus that are distinctive and relevant to the conceptual and practical development of scenography. As might be imagined, there is considerable overlapping of concern between their preoccupations.

Adolphe Appia (1862–1928)

Pioneers of theatre are often labelled as such because their inspiration, thinking and achievement often occur as a result of dissatisfaction with existing theatrical conditions. In the case of Adolphe Appia his frustration lay with the convention of elaborately detailed sets, created from a combination of painted flats, borders and backdrops that fringed the stage and purported to create the illusion of a real place and, in fact, did nothing of the kind. Around 1902, Appia, in translation, wrote:

> Our present stage scenery is entirely the slave of painting – scene painting – which pretends to create for us the illusion of reality. But this illusion is in itself an illusion, for the presence of the actor contradicts it. In fact, the principle of illusion obtained by painting on flat canvas and that obtained by the plastic and living body of the actor are in contradiction.[1]

For Appia there needed to be fusion between the actor and the performance space. Effectively, he considered that the three-dimensional actor performed against a two-dimensional painted backdrop in which the occupied space was not considered. Such settings with their so-called naturalistic details only served to deny the theatrical illusion that they were supposed to create. Appia thus became involved with elements of scenography that were capable of producing the necessary three-dimensional harmony to realise his vision.

> 2   IN EVERY WORK OF ART there must be a harmonious relationship between feeling and form, a perfect balance between the idea which the artist wishes to express and the means he uses to express it. If one of the means seems to us clearly unnecessary to the expression of the idea, or if the artist's idea – the object of his expression – is only imperfectly communicated to us by the means he employs, our aesthetic pleasure is weakened, if not destroyed.
>
>   Adolphe Appia in Barnard Hewitt (ed.), *Adolphe Appia's Music and the Art of the Theatre*, p. 2

Appia's developing vision became inextricably linked to the work and thinking of Richard Wagner (1813–1883). His early ideas about scenography were developed through his work on detailed scenarios and designs for Wagner's operas, which although rejected by the Wagner family,[2] form the basis of his theoretical writing. For Appia, the strength of Wagner's work lay in the location of 'the center of gravity in the *internal* action, to which music and *only* music holds the key, but of which, nevertheless, the actor must remain the corporeal embodiment on the stage'.[3] Even so, realisation of this relationship only served to exacerbate a much deeper and pivotal contradiction which was that 'during performance, there is a continual compromise between the music and the actor, between the art of sound and rhythm and the art of plastic and dramatic movement, and any attempt at traditional stage setting for this drama can rest only on a compromise, a compromise which must somehow be transcended if aesthetic truth is to be attained'.[4] The value of music to Appia's conception of the life of the drama was summed up by the notion that 'a dramatic idea requiring musical expression in order to be revealed must spring from the hidden world of our inner life, since this life *cannot be expressed* except through music, and music can express only that life'.[5] Appia considered that the musical score, the actor, the spatial arrangement and lighting constituted an organically composed hierarchy in which 'music, the soul of the drama, gives life to the drama, and by its pulsations determines every motion of the organism, in proportion and sequence. If one of the links of this organic chain breaks or is missing, the expressive power of the music is cut off there and cannot reach beyond it.'[6] For Appia, Wagner's vision of the *Gesamtkunstwerk*, or integration of the arts of music, drama and painting through theatre, was hampered by the staging practices of the time and so there was still the problem that the stage settings, no matter how well executed, offered nothing to fuse with Wagner's powerful and 'wondrous' scores.

Appia's concerns therefore focused upon the relationship between the actor, space, light and music. The most important of these points of focus was the actor. Three-dimensional reality created by the actor's body was the most critical starting point in Appia's consideration of the three-dimensional stage. Whatever happened on stage, according to Appia, needed to make its own contribution to creating three-dimensional harmony through the actor.

Space may be differently conceived by different cultures at different times for different purposes. Appia's preoccupation with space was not merely concerned with an abstract concept but with its physicalisation. How was space to be demarcated if the two-dimensional, painted backdrop settings of late nineteenth-century theatre were considered to be inadequate? The key to the definition of space for Appia lay with the actor in motion and the spectator's perception as determined by use of light and timing as dictated by the structure and rhythms of music.

3   Of the three elements of production, painting is without any question the one subject to the narrowest conventions. It is incapable of revealing any living and expressive reality by itself, and it loses its power of signification to the extent that the rest of the setting plays an active part in the scene; that is, to the extent that lighting and the spatial arrangement are directly related to the actor. Therefore, lighting and the spatial arrangement of the setting are more expressive than painting, and of the two, lighting, apart from its obvious function of simple illumination, is the more expressive. This is so because it is subject to a minimum of conventions, is unobtrusive, and therefore freely communicates external life in its most expressive form.
   Adolphe Appia in Barnard Hewitt (ed.), *Adolphe Appia's Music and the Art of the Theatre*, p. 22

Although selective use of light helped to contribute to the harmony of the actor in space, the concomitant use of shadow also aided three-dimensional definition of that harmony. Light not only helps to give life to the actor but it is also the means of bonding the actor with his space. Just as the actor's motion conditions definition of scenographic space, so does music help to define the time-scale and its delineation by which fused harmony may occur.

Appia proposed that the domination of painted flats be relegated. Effort was required to direct attention away from the depiction of a scene towards creation of the scene's atmosphere. Starting from the actor's presence and movement, light and space were envisaged to provide a suggestive, flexible and expressive environment. Describing his suggestions for the staging of the second scene of Wagner's *Siegfried*, he says:

> we shall no longer try to give the illusion of a forest, but the illusion of a man in the atmosphere of a forest. Man is the reality, and nothing else counts. Whatever this man touches must be intended for him – everything else must contribute to the creation of a suitable atmosphere around him. And if, leaving Siegfried for a moment, we lift our eyes, the scenic picture need not give a complete illusion. It is composed for Siegfried alone. When the forest, gently stirred by a breeze, attracts Siegfried's attention, we – the spectators – will see Siegfried bathed in ever-changing lights and shadows but no longer moving among cut-out fragments set in motion by stage tricks.[7]

The visual clutter provided by the content of two-dimensional painted backdrops in the theatre of the late nineteenth century was replaced in Appia's thinking and practice by simple organisation of three-dimensional space. Simplicity governed the intended synthesis of concerns for the actor, space, light and music through definition of volumes of space, the relationship between light and shadow and timing as dictated by music. Horizontal, vertical and diagonal lines and planes delineated the respective spaces which were frequently designed to lead the eye to focus on the horizon. In spatial terms, Appia's stage most often became graduated through a number of receding levels to the horizon. The more the actor moved towards the back of such vistas (up stage), the more possible it was to conceive of the actor/character being involved with larger or more universal issues. The more the actor came down stage towards the audience, the more personal, intimate or domestic he could become with and to it.

Although Appia was profoundly influenced by the work and thinking of Wagner, he considered that Wagner 'could not resolve the cruel conflict in which he struggled, even with some degree of awareness: the conflict between music for which there was no suitable expression in the living body of the performer, music which *could not achieve such externalization* without the risk of having its own identity suppressed – and the necessity, nevertheless, of presenting the music and the human body *simultaneously*'.[8] Such an apparent predicament was addressed and resolved through Appia's application of the ideas of Émile Jaques-Dalcroze. Appia was particularly influenced by *Eurhythmics*, a system of exercises devised by Jaques-Dalcroze to help musicians develop their feel for playing rhythmically. After witnessing a lecture-demonstration by Jaques-Dalcroze in 1906 Appia records that: 'I found the answer to my passionate desire for synthesis!' He goes on to say:

By closely following this musical discipline of the body, I discovered the living germ of a dramatic art, in which music is no longer separated from the human body in a splendor which is after all illusory, at least during performance, nor subjugated to it, a dramatic art which will direct the body towards an externalization in space, and thus make it the primary and supreme means of scenic expression, to which all other elements of production will be subordinated.[9]

In response, he developed the idea of 'rhythmic space' and presented designs to Jaques-Dalcroze which explored the use of three-dimensional space through the use of architectonic mass (steps, platforms, pillars, walls) and light to create environments which would work in contrast to the human body:

Their rigidity, sharp lines and angles, and immobility, when confronted by the softness, subtlety and movement of the body, would, by opposition, take on a kind of borrowed life. The spectator himself could imaginatively sense the designs' physical quality as the body of the performer moved amongst them; and, moreover, because of the qualities of architectural harmony and proportion with which Appia imbued them, though lacking any element of time or movement themselves, as the eye surveyed them they could nevertheless visually provide a strong sense of rhythm.[10] (Figure 1.)

In 1910 Jaques-Dalcroze established an institute at Hellerau, near Dresden, that was specifically built for his work. Appia became involved with the institute in a consultative capacity and effectively designed the layout of the Hellerau Festival Auditorium. In his design there was no separation between stage and auditorium. The overall length of the hall was fifty metres, the width was sixteen metres and the height was twelve metres. Thus an open space was created with no raised stage or hidden orchestra.[11] The inaugural festival of eurhythmics was presented in July 1912. A scene from Gluck's *Orpheus and Eurydice* showing Orpheus descending to the Underworld was particularly successful and demonstrated how Appia's theories on space, light and the performing body could work in practice:

Orpheus entered at the highest point of the scenic structure, in a glare of light, and slowly descended a great monumental staircase into ever-greater darkness, confronted and opposed by the Furies. Dressed in dark tights, they were in constant motion, carefully coordinated with the ebb and flow of the music. Arranged along the steps and platforms, their naked arms and legs seemed like snakes, and formed a veritable moving mountain of monstrous forms, before being overcome and subdued by the sound of Orpheus' playing and the poignancy of his pleas. The whole scene was bathed in an otherwordly blue light: the glow of Hades.[12] (Figure 2.)

1. Adolphe Appia, Rhythmic Space, *The Staircase*, 1909

Appia's vision for the role of lighting is summed up by his translated statement that 'Light is to production what music is to the score: the expressive element in opposition to literal signs; and, like music, light can express only what belongs to "the inner essence of all vision".'[13] Even though Appia was not privy to the technical advancements that enabled the control, power and sensitivity of modern lighting, he was still able to distinguish between qualities of light and the manipulation of their perceived functions. When he worked at Hellerau in conjunction with Alexander von Salzmann[14] he was able to put his theories into practice. Appia defined two principal qualities of light required for it to become an expressive medium as 'diffused light' and 'formative' or 'living' light'.[15] Diffused lighting offered a general illumination or 'luminous under-coat'[16] for the more defined effects of formative light. Diffused light was to be achieved through fixed lighting instruments (arranged in battens and ground-rows) and placed behind and between 'screens of varying transparencies, designed to cut down any extreme degrees of brightness thrown on the nearest objects, or on the actors as they come into these lights'.[17] At Hellerau, these screens were constructed using semi-transparent linen dipped in cedar oil to intensify the glow. Living light was achieved by mobile apparatus producing

2. Adolphe Appia, *Orpheus and Eurydice*, by C. W. Gluck. Hellerau,
Jaques-Dalcroze Institute, 1912–13

more intense light and positioned carefully to produce shadow as well as light. Living or formative light, Beacham claims, provided an 'extraordinarily subtle tool' for the scenographer:

> With it he could highlight objects or cause them to disappear; he could, like a sculptor, build up or take away; distort, give mass to or dematerialise the physical objects on stage, including the performer. Indeed, the very scenic space itself could be animated when this light passed through: expanding or contracting, the space could be made to advance or retreat, to swallow up objects or bring them forth, to take on form and move.[18]

These distinctive qualities of light were premised by Appia through his understanding of the ways in which it behaves: 'But the direction of light can only be sensed by means of shadow – it is the quality of the shadows which expresses the quality of light. Shadows are formed by the same light which illuminates the atmosphere.'[19] Appia understood clearly the notion that no three-dimensional object, animate or inanimate, was capable of dispensing with shadow: 'If there is no shade, there is no light; for light is not simple "visibility" … light is distinguished from visibility by virtue of its power to be expressive.'[20] (Figure 3.)

3. Adolphe Appia, Rhythmic Space, *The Shadow of the Cypress Tree*, 1909

Understanding of the qualities of these two distinctive kinds of light helped to determine and influence the principles upon which modern lighting is conducted. Instruments such as fresnel lanterns and profile spotlights are capable of producing the distinctive qualities of light first identified by Appia as a means of contributing to the sought harmony of the actor, space, light and music.

True to his spatial concerns, Appia sought to delineate space by intersecting it with planes juxtaposed at different angles. Spatial distance could be nearer or further from the viewer not merely in terms of physical distance but through the way that such planes created perspective. Flights of stairs could start down stage and recede upwards into the flies at the back of the stage. This kind of treatment was capable of producing a sense of infinity. In addition to strategic use of stairs Appia made much use of blocks, ramps and screens to produce spatial dimension. The example of the receding flight of stairs that starts its rise in front of the audience points to a developing concern that relates to the space occupied by the stage set and that taken up by the auditorium. Appia's radical vision of the use of stage space could not find its logical conclusion if it was restricted to the stage space alone. This notion, coupled with Appia's dissatisfaction that stage space and audience space were divided by the barrier, both literal and metaphorical, of the proscenium arch, inspired such thinking as to extend the flight of stairs into the previously designated audience space. Such a barrier was anathema to Appia.

Concern for the stage and auditorium filling a common space was part of and consistent with Appia's prophetic vision that the theatre of the future would not make distinctions between performers and audience but all would be participants in developing social events. Some of Appia's thoughts written in 1918 and translated in 1962 determine that:

> The term *production* will gradually become an anachronism, and finally even meaningless. We shall wish to act in harmonious unity. The dramatic art of tomorrow will be a *social act*, in which each of us will assist. And, who knows, perhaps one day we shall arrive, after a period of transition, at majestic festivals in which a whole people will participate, where each of us will express our feelings, our sorrows, our joys, no longer content to remain a passive onlooker. Then will the dramatist triumph![21]

The design of the Hall at Hellerau effectively abolished the distinction between stage and auditorium. This invited active engagement from the audience and the possibility that theatre could become a 'living art', a collective discipline based on the bodily sensibility of all who participate.[22]

Edward Gordon Craig (1872–1966)

The thinking, work and vision of Edward Gordon Craig are often compared with that of Adolphe Appia. Indeed, because the work and vision of both men shared many similarities it is often suggested that Craig copied his ideas from Appia. However, this is not the case. Craig first became aware of Appia's work in 1908 when he was shown some designs for Wagner's operas. Craig was immediately struck by Appia's designs and wanted to meet him. Unfortunately, Craig was informed, wrongly as it happens, that Appia was dead.[23] It was not until 1911 that Craig found out that Appia was still alive and the two men finally met in 1914. Both Craig and Appia had been invited to present work at the Theatre Exhibition at the Kunstgewerbemuseum in Zurich. Up to this point the theatrical experience of the two men had been quite different. Consideration of similarities and differences in the theatrical drive and output of both men up to 1914 is a useful means of establishing what drove them individually.

Craig was the son of the actress Ellen Terry, and he spent much of his early theatrical life from 1889–1897 as an actor in Sir Henry Irving's company at the Lyceum in London. He was not tied exclusively to Irving's company for during this period he took on *Hamlet* in September 1894 at Hereford and was again engaged to stand in as Hamlet in a production in 1897. He was highly regarded as an actor. In 1897 he stopped acting and this coincided with growing feelings of dissatisfaction about the state of the English theatre. His revived interest and commitment to the theatre occurred through a number of productions between 1900 and 1903. By 1914 Craig had not only been an accomplished actor but he had designed and directed several plays and published several books and essays.[24] In Appia's case, his experience in the theatre up to 1914 had been largely filtered through his response to the operas of Richard Wagner and his association with Émile Jaques-Dalcroze, and he had published his two books: *La Mise en Scène du Drame Wagnérien* (1895) and *Die Musik und die Inscenierung* (1899).[25]

After their first meeting, Craig wrote in his diary, *Daybook III*:

> Yesterday Appia and I had our first talk. It was *very good*, very enjoyable.
> Today our second talk, and it was *exciting*.
> He spoke much of Wagner and of Hellerau and Jaques-Dalcroze.
> Yesterday – less today.
> I let him talk – although I told him that for me the *human* body in movement seemed to signify less and less.
> Today he spoke of Wagner and the Art of Theatre. I had to say that Wagner hated the Theatre and used it as a Prostitute is used.
> This made him divinely angry.
> I tried to show him, without saying so, that he was searching for – for what I believe I have found – The true and sole Material for the Art of the Theatre, *Light* – and through light *Movement*.
> The veils of *music* and *the human form* made mist for his eyes and he could not see through.
> I thought I caught him trying once or twice to push the veils aside, but he laughed on ... A fine man – seeing very clearly – many things.
> One weakness (his strength perhaps) that first he 'needed' Wagner to hang upon – now he 'needs' Dalcroze.
> Last night he saw the marionettes here (he says for the first time), and was amazed.
> Well then – let's believe that they will lead him somewhere away from Dalcroze and Wagner.[26]

It is clear that a deep admiration for each other's work developed and after 1914 they corresponded frequently. Appia summed up their similarities and differences in a letter to Craig: 'In the depths of our souls we have *the same vibration and the same desire*; only expressed differently, owing to our different temperaments and our very different circumstances. What matter! We are together, for always. That is enough.'[27] One of the most important tenets of Craig's developing philosophy on the nature of theatre was that expressed in his paper 'The Actor and the Über-Marionette'. The article was first published in the magazine, *The Mask*, edited by Craig in April 1908, and was later reproduced in his book *On the Art of the Theatre* in 1911. The thrust of this paper has been frequently misunderstood for it has been interpreted to mean that Craig wanted a theatre in which the actor was replaced by the marionette. The crudity of this suggestion belies a deeper principle with which Craig was concerned. Because Craig had spent a good deal of his life as an actor he knew of the role of the ego for the actor. He considered that the actor's ego got in the way and loosened the actor's control of what he was required to do. The significance of this concern is referred to in 'The Actor and the Über-Marionette':

> Acting is not an art. It is therefore incorrect to speak of the actor as an artist. For accident is an enemy of the artist. Art is the exact antithesis of pandemonium, and pandemonium is created by the tumbling together of many accidents. Art arrives only by design. Therefore in order to make any work of art it is clear we may only work in those materials with which we can calculate. Man is not one of these materials.[28]

Craig considered that the actor was enslaved by his emotions and because of this was unable to maintain control over his bodily expression. Thus, movement and speech were susceptible to uncontrolled use and prone to accidental expression. Craig was searching for a form of acting that did not mimic reality and was not measured by accuracy of verisimilitude. He did not like the pursuit of realism. Instead, he sought a kind of acting that removed internal emotion, mimicry and what amounted to 'real life' on stage. He wanted to remove actors' attempts to impersonate. The actors, he declared, 'must create for themselves a new form of acting, consisting for the main part of symbolical gesture. To-day they *impersonate* and interpret; to-morrow they must *represent* and interpret; and the third day they must create. By this means style may return.'[29]

> 4   The actor must go, and in his place comes the inanimate figure – the Über-marionette we may call him, until he has won for himself a better name ... The über-marionette will not compete with life – rather will it go beyond it.
> Edward Gordon Craig, *On the Art of the Theatre*, pp. 81, 84

The notion of the 'Über-Marionette' was the most precise term that Craig could specify in attempts to define a different role for the actor as one who 'represents' rather than 'impersonates' on stage. He knew this term to be inadequate[30] to its purpose but the inanimate properties of the marionette drew Craig closer to what he was trying to express. He was trying to express, in some new way, a kind of detachment of actors from what they try to portray in a way that Brecht, for different purposes, might well have recognised. Like Brecht, he sought examples and reference points for such identification in Asian theatre. He admired what he saw in the art of oriental and ancient civilisations as a pursuit of 'simple truths', that is, an abstracted, refined and carefully controlled reflection of the essence of life.[31] His interest in masks and puppets focused on their capacity to express a calm and transcendent clarity which could be used as a 'faithful medium for the beautiful thoughts of the artist'.[32] As an artist himself, he considered the whole stage to be his medium. The actors, therefore, needed to be considered as part of the entire composition of the stage and subsumed under it. The distinction between 'impersonating' and 'representing' was therefore not only an issue for the actor but also for the context in which the actor operated. Craig sought to remove all elements of realism from the stage. A principal means of achieving this was to conceive of a kinetic stage which could be manipulated to create dramatic space through abstract compositions. Craig experimented using models and various combinations of stage space for well over a decade. Some of the outcomes of these experiments were able to be translated directly to the stage whilst others remained ideals. His *Screens* were developed not only for his own productions, but also as something that other directors might use, and these were patented in 1910. The construction of them was not particularly innovative. They consisted of self-supporting double-hinged flats made of canvas stretched over wooden frames (which varied in width but not height) and moved by means of castors.[33] It was the way that Craig conceived of their use that was new: 'The object of my invention is to produce a device which shall present the aesthetic advantages of the plain curtain but shall further be capable of a multitude of effects which although not intended to produce an illusion shall nevertheless assist the imagination of the spectator by suggestion.'[34] He had replaced the 'pictorial scene' with the 'architectonic scene'.[35] However, this architectonic space was not to work independently from performers. Beyond initial sketches, designs for the *Screens* always included figures of performers in clearly defined dramatic poses and arranged in groups among the screens to show the way these two elements were to interact.[36]

Spaces created by the *Screens* were infinitely variable and additional use of light multiplied the flexible features of the schemes. The relationship between the ideas of Craig and Appia can be seen through these proposals. Craig saw that his *Screens* could be animated by changing intensities and colours of light. Filiberto Scarpelli, a visitor to Craig's studio at the Arena Goldoni in Italy in 1913, was amazed by the effects that Craig could produce, apparently from nothing:

He sets upon the stage of his little theatre (no bigger than a child's marionette theatre) his tiny screens, and while you look on, with a rapid movement of the hands, arranges them in a certain way: a ray of electric light comes to strike between those simple rectangles of cardboard, and the miracle is accomplished; you behold a majestic scene: the sense of the small disappears absolutely; you forget the dimensions of the theatre, such is the scrupulous equilibrium of the lights and of the lines which Craig knows how to give to the scenes ... He paints with light, he constructs with a few rectangles of cardboard, and with the harmony of his colours and of his lines he creates profound sensations.[37]

In retrospect, the difficulties, artistic conflict, and visionary polarity experienced by Craig and Konstantin Stanislavsky during their production of *Hamlet* in Moscow (1912) might well have been anticipated in advance of their collaboration. However, they both wanted to respect each other's reputations and it is only during the process of the collaboration that understandable and perhaps inevitable differences emerged. Craig's insistence on the requirement of the actor to 'represent' was diametrically opposed to Stanislavsky's need for the actor to 'impersonate' in order to produce psychological realism. At this time Stanislavsky's search for realistic perfection from the actor was still gathering momentum. At the same time, he was aware that arts other than theatre were focusing on forms of expression other than imitation. He thought that the theatre should also reflect these changing forms. Hence, his openness to the work of Craig and the invitation to him to work in Moscow.

Stanislavsky was not impressed with abstraction and therefore struggled imaginatively and intellectually with Craig's versions of it. He similarly thought that some of Craig's theories were hazy and at odds with each other. However, he too had come to disparage what might be regarded as traditional scenery and welcomed the simplicity of some of Craig's designs. He particularly embraced Craig's emphasis upon three-dimensional architectural features instead of painted backdrops.

Craig was appointed as a stage director at Stanislavsky's Art Theatre for a year and it was agreed that Craig should stage the production of *Hamlet*. Many detailed and visionary conversations took place in respect of the nature of the play, what Shakespeare required of the play and how it should be staged. These were not just discussions between Craig and Stanislavsky but between all the people involved in the production. The gulf between Stanislavky's concern for psychological realism and Craig's vision of representation is clearly alluded to in the following statement:

> I should like the play to begin without a curtain – in fact to have no curtain at all. So that the public on coming into the auditorium should

have time before the beginning of the play to take in *these new lines*, and this for them, new appearance of the stage. It would be good also if each scene began by people in special costumes, coming onto the stage, arranging the scenery, seeing to the light and so on; in this way making the audience feel that this is a performance.[38]

This is an extraordinary statement in relation to modern practice, in which such behaviour and vision is conventionally attributed to the influence of Brecht. In the event, however, the screens as constructed were not stable enough to be moved in full view of the audience and a curtain had to be used between scenes.[39]

The interpretation and orientation of the production were such that the unfolding events were to be understood as seen through Hamlet's eyes. Senelick's account of the second scene demonstrates:

> The stage picture supported Craig's concept of *Hamlet* as a monodrama: everything that took place within the scene until the exit of the Court was Hamlet's nightmare. At back, arranged in a semicircle stand the high screens covered with gilt paper, and up center a raised platform, approached by steps, surmounted by the gold half-moon of a throne. There sit Claudius and Gertrude ... From their shoulders spreads a cloak of gold brocade that fans out to occupy the whole width of the stage ... Out of this shimmering expanse jut the heads of the courtiers ... Hamlet sits facing the audience, lost in a revery, isolated from the image of molten gold behind him.[40] (Figure 4.)

Development and realisation of the production were fraught with difficulties and misunderstandings. Both director and designer considered that they had made compromises. The reviews were of mixed quality; some reviewers thought the work was innovative and brilliant; others found the design concept stifling and use of the screens monotonous.[41] However, *The Times* special correspondent declared that:

> Mr Craig has the singular power of carrying the spiritual significance of words and dramatic situations beyond the actor to the scene in which he moves. By the simplest of means he is able in some mysterious way to evoke almost any sensation of time or space, the scenes even in themselves suggesting variations of human emotions.[42]

Alongside his commissioned work in the theatre, he continued to develop the idea of 'The Thousand Scenes in One Scene'; a design for a single setting which could be infinitely flexible and capable of different expressions and moods – as mobile and responsive as a human face.[43] (Figure 5.) One version of this extended experiment was a stage composed of sections which could

4. Edward Gordon Craig, design for Act 1, Scene 2, *Hamlet*, by William
Shakespeare. Director Konstantin Stanislavsky, Moscow Art Theatre,
1910

rise and fall, creating steps, platforms, open spaces and voids. This experiment
was inspired by Sebastiano Serlio's *Treatise on Perspective*[44] and here Craig
conceived of ways in which the volumes of objects and space could create
endless movement opportunities through their changed arrangements. The
floor could be raised or lowered in sections and a roof composed in the same
way could further extend the possibilities. Such potential movement could be
increased further through careful and selected use of light to create both
light and shadow to the surfaces and strengthen the planes and angles
or alternatively soften definition. Such concerns are well illustrated by the
painter, Piot, who wrote to Jacques Rouché to report on a meeting with
Craig in 1910:

> He showed me a stage design, the interest of which lay in the fact that
> he is trying to make the stage space infinitely changeable … By means of
> a number of cubes which can shrink or expand, the cube of the stage
> becomes either square, oblong, or tall in proportion to its width – thus
> giving unlimited variety to the cubic volume of the stage, just as a painter
> selects a square, wide or tall canvas to suit his subject. The scenery is so

5. Edward Gordon Craig, *Scenes* (Hell), copper engraving, 1907

greatly simplified that it takes its expression chiefly from changes in the lighting as it strikes a number of different shapes. In short, Craig's aim seems to be to achieve, by means of simplification, a musical ebb and flow of the scene, bringing it into the time-scheme so as to link it with the play. Up to now the scenery designed by painters, or self-styled painters, has consisted of motionless rags, dangling round the moving figures on the stage. Craig wants his scenery to move like sound, to refine certain moments in the play just as music follows and heightens all its movements; *he wants it to advance with the play.*[45]

Craig's ideas went far beyond pragmatic ideas and the convenience of moveable scenery; the fluidity of movement and endless spatial possibilities conceived by him provided an instrument of artistic expression. He even imagined that it might be possible for the director/designer to operate the stage as a live instrument with the audience and so respond to its emotions.[46]

Oskar Schlemmer (1888–1943)

Although Oskar Schlemmer was well-known as a teacher throughout his adult life, it is his work at the Dessau Bauhaus between 1925 and 1929 for which he is better known. Indeed, Schlemmer's influence from this period has had such an enormous impact on the theatre of Western Europe and North America that it continues to be experienced in the theatre of today. Like other pioneers in the thinking and conduct of theatre, Schlemmer's views and vision cannot be reduced to simple theory. His thinking developed in such a way as to inhibit any description of his work as fixed. However, it is clear that he was driven by recurring artistic, philosophical and social concerns visible in his drawing, painting, sculpture, dance and theatre.

Schlemmer's experience in the First World War, where he was twice wounded, clearly affected his outlook and desire to re-establish links between the human figure and its habitation in a developing mechanical world. Due to this concern he did not wish to present the human figure clothed in costume dictated by the aesthetics of the machine, in the way that the Dadaists or the Futurists had done, but he regarded the relationship between the actor/dancer and the costume somewhat differently. He considered costume to be the wearer of the actor/dancer (and not the conventional way round) in attempts to reach out to the surrounding space. His observation and recognition of parts of the human body and their representation as squares, circles, triangles, spheres, cylinders and cubes formed the basis of his concern for abstraction. He regarded abstraction as fulfilling a unifying principle. The focus was upon simplification, paring down of essentials and concern for the elemental or fundamental in such a way as to create unity. For example, in his diary for October 1915 he delineated the geometry of the human body as:

> The square of the ribcage.
> the circle of the belly,
> the cylinder of the neck,
> the cylinders of the arms and lower thighs,
> the circles of the elbow joints, elbows, knees, shoulders, knuckles,
> the circles of the head, the eyes,
> the triangle of the nose,
> the line connecting the heart and the brain,

the line connecting the sight with the object seen,
the ornament that forms between the body and the outer world,
symbolizing the former's relationship to the latter.[47]

Schlemmer regarded these shapes and volumes to be organic to natural body shapes. Extension of these defined features was articulated by him thus:

Let us take as our starting point the human body moving through space … let us imagine this space as being filled with a putty-like substance, which becomes hard once the movement has been completed. Bodily movements – twisting, stretching out, etc. – then take the shape of plastic forms of the body, frozen in the solidified mass. For example, if I move an arm or a leg parallel to the axis of the body, the result is a disc-shaped figure; if I stretch out an arm or a leg and rotate it, the resulting shape is that of a cone or funnel. Other shapes which can result from dividing up space in this way are (spinning) tops, volutes, spirals, figures resembling technical organisms.[48]

5   The recipe the Bauhaus Theater follows is very simple: one should be as free of preconceptions as possible; one should act as if the world had just been created; one should not analyze a thing to death, but rather let it unfold gradually and without interference. One should be simple, but not puritanical. ('Simplicity is a noble concept!') One should rather be primitive than over-elaborate or pompous; one should not be sentimental; one should be sensitive and intelligent. That says everything – and nothing!
Oskar Schlemmer in Tut Schlemmer (ed.), *The Letters and Diaries of Oskar Schlemmer*, p. 243

6   Furthermore: one should start with the fundamentals. Well, what does that mean? One should start with a dot, a line, a bare surface: the body. One should start with the simple, existing colors: red, blue, yellow, black, white, gray. One should start with the materials, learn to feel the differences in texture among such materials as glass, metal, wood, and so on, and one should let these perceptions sink in until they are part of one. One should start with space, its laws and its mysteries, and let oneself be 'captivated' by it. This again says a great deal – or it says nothing, if these words and concepts are not felt and made reality.
Oskar Schlemmer in Tut Schlemmer (ed.), *The Letters and Diaries of Oskar Schlemmer*, p. 243

Schlemmer was continually absorbed and affected by what he considered the 'Apollonian' and the 'Dionysian' views of life.[49] Much of his work attempted to reconcile these apparently opposing stances. He explained what he meant in his diary in an entry from September 1915:

> I vacillate between two styles, two worlds, two attitudes toward life. If I could succeed in analyzing them, I think I would be able to shake off all these doubts. Characteristics of the first type are: discipline, ruggedness, reserve, restraint, exclusivity, profundity. The effect does not lie on the surface; a first look leaves one cold, but gradually something is revealed to the beholder, by delayed action, as it were. These are probably the essential characteristics of ancient Greek and Roman art. The characteristics of the other type, then, are diametrically opposed to the art of Antiquity; what contrast could be greater than the Gothic? Or mysticism. In short, anything supernatural, gigantic, Dionysian, intoxicated, enraptured, dynamic. The effect is direct, abrupt, casting an immediate spell, imprisoning one, 'bedazzling the senses', overwhelming. These are the great contrasts represented by Antiquity and the Middle Ages. But within them, too, contradictions exist … Everything should merge into one great current. Mysticism, the primitive, the most recent, Greece, Gothic – all the elements must be drawn upon.[50]

Much of this thinking was to find expression in Schlemmer's *Triadic Ballet* which he developed in 1912 and performed with changes in 1915, 1922 and 1923. For Schlemmer, 'dance is not intellectual but Dionysian in origin'.[51] In his diary for September 1922, he writes of the way in which the Dionysian and the Apollonian were to be fused through the *Triadic Ballet*:

> The 'Triadic Ballet': dance of the trinity, changing faces of the One, Two, and Three, in form, color, and movement; it should also follow the plane geometry of the dance surface and the solid geometry of the moving bodies, producing that sense of spatial dimension which necessarily results from tracing such basic forms as the straight line, the diagonal, the circle, the ellipse, and their combinations. Thus the dance, which is Dionysian and wholly emotional in origin, becomes strict and Apollonian in its final form, a symbol of the balancing of opposites.[52]

The *Triadic Ballet* was constructed in three parts, the first of which consisted of 'a burlesque, picturesque mood; not an earnest, festive one'[53] and the third section was of 'heroic monumentality'. Schlemmer found the second section 'hard to pin down'.[54] There were twelve distinct dances involving one female and two male dancers who operated alternately in eighteen different costumes formed out of padded cloth and papier-mâché and painted.[55] In a letter to Hans Hildebrandt of 4 October 1922, Schlemmer stressed the importance of the 'floor geometry' of the piece. Delineation of both two- and three-dimensional space was fundamental to all of Schlemmer's theatre. In the letter he describes what may be interpreted as a key element in a personal manifesto concerning the fundamental issues as they affect delineation of space:

the 'floor geometry', the configurations which determine the paths of the dancers; they are identical with the forms of the figurines [the dancers in padded costumes]. Both are elemental, primal. I should like to do more with the choreography; I mean the graphic representation of the dancers' paths, a problem which has not yet been satisfactorily solved because too much would have to be portrayed within too small a space, resulting in either confusion or lack of completeness. For instance, one dancer might move only from back to front, following a straight line. Then come the diagonal, the circle, the ellipse, and so on. This idea was not based on any particular 'intellectual' considerations. It grew rather out of inventive, aesthetic pleasure in mixing opposites of form color, and movement and shaping the whole into something which conveyed significance and an underlying concept.[56]

The fundamental spatial considerations referred to here were to find further expression, development and clarification in a lecture-demonstration that Schlemmer offered to Bauhaus colleagues on 16 March 1927. In some respects, the content of this lecture-demonstration synthesised and defined many of Schlemmer's fundamental concerns in theatrical experiments. Here, he was concerned with the delineation of stage space: 'The art of the stage is a spatial art … The stage, including the auditorium, is above all an architectonic-spatial organism where all things happening to it and within it exist in a spatially conditioned relationship.'[57] These experiments addressed what Schlemmer called *Bühnenprobleme*, or stage problems,[58] and the possibility of discovering the fundamental elements and properties of the stage. He regarded form as an aspect of space in respect of surface (i.e. two-dimensional) form and plastic (i.e. three-dimensional) form. He also considered colour and light to be aspects of form. The demonstration parts of this presentation began with the process of dividing up the square surface of the floor by bisecting axes and diagonals. A circle was also marked out. This established a geometry of the floor. From this, a man was required to travel along these lines, changing direction at the intersections. The three-dimensional space was delineated by a number of taut wires that joined and defined the corners of the cubical stage space. A mid-point was achieved at the intersection of these wires and the human figure was placed at their centre. After establishing the three-dimensional geometry of the space, Schlemmer considered that it was possible to explore fundamentally different routes from this point. One consisted of 'psychic expression, height-ened emotion and pantomime'[59] and the other was 'that of mathematics in motion, the mechanics of joints and swivels, and the exactitudes of rhythmics and gymnastics'.[60] These respective paths found focus in the lecture demon-stration as the *Space Dance*, the *Form Dance* and the *Gesture Dance*.

In the *Space Dance* the actors/dancers wore padded tights and masks. The purpose of this costume was to dress the actors/dancers in such a way as to unify the different parts of the body into simple identifiable form. The three actors/dancers were each dressed in one of the primary pigment colours of red, yellow and blue and given different rates of walking. They alternated between a slow walk, a normal walk and a 'tripping gait'.[61] These rates of motion were timed in relation to sound from a kettledrum, a snare drum and wooden blocks. Each actor/dancer produced a changing sequence to the sound stimulus as they moved along the demarcated lines that were laid out on the floor. The space in which this took place was thus delineated.

Development of the basic *Space Dance* was extended to produce the *Form Dance*. Here, each actor/dancer was given an object whose form was permitted and required to affect instinctively the nature of the movement according to the identity of the object. For this purpose objects such as a ball, a club, a cane and a pole were held in such a way as to condition imitated shapes of movement.

A further development of the basic criteria established by the *Space Dance* and the *Form Dance* was to provide the actors/dancers' masks with moustaches and glasses and to give them gloves and dress their upper bodies with stylised dinner jackets with tails. This was known as the *Gesture Dance*. In addition to the ways of walking in the space that were established by the *Space Dance*, there were now fixed places to sit down on a swivel chair, an armchair and a bench. Further elaboration occurred through use of sound such as 'murmuring and hissing noises; double-talk and jabbering; an occasional bit of pandemonium; perhaps also a phonograph, piano, and trumpet'.[62]

These three dances, or plays, existed without narrative plots. The pure motion of forms, colour and light conditioned and directed development of the respective pieces. Conventional narrative did not drive these works. The relative precision with which these dances were conducted might lead to the proposition that they were somewhat mechanical in their execution. However, Schlemmer was not interested in pursuing such mechanical perfection for he considered that the human being should remain at the centre and as purpose of such work.

Additional dances were created that further investigated the relationship between the actor/dancer and the spatial environment. The *Pole Dance* (Figure 6) was developed by a dancer whose limbs were extended by 12 poles. Thus, the space that the figure moved in was greatly enlarged. The poles were permitted to reflect light while the dancer, costumed in dark material, lost his normal identity to that of the exaggerated figure, defined by the extended lines of movement evident through the poles. The movement of the dancer through space was

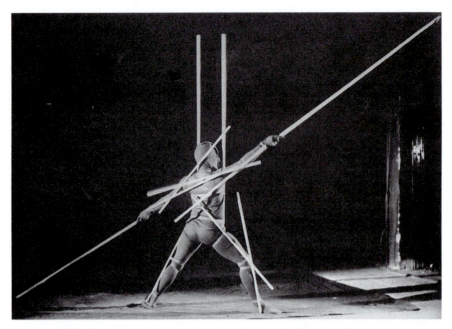

6. Oskar Schlemmer, *Pole Dance*, Dessau Bauhaus, 1927

what was registered, whilst the body of the dancer became subliminal. A similar spatial experiment was the *Hoop Dance* (Figure 7). This performance made use of hoops of different sizes which were similarly lit. The hoops were used to explore the space around the darkened figure of the dancer through curvilinear shapes radiating from the body of the performer. Another spatial dance was the *Flats Dance*. Here, three flats painted in the primary colours of blue, red and yellow were moved into different positions to create different spatial dynamics. The dancers played among the flats thus creating new spatial dimensions. In the *Game of Bricks*, differently coloured wooden blocks were turned, lifted, thrown and carried into different spatial positions and arrangements. The range of colours affected the spatial choices. The *Chorus of Masks* required the dancers to wear masks that removed all that was private and individual. All identity was taken away. The masked figures were no longer human or alive but inanimate and impersonal. Only the masks reflected light so that the dancers' bodies were relegated to relatively unseen ones.

Throughout his work, to date, Schlemmer had cautiously avoided the potential problems imposed by the use of language. The *Space Dance*, the *Form Dance* and the *Gesture Dance* did not employ language. Sound was used

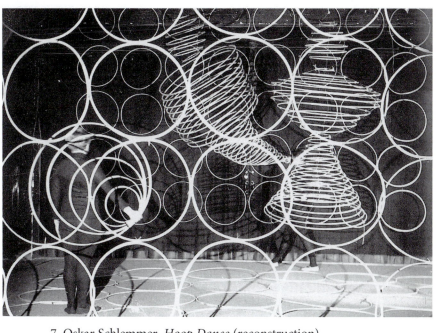

7. Oskar Schlemmer, *Hoop Dance* (reconstruction)

as a stimulus to motion and sporadic words were used in the *Gesture Dance* but these did not amount to use as language. Schlemmer did not want to disregard language but, aware of its potential significance, he wanted to control its use and development. He considered that mastery over the relative silence of motion and gesture would lead to an automatic development of the word and its use. Essentially, he was concerned with using the word in its primary state without its implicit loading of literal and/or literary meaning. This concern was to find its focus and articulation in an experimental play that Schlemmer called the *House of Pi* (π). In a letter that he wrote to his wife on 27 May 1927 Schlemmer said: 'We are working on a "play": *The House of Py*. Wrote it myself. The structure will do nicely. Very difficult to find the "word". Everyone was looking for a story.'[63] This latter notion seems to have been a typical response, even from some of his close colleagues, and indicates something of the normal cultural dependency on the use of narrative. He too must have found it difficult to remove narrative elements in order to concentrate on the logic and development of abstract content. In another letter to his wife, dated 1 June 1927, he outlined 'The roles in the play: astrologer, female dancer, young man, revolutionary, passer-by, general, his wife, their child, the mysterious one, three thieves'.[64] These figures operated within the following spatial context:

> Starting with a prepared stage with its own set of spatial relationships (involving various levels constructed of movable skeletal boxes with flooring where needed), and with experimental light effects, it was possible to obtain through pure chance, inspiration, and the extemporizing of the participants an 'extract', which, as it developed, became more fascinating, the clearer the possibility became of giving the action a definitive form. It was demonstrated here, too, that the growth of a scene must follow ultimately a rhythmical and somehow mathematically determinable law, perhaps most closely akin to the laws of music, without, however, its involving music as such.[65]

The development of Schlemmer's short plays did not progress through developed narrative but through juxtaposition of action, image, colour, light and sound. Each piece constructed its own organic logic which was organised through juxtaposed and sequential action.

Antonin Artaud (1896–1948)

Artaud was a poet, an actor and a director; a visionary of modern theatre whose theories, rather than his practice, have been extremely influential, especially in experimental theatre. His contribution to ideas about scenography is contained in his emphasis on the physical, material experience of the theatre as the principal means by which it could communicate to the audience. In his concept of the *Theatre of Cruelty*, he envisaged audiences being surrounded by the physical and plastic properties of the stage including costumes, large masks and puppets, lighting and sound. These were intended to contribute to a theatre event which aimed 'to exalt, to benumb, to bewitch, to arrest our sensibility' through distillations which are 'spatially amplified'.[66]

Artaud's concern for the theatre was that it should be a transcendent and transformative experience: 'I believe that the aim of true theatre is to reconcile us with a certain idea of action, of immediate effectiveness … it ought to seek to reach the deep-seated regions of the individual and create in him a real transformation, although hidden, and the consequences of which he will only perceive later.'[67] And the means by which theatre could achieve this transcendence were by a direct appeal to the senses through the physical aspects of performances, including gestures, sounds and images. The 'excessive logic' of text was a hindrance to this 'direct action' on the nervous system. Artaud did not argue for the abandonment of text, but he was wary of the emphasis on 'purely psychological and naturalistic theatre'.[68] He also believed that words alone were incapable of conveying intense, inner feelings. His suggestion was that text could be used in ways that refer back to older forms of theatre and ritual and 'give words something of the significance they have in dreams'.[69]

The text, therefore, was exploited for its physical qualities. Artaud envisaged that delivery of the text, through an emphasis on patterns of breathing, intonation and inflection, was to be subsumed under staging conditions which themselves were intended to provide focus for an 'archetypal theatre language'. In his influential collection of essays, *The Theatre and its Double*, Artaud describes how the components of this language were to be sound, movement and colour as expressed through the work of actors, costume, lighting and objects that appeared on stage. In short, a material, physical language:

> Every show will contain physical, objective elements perceptible to all. Shouts, groans, apparitions, surprise, dramatic moments of all kinds, the magic beauty of the costumes modelled on certain ritualistic patterns, brilliant lighting, vocal, incantational beauty, attractive harmonies, rare musical notes, object colours, the physical rhythm of the moves whose build and fall will be wedded to the beat of moves familiar to all, the tangible appearance of new, surprising objects, masks, puppets many feet high, abrupt lighting changes, the physical action of lighting stimulating heat and cold, and so on.[70]

Artaud attempted to develop a language of the senses in which 'spatial poetry' could replace the poetry of language.[71]

7   I maintain the stage is a tangible, physical place that needs to be filled and it ought to be allowed to speak its own concrete language.
   I maintain that this physical language, aimed at the sense and independent of speech, must first satisfy the senses. There must be poetry for the senses just as there is for speech, but this physical tangible language I am referring to is really only theatrical in as far as the thoughts it expresses escape spoken language …
   The most urgent thing seems to me to decide what this physical language is composed of, this solid, material language by which theatre can be distinguished from words.
   It is composed of everything filling the stage, everything that can be shown and materially expressed on stage, intended first of all to appeal to the senses, instead of being addressed primarily to the mind, like spoken language.
   Antonin Artaud, *The Theatre and its Double*, p. 27

Exposure to Balinese theatre at the Paris Colonial Exposition in 1931 helped to crystallise Artaud's thoughts on this theatrical language. He was mesmerised by the theatricality of the presentation, the stylised, angular movement of the dancers, the unfamiliar (to Artaud) sounds created by the musicians and the dancers themselves. He records that he became aware of a sort of 'spatial density' produced by a network of non-verbal signs where sound, image and movement worked in a 'constant play of mirrors'.[72] The costumes extended the sense of the dancers and their gestures as 'hieroglyphs' or recreations of life rather than imitations of it.[73]

> Those actors with their asymmetrical robes looking like moving hieroglyphs; not just the shape of their gowns, shifting the axis of the human figure, but creating a kind of second symbolic clothing standing beside the uniforms of those warriors entranced and perpetually at war, thus inspiring intellectual ideas or merely connecting all the criss-crossing of these lines with all the criss-crossing of spatial perspective. These mental signs have an exact meaning that only strikes one intuitively, but violently enough to make any translations into logical, discursive language useless.[74]

Artaud's reading of this work was highly subjective and took no account of the cultural context of the work or its inherent conventions. It did, however, seem to act as a moment of inspiration for him as to how theatre should work on the spectator. The costumes appeared to him to be at times part of, and at times separate from, the dancers. The feathered tiers of the head-dresses 'tremble rhythmically, seeming *consciously* to answer the trembling bodies'[75] but the costumes also served to contain and define the movements of the dancers within the geometry of the stage: 'the folds of these robes curving above their buttocks, holding them up as if suspended in the air, as if pinned onto the backdrop, prolonging each of their leaps into flight'.[76] The scenic presence created by use of these costumes was powerful for Artaud.[77] The effect of a 'pure' or 'total' theatre which transcended mere entertainment was capable of directly tapping into the 'secret psychic impulse': 'This theatre vibrates with instinctive things but brought to that lucid, intelligent, malleable point where they seem physically to supply us with some of the mind's most secret perceptions.'[78] Another influential experience for Artaud was his encounter with Lucas van Leyden's painting *Lot and his Daughters*. He was struck by the 'visual harmony' of the composition and the drama that was revealed through the spatial poetry of the painting. Artaud responded to the material, spatial qualities of the work as much as to the representational details:

> there is an idea of change in the different landscape details and the way they are painted, their levels annulling or corresponding to one another, leads us into the mind in painting the same way as in music … There is another idea about Fate, revealed not so much by the appearance of that sudden fire as by the solemn way in which all forms are arranged or

disarranged beneath it, some as if bent beneath a gust of irresistible panic, the others motionless, almost ironic, all obeying a powerful intelligent consistency, seemingly nature's mind externalized.[79]

Artaud found it hard to determine how the painting achieved such a tangible and direct effect but he concluded that 'this painting is what theatre ought to be, if only it knew how to speak its own language'.[80] He saw theatre, like the painting, as physical and material where three-dimensional space and the movement within it could create a language of movement in space.[81]

In his 'First Manifesto' for the *Theatre of Cruelty*, Artaud described how the stage could evoke sensations through the interaction of strange and striking objects: 'No décor. Hieroglyphic characters, ritual costume, thirty foot high effigies of King Lear's beard in the storm, musical instruments as tall as men, objects of unknown form and purpose are enough to fulfil this function.'[82] He favoured costumes 'of ritual intent', that is, costumes with a history which carry with them something of the tradition from which they they spring. Puppets, huge masks and objects of strange proportions provided a visual language of images and non-verbal signs. Musical instruments and other means of creating sounds were to be used as part of the set to provide a deep and direct sensory experience for the audience. He advocated research into new sounds and new materials to create excruciatingly penetrating sounds. Lighting was also conceived as having great potential to move or disorientate the spectator, but like sound, needed technological development. Artaud wanted to be able to manipulate the 'special tonal qualities' of light and create 'sensations of heat, cold, anger and fear'. He envisaged the opportunity to explore the oscillation and diffusion of light, creating, for example, 'sheet lighting like a flight of fire-arrows'.[83] Perhaps the most important property of stage light was its ability to operate as an active force capable of unlocking primal responses through the transposition of stage action.[84]

He also called for a new form of auditorium: 'a single, undivided locale without partitions of any kind'.[85] He envisaged that the large auditorium could reflect the architectural logic of certain churches or Tibetan temples, suggesting that particular ratios of interior height and depth accorded spaces with special qualities. Members of the audience were to be seated in the centre on swivel chairs so that they might look up and around at the action which would extend to all parts of the auditorium. Thus the action was intended to surround the audience at all levels.[86]

Artaud's outline for *The Conquest of Mexico*, a play which was never completed, but which aimed to show Montezuma's 'inner struggle, and his symbolic discussion with visualised astronomical myths in a pictorial, objective manner',[87] gives an idea of what he hoped the *Theatre of Cruelty* would achieve in scenographic terms. In Act Three:

> The wall of the stage is crammed unevenly with heads, with throats:
> cracked and strangely sliced melodies, answers to these melodies appear
> truncated. Montezuma himself seems split in two, appears double; with
> some pieces of him half-lit; others dazzling with light, with manifold
> hands sticking out of his costume, with faces painted on his body like
> a multiple meeting point of consciousness ...

And in Act Four as the revolt breaks out:

> the stage space looks as if it is stuffed with a shrieking mosaic either of
> men, or of compact troops in man-to-man formation, clashing frenetically.
> The space is stacked high with swirling gestures, horrible faces, glaring
> eyes, closed fists, plumes, armour, heads, bellies falling like hailstones
> pelting the earth with supernatural explosions.[88]

The apparent gap between Artaud's widely cited theories and the evidence of his practice, albeit limited, prompts concern as to whether Artaud was a true innovator.[89] *The Cenci* (1935), his only full-length play, was an exploration of *Theatre of Cruelty* principles. Christopher Innes' investigation of the production reveals the extent to which the production was able to realise the promise of the theory.

Count Cenci is the embodiment of evil who murders his rivals (including his own sons) and rapes his adolescent daughter, Beatrice. She has Cenci murdered, and is then arrested, tortured and beheaded. The aim was for audience members to be agitated, excited and drawn into the work, participating, as it were, through their souls,[90] and towards this end the performance was intended to be filled with a particularised language of gestures and signs capable of embodying contemporary anxieties in a violent consummation of feeling.[91]

The painter Balthus Klossowski designed the sets and costumes. Photographs from the production suggest that Artaud relied far more on a symbolic use of setting than his theories suggest. The costumes consisted of a suggestive mix of medieval styles and symbolic elements such as those to outline muscle definition on the men's costumes. Human dummies were also included to stand for the things that could not be spoken about and to 'formulate all the reproaches, rancour, remorse, anguish and demands'.[92] Cenci's castle reflected his persona[93] and made use of towering and abstracted architectural references. Scaffolding levels and distorted perspectives led one reviewer to comment that the set was 'essentially architectonic and is reminiscent of a gigantic prison palace by Piranese'.[94] One clear connection between the scenography of *The Cenci* and theories of the *Theatre of Cruelty* is in the way that certain scenes develop a momentum through use of space, movement and rhythm. In the opening scene, the multiple levels of the set reveal a spiral gallery, suggesting an unending circular rotation which develops as the play progresses. Guests in the banquet scene dance in circles, Beatrice's circular movements echo the spiral gallery (as do the guards who come to arrest her) and prefigure the wheel on which she will be tortured. These spatial and geometric patterns create a powerful pull towards the awful and inevitable events.[95]

But perhaps the most successful evocation of the *Theatre of Cruelty* through scenographic means can be discerned in the use of sound. Sound in *The Cenci* was driven by the same impulses as the visible ones involving intensified aspects of reality.[96] Dialogue spoken by the actors was exaggerated and formalised to emphasise rhythm. Carefully orchestrated movement of the cast was underscored by recorded, amplified footsteps and punctuated with rhythmic breathing and silences. A recording of church bells (from Amiens Cathedral) was amplified to deafening levels and played through speakers around the auditorium. The musical composition by Roger Désormière made use of an electronic keyboard which could produce sounds as well as notes and managed to suggest, for Beatrice's final scene, contemporary factory machinery and a medieval torture chamber.[97] Artaud claimed that the audience was intended to be 'in the centre of a network of sound vibrations'.[98] A review of the production suggests that the scenographic aspect of *The Cenci* was successful in conveying the spatial poetry of the stage: 'Complex lighting, individual and mass-movement, sound, music, revealed to the spectator that space and time form an *affective* reality.'[99]

Vsevolod Emilievich Meyerhold (1874–1940)

Vsevolod Meyerhold was an actor and director and not a designer. Yet his work, in collaboration with several different artists and designers, explored important scenographic principles.[100] His writing on the scenographic aspects of his work also provides useful material in this context and shows a line of development from naturalism through to Constructivism where scenography is central and where it has social as well as aesthetic impact.

In *The Government Inspector* (1926), Meyerhold was credited as the 'author of the production' to signify the extent that the production, through its mise-en-scène, had reinterpreted the original Gogol text. Through his production, Gogol's farcical satire of provincial corruption became a darker, more foreboding reflection of the degradation of life underlying Soviet Russian

society.[101] The interaction of the scenic environment and the actors' movements were orchestrated by Meyerhold to reveal a subtext of the play which
could engage and involve the audience. He was interested in a theatre which,
through 'mysterious allusions, deception and transformation', transcended
everyday life.[102] He explored and exploited the non-textual aspects of the
stage to achieve this transcendence. He frequently used music as a means of
expressing unspoken but significant undercurrents in his productions, and the
scenographic concerns of space, movement and composition were central to
his work.

His early career between 1898 and 1902 was as an actor in Stanislavsky's
company at the Moscow Art Theatre. The staging practices and the particular
brand of naturalistic design employed by the theatre initially excited him. For
The Merchant of Venice (1898), Viktor Simov's set design was seen to make an
important contribution to the performance. Describing the model of the set
design, Meyerhold reported:

> Old Venice will rise as a living thing before the audience … On one
> side the old Jewish quarter, dark and dirty, on the other the square in
> front of Portia's palace, poetic, beautiful with a view over the sea … There
> darkness, here light; there despair and oppression, here gaiety and light.
> The set outlines the idea of the play all by itself.[103]

Stanislavsky and his collaborator, designer Viktor Simov, often travelled to
what they imagined would be actual locations of the play in order to immerse
themselves in the particular atmosphere and obtain authentic furniture, props
and costumes. For a production of *The Three Sisters*, Simov carefully selected
materials and props to reflect Russian provincial life. The rug was worn, the
floors were yellowed, the cuckoo clock 'was slow to strike and then counted
out the time hurriedly, as if embarrassed'[104] and, together with the rest of the
setting, built up a claustrophobic and stultifying atmosphere.

But Meyerhold recognised that this approach to naturalism could become
obsessed with the trappings of verisimilitude. Simov's design for *The Snow
Maiden* (1900), which incorporated 'authentic objects of folk art' and many
effects including avalanches and snowstorms, was judged to be intricate but
uninteresting with characters submerged by painstaking detail.[105] Meyerhold's
disappointment focused on the inability of the theatre to respond to the
turmoil of pre-revolutionary Russian society. He wrote to Anton Chekhov:
'[The] Snow Maiden is simply old-fashioned. It's obvious that in troubled
times like ours, when everything is falling apart around us, a simple appeal to
beauty is not enough.'[106] Meyerhold was convinced of the power and capacity
of theatre to play a powerful role in the transformation of human existence[107]

and his own work as a director represented a series of explorations of form and function in the theatre.

In 1905 Meyerhold became the artistic director of the Theatre Studio at the Moscow Art Theatre which was a kind of laboratory, whose purpose was to develop new forms and techniques of staging in order to enable the theatre to respond to nuanced changes in society.[108] Here Meyerhold started to develop his concept of 'stylisation',[109] a technique which allowed his productions to look beyond the surface of reality to reveal what lay beneath. Although the Studio turned out to be a short-lived experiment, Meyerhold realised that the core of human relationships was determined by gestures, poses, glances and silences. As such, he discerned that words were not always adequate to their purpose in communication.[110] As well as influencing the style of acting, this discovery presented immense implications for the design of the stage. Working with young artists rather than scene painters, Meyerhold invited them to contribute their artistic vision to the productions. Through use of colour, line and suggestion, the aim was to create performance space which harmonised with and facilitated the actor's work. The overarching sensibility of stylisation was one of musical composition. Meyerhold describes Nikolai Ulyanov's designs for one of the Studio productions, Hauptmann's *Schluck und Jau*: 'Crinolines, white periwigs, and the characters' costumes are blended with the colours of the setting into a single artistic design, a symphony in mother-of-pearl ... Everything conveys the musical rhythm: movements, lines, gestures, dialogue, the colours of the setting and costumes.'[111] Nikolai Sapunov's designs for *Hedda Gabler* (1906), directed by Meyerhold for Vera Komissarzhevskaya's company, further developed the concept of stylisation for the stage. Although the design included a painted backdrop of pale blue sky seen through vast windows, the stage did not conform to architectural reality. The acting area was wide but shallow, pushing the action towards the front of the stage, and this facilitated carefully choreographed sequences of a non-naturalist delivery of Ibsen's text. Enormous tapestries and screens in autumn shades contrasted with the blue sky beyond. A white piano and an enormous chair covered in white fur, like a throne, were said to add to the impression of Hedda's inner character. The costumes aimed to present a synthesis of the period and society of the play rather than accurate colour and were conceived to harmonise with the setting which reflected the response of the designer, Vasily Milioti, to the character's inner nature. Tesman, dressed in dull grey with a wide tie and trousers, sought to express 'the essence of Tesmanism'.[112]

Meyerhold's desire to produce 'transforming' theatre was not realised predominantly through overtly political texts, but through the relationship which his productions sought to develop with the audience. Where Stanislavsky had insisted on the primacy of the actor and the stage as the focus, Meyerhold sought to locate the theatrical event as a joint enterprise between performers and audience: 'We produce every play on the assumption that it will be still unfinished when it appears on the stage. We do this consciously because we realize that the crucial revision of a production is that which is made by the spectator.'[113] This 'crucial revision' was one that was built on the audience's capacity to respond imaginatively and creatively. The audience was not intended to observe passively, but to 'participate in a *corporate* creative act'.[114]

One way in which Meyerhold attempted to engage the audience was to blur the boundary between the auditorium and the acting area. This was achieved by throwing action forward onto the forestage and even extending the stage into the auditorium in attempts to bring an immediacy and vibrancy to the performance. In *The Fairground Booth* (1906), a piece by Alexander Blok which consisted of farce and absurd images intended to poke fun at the more pompous tendencies of Symbolism, the spirit of Commedia dell'Arte was evoked through the physicality of the actors and through playful use of deliberately contrived theatrical props and costumes. For the opening scene, the stage was hung with blue drapes at the back and sides and was empty except for a little booth or theatre in the centre:

> This booth has its own stage, curtain, prompter's box, and proscenium opening. Instead of being masked with the conventional border, the flies, together with all the ropes and wires, are visible to the audience. When the entire set in the booth is hauled aloft, the audience in the actual theatre sees the whole process. In front of the booth, the stage area adjacent to the footlights is left free. It is here that the 'Author' appears to serve as an intermediary between the public and the events enacted within the booth.[115]

The character of the irate Author, who protested throughout at the misrepresentation of his text, was prevented from interfering by being tethered to the forestage by a rope. He provided a direct physical link between the audience and the action further up the stage. In Molière's *Don Juan* (1910) Meyerhold and designer Alexander Golovin sought to further dissolve the division between auditorium and stage by extending the stage area out over the deep orchestra pit and into the first row of seats. Additionally, the auditorium was as brightly lit as the stage. At one point, the Sganarelle character walked along the front of the stage projecting a light at the dignitaries in the front row and making humorous comments about them.[116] Use of the forestage in this way, where events on stage and real lives of the audience start to overlap, may be seen to operate as a literal and metaphorical meeting place between stage action and audience.[117] Such use of the forestage affords actors greater physical freedom and allows them to exist concurrently within and beyond the scenic devices further upstage. For audience members it provokes a heightened awareness of their presence at a theatrical event and, at the same time, their involvement in it. This sets up a productive theatrical tension between performers and audience.[118] However, Meyerhold's use of theatre imagery was also part of such creative tension. Designs for Meyerhold productions can be seen as a series of explorations towards a design approach which suited his intentions for the actor:

> if the actor, in order to encourage the audience's active participation in the creation of the work, was going to emerge on to the forestage, then a type of *mise-en-scène* had to be devised to complement rather than negate this. The old decorative or illusory set was unacceptable: the *mise-en-scène* needed the capacity for independent intervention.[119]

Sapunov's designs for *The Fairground Booth* made a major contribution to its performance. The little theatre booth with its exposed workings offered 'a further dimension to the play's irony'.[120] In the opening scene, a group of Mystics sat behind a table and they were revealed on the stage of the booth while they awaited the arrival of Death: 'Frightened by some rejoinder, they duck their heads, and suddenly all that remains at the table is a row of torsos minus heads and hands. It transpires that the figures are cut out of cardboard with frock-coats, shirt-fronts, collars and cuffs drawn on with soot and chalk.'[121] As well as marrying the text to the mode of performance, Sapunov's design made a comment on the restrictions of a tatty and superficial everyday existence.[122]

The Fairground Booth, with its uneasy mix of tragedy and comedy, its incorporation of popular theatre styles, its challenging and often incongruous imagery, provided Meyerhold with the basis for his concept of the 'grotesque':

> The grotesque mixes opposites, consciously creating harsh incongruity, *playing entirely on its own originality* … The grotesque deepens life's outward appearance to the point where it ceases to appear merely natural … The basis of the grotesque is the artist's constant desire to switch the spectator from the plane he has just reached to another that is totally unforeseen.[123]

This sort of thinking referred to theatre which unsettled and surprised; theatre which was overtly theatrical and which borrowed from other theatre forms; theatre which challenged perceptions and theatre which was playful and satirical. It was a development from the stylisation of earlier productions and it also signalled new possibilities for design. Meyerhold explained that 'The art of the grotesque is based on the conflict between form and content ... That is why in every theatre which has been dominated by the grotesque the aspect of design in its widest sense has been so important.'[124] By design 'in its widest sense', Meyerhold considered the whole organisation of the stage environment, including the spatial relationship of performers to audience, and the relationship of actors through gesture and movement to performance environment.

One of the borrowed forms was that of the *kurogo*, the black-clad stage figure of traditional Japanese theatre. The traditional function of the *kurogo* is to hand properties to the actors and clear the stage. Dressed in black clothes, the convention renders the *kurogo* invisible. In Molière's *Don Juan*, Meyerhold employed a crew of blacked-up and liveried 'proscenium servants' to assist with the theatrical creation of 'the perfumed, gilded monarchy of Versailles'.[125] These servants appeared on stage alongside the action proper. They performed a host of duties including 'sprinkling intoxicating perfumes from crystal bottles ... picking up a lace handkerchief dropped by Dom Juan, offering a stool to a tired actor ... fastening Dom Juan's shoelaces as he argues with Sganarelle ... summoning the public with tinkling silver bells and announcing the intervals (in the absence of a curtain)'.[126] Like the actors, they performed a role which drew the audience into Versailles, but at the same time, by means of an unfamiliar scenic convention, they drew attention to the theatre event itself, within which audience members were active participants. In *The Unknown Woman* (1914) proscenium servants, using simple objects, performed scenic transformations with rhythmical ease. A shooting star was presented by one servant with a burning flame on the end of a long bamboo cane describing an arc across the stage. The flame was extinguished when the cane ended its journey in a cup of water, provided by another servant. Later, a character caught in a snowstorm was wrapped in a white muslin shawl.[127]

During the decade following the Russian Revolution many Soviet artists and intellectuals felt it important to sever all ties with pre-revolutionary Russian culture and establish new forms which would be appropriate to the Soviet project. The theatre, particularly, was seen as a 'laboratory' for new ideas, not just for the form and function of theatre, but also for the task of reforming society.[128] Meyerhold, along with other directors such as Evgeny Vakhtangov and Alexander Tairov, enthusiastically embraced this new role for theatre and found collaborative partners such as Lyubov Popova and Alexandra Exter, who were Constructivist artists and were similarly inspired by the task of creating what was considered to be a new reality.[129]

Popova's design for Meyerhold's 1922 production of *The Magnanimous Cuckold* by Fernand Crommelynck was a radical departure from the original text. Popova stripped away the decorative detail suggested by the text and

8. Lyubov Popova, *The Magnanimous Cuckold*, by Fernand Crommelynck. Director Vsevolod Emilievich Meyerhold, The Actors' Theatre, Moscow, 1922

arrived at a skeletal structure consisting of several platforms connected by stairs and ramps and backed by three enormous wheels. The resulting structure retained the trace of the mill in which the play is set but also alluded to other possibilities such as a playground, a machine or a factory.[130] (Figure 8.)

The costumes consisted of blue boiler suits which resembled workers' uniforms. This unified the actors as a group, almost like components in a machine which in turn emphasised the actors' movements. The company had been trained in the use of a repertoire of technical exercises which Meyerhold termed 'biomechanics'. It was an approach that developed control of the body and a range of possible movement for use on stage. Action was stylised and exaggerated, but also light and athletic.[131] Various levels of Popova's set provided strong choreographic and kinetic possibilities for placing actors in space while the linear, angular aesthetic of the structure underlined the extremity of the actors' gestures and expressions.

Much of the impact of this production came from the tension between the original text and the way it was staged. The skeletal set suggested a stripping away of the surface so that the underlying workings of society could be revealed. The set and costumes became a means of examining redundant social values and the play offered an alternative vision based on the common creative endeavour of performers and audience.

Bertolt Brecht (1898–1956) and Caspar Neher (1897–1962)

Bertolt Brecht's approach to staging, which was in large part developed as a result of his longstanding collaboration with artist and designer Caspar Neher, has had a lasting influence on Western theatre-design practice. The term 'Brechtian' suggests economy of image, with nothing on the stage that is superfluous to the telling of the story. The austere beauty of this pared-down approach was enhanced by selective use of real materials and objects in preference to the provision of elaborate scenic illusion. Materials such as wood, leather, metal, calico and earth pigments were often used, while props and costumes were chosen for their capacity to suggest a life beyond the stage. Use of half-height walls, curtains and visible lighting instruments pointed to a conscious theatricality where spectators were always aware of the context of the theatre. Since the 1960s a Brechtian aesthetic has been widely adopted and incorporated into mainstream theatre design, but largely as a stylistic device rather than a set of practices and principles which articulate scenography as an intervention in the process of performance. What is crucial to Brechtian scenography is not simply the way it looks but how it is able to comment, intervene and perform as part of the production.

8   The words 'picture' and 'stage' are incompatible … A picture is never realistic, the stage is always realistic. That's why I maintain that the 'realistic stage picture' is a nonsense. Nor can I imagine what can possibly be meant by it. A marble pillar can only be translated, i.e. at best hinted at; while if a turbine were a real one it would break the stage floor. This means that one always has to allow the audience to set their imagination to work in order to believe it could be a turbine, or might be a marble pillar. So you have to have an element of conjuring, of illusion. And in order to guide illusion along a track corresponding to some reality or other you may be able to dispense with reality itself. Perhaps reality is expressed in the proportions: a small house, a big hall, a stable and so on.
Caspar Neher in John Willett, *Caspar Neher: Brecht's Designer*, p. 76

Although both Brecht and Neher worked with other collaborators, their work together represents a fascinating model for scenography. Brecht's writing on design for the stage reflects their longstanding collaboration.[132] They were schoolboys together in Augsburg and later Neher helped Brecht by making drawings which visualised his first plays. These were not designs as such, but images which complemented and extended ideas in the text. Neher's designs were always more of a poetic visualisation of the text than a detailed, technical specification[133] and they were developed simultaneously with the actors' rehearsals rather than ahead of them. It was an approach in which design was integral to the production rather than simply the background and one which challenged the traditional role of the designer.

Brecht and Neher adapted the usual German word to describe a stage designer, *Bühnenbildner* (stage painter), and coined the term *Bühnenbauer* (stage constructor or scene designer) to distinguish the way they worked from the way in which designers were generally expected (or expected themselves) to work. This new term laid emphasis on the three-dimensional quality of the work and pointed not simply to the way that Neher's designs were structural rather than decorative, but to the way in which the designs developed during the rehearsal period and the way they were intended to be viewed as part of the performance. Key principles of Neher's process of designing for the stage are illustrated in this translated extract from Brecht:

> The good scene designer [*Bühnenbauer*] proceeds slowly and experimentally. A working hypothesis is based on a precise reading of the text, and substantial conversations with other members of the theatre, especially on the social aims of the play and the concerns of the performance, are useful to him. However, his basic performance ideas must still be general and flexible. He will test them constantly and revise them on the basis of results in rehearsals with the actors. The wishes and opinions of the actors are wells of discovery for him. He studies to what extent their strengths are adequate and intervenes … This is how a good stage designer [*Bühnenbauer*] works. Now ahead of the actor, now behind him, always together with him. Step by step he builds up the performance area, just as experimentally as the actor.[134]

Of course, the designer needs to proceed from a shared understanding of and commitment to the aims of the performance. For Brecht this was bound up with his political philosophy and his commitment to a Marxist view of history and political change. What was crucial for Brecht in his desire for political change was that things needed to be seen as they were in reality. Brecht's theatre, and Neher's scenography, aimed to present social reality and allow audiences to see it more objectively, leaving open the possibility for challenge and change. The contribution of Neher's scenography was central to the process of presenting truthful renditions of human society on stage in ways which invited reappraisal of the status quo.

Neher's designs for Brecht arose from a shared ideological pursuit of the production. The stage environment was constructed alongside and in response to rehearsals. In the rehearsal room Brecht and Neher sat side by side and ignored the usual distinction between designer and director or designer and playwright. Neher did not begin designing until he understood the play and how it might be presented by the particular company with whom he worked. In rehearsals he made sketches which responded to the actors' physical characteristics and movements, developing what he saw and suggesting ways that items of costume or the addition of selected scenic elements could extend or 'comment' on their work. These sketches helped to crystallise the 'scenic instant'[135] and gave the actors guidance on the development of their characters and ways of presenting them:

> We often begin rehearsing without any knowledge of the stage designs, and our friend merely prepares small sketches of the episodes to be played … he shows us the essential … In his designs our friend always starts with 'the people themselves' and 'what is happening to or through them'. He provides no 'décor', frames and backgrounds, but constructs the space for 'people' to experience something in.[136]

These drawings, or *Arrangementskizzen*, were an important part of the rehearsal process of Brecht's company and were adopted by Karl von Appen, the designer who succeeded Neher at the Berliner Ensemble. The drawings did more than just indicate how the design was to develop. They 'drew strength from the actors, were fed back to them and served as models for stage blocking and textual development'.[137] So they were viewed as a dialogue between the actors and Neher. In turn, Neher's considerations of the spatial arrangements for the production became, for the actors, a way of understanding and developing their performances. Egon Monk records a particular instance during rehearsals:

> Unforgettable: Friedrich Maurer as Wenzeslaus the Schoolmaster in scene II of *The Tutor*. One hand holding Neher's sketch, the other holding the long quill pen with which the sketch shows him driving Count Vermuth and the Major's armed domestics from the room. A most impressive moment, clarifying the scene as no subsequent performance could do.[138]

In a drawing for *Puntila*[139] (Figure 9) the restrained addition of a few items of costume, such as a feathered hat, tail-coats and pince-nez, extended the gestures of the actors. Here, costume was more than a sociometric or historical detail or

9. Caspar Neher, *Puntila*, Scene 9 (Puntila betroths his daughters), by Bertolt Brecht. Directors Bertolt Brecht and E. Engel, Berliner Ensemble in Deutsches Theater, 1949

sign of character. Actors were able to use Neher's drawings as clarification and inspiration, even when they defied logic, as Monk reports: 'Occasional uncertainty. The drunken Puntila blessing his four fiancées: in Neher's drawing he has four arms. Where were the two extra arms to come from? Steckel invented a gesture that almost made one see Neher's four arms.'[140] Monk also describes the way Neher ensured that furniture on stage created attitudes. 'Neher-height' was a reference to his practice of subtly altering the way actors related to furniture. He ensured that chair and table legs were cut down by about 5–10 centimetres below normal to provoke subtle exaggerations in the actors' stances and gestures: 'One's back bends when one props one's elbows on the table, and one has to tilt one's head back in order to address one's neighbour.'[141]

Neher's designs shaped the performance space and were an integral part of the action. The adjustment of door heights and chair legs served to provoke and extend the actor's physical and emotional energy on stage. Brecht, in translation, suggested that 'the set needs to spring from the rehearsal of groupings, so in effect it must be a fellow-actor'.[142]

Brecht and Neher were committed to the exploration of 'representation' of reality on stage. They were united in their opposition to illusion. Comments from Neher on the relationship of the set to the action addressed notions of reality: 'Too little attention is paid these days to the life of reality. The things we put on the stage are dead, never mind how real they are, if they have no function – if they are not used by the actors or used on their behalf.'[143] Neher was concerned here with the 'life' of reality, and drew a distinction between a process of exposing the real world through a theatrical performance and the inclusion of real, or apparently real, things which have no dramaturgical purpose. He rejected the idea of 'realist stage design' because the stage is only ever an illusion of reality. In the theatre 'a marble pillar can only be translated … while if a turbine were a real one it would break the stage floor'.[144] The reality which principally interested him was the reality of the stage and the theatrical process whereby scenography worked simultaneously with actors at the point of performance. What was real was the two or so hours of a production where performers worked within a temporary and provisional environment in order to offer insights into and questions about the world beyond the theatre. References to the real world found their way into Neher's settings as mere indications through the contrast of architectural proportions, or a single colour or isolated details in particular costumes and props. For the 1948 production of *Antigone*, Neher created a semicircular space with posts topped with horses' skulls, which Brecht described as 'barbaric war emblems', and ox-blood-coloured canvas screens 'reminiscent of sails and tents'.[145] Beyond these carefully selected elements, the set created an arena in which the presentation of characters took place. Actors waited for their turn to perform on benches placed between the posts (Figure 10).

10. Caspar Neher, *Antigone*, by Bertolt Brecht (after Sophocles). Directors Bertolt Brecht and Caspar Neher, Stadttheater, Chur, 1948

Brecht and Neher both recognised the beauty and potency of authentic objects on stage, but the beauty of stage objects extended beyond simply importing real things into the theatre; it also applied to the way in which everything was selected and constructed in order to take an appropriate place in the overall statement and not simply to operate in support of it. Egon Monk describes the care with which Neher supervised the process of constructing Helen Weigel's blouse for *The Mother*:

> It was to be blue, but blue like calico that has been to the wash a couple of hundred times. Had it once had a pattern? Was this still visible? Had it picked up a blue or grey dye? [Kurt] Palm made tests and juggled the blouse through every conceivable stage. Luxury with unluxurious material. In the end it was the most beautiful blouse in theatrical history.[146]

Neher's impulse as an artist was crucial to his work. His sketches, created as part of the rehearsal process, were expressive and evocative and suggested in a few lines the gestural relationship of one character to another. It is possible to see links between his pen and ink sketches and the eventual staging. His use of wood, canvas and stage paint was imbued with 'a softness of definition similar to the undogmatic, thought-provoking effects achieved by drawing with ink upon damp watercolour washes'.[147] Incorporation of his paintings as part of the scenography offered another dimension to the presentation of text and character. For the *Life Story of a Man Called Baal* (1926), 'about the decline of a mere sensualist and his eventual incapacity to enjoy his senses'[148] (Figure 11), Neher painted canvas flats to reflect not only a suggestion of location, but more significantly, the 'world's diminishing interest in such types'.[149] The spare quality of brushstrokes which, for example, rendered trees simply, was said to indicate both reflection and judgement on Baal's degenerate state.

Despite their collaborative creation, Neher's designs possessed qualities which enabled them to be considered as statements in their own right. In *Fear and Misery of the Third Reich* (1947) (Figure 12), Neher created paintings which were projected above the action. One image was of people hiding in a primitive shelter from a gas attack, their gas masks making their faces look like skulls. This was not a location from the text. It was clearly Neher's own personal interpretation of the horrors of war, drawing perhaps on his experiences at the front in the First World War. It worked in parallel to the text and the actors and adding additional meaning.

Brecht's dismissal of Wagner's notion of the *Gesamtkunstwerk* [integrated work of art] was based on a concern that it bewitched or hypnotised the audience into becoming passive.[150] His use of the term *Verfremdung*

11. Caspar Neher, *Life Story of a Man Called Baal*, by Bertolt Brecht. Directors Bertolt Brecht and Oskar Homolka, Deutsches Theater, Berlin, 1926

12. Caspar Neher, *Fear and Misery of the Third Reich*, by Bertolt Brecht. Director E. Ginsberg, Stadttheater, Basel, 1947

(defamiliarisation), described his approach to the creation of theatre as one which made the world appear strange so that it might be considered afresh and 'help the oppressed recognise the form of their oppression, and so overcome it'.[151] Likewise, the rejection of the term *Bühnenbildner* was for Neher a sign of his contempt for theatre practices which sought to offer a complete, uncomplicated view of the world. For Neher, this was a 'Nazi-like' term because it presented a version of the world which was uncontested. By contrast, the approach of the *Bühnenbauer* was to present fragments of reality in ways which worked in parallel with other elements on the stage. Rather than a fused and harmonious presentation of text, actor, scene and music, the effect was one of multiple viewpoints. Brecht called this the 'separation of the elements'.[152] The idea was that each aspect of the staging operated independently in order to comment on the other aspects or elements: 'Neher's projections adopt an attitude towards the events on the stage; as when the real glutton sits in front of the glutton whom Neher has drawn. In the same way the stage unreels the events that are fixed on the screen.'[153] Separation of elements suggests that the concept of *Bühnenbau*, as well as referring to the way scenography is built up, step by step, also extends to the way an audience experiences scenography. In a Brechtian performance, the world is exposed using simultaneous presentation of images, text and gestures which require active attention by the audience. The absence of a unified stage picture opens up gaps between one element and another which invite the audience to become imaginatively and critically involved in interpretation of the performance. Like the process of developing the design, the process of interpretation is active and dialectical: 'The final, live act of performance becomes the setting in motion of a multi-dimensional structure consisting of many components, which engage and inter-mesh in complex semiotic formations across both space and time.'[154] The idea of a stage construction (rather than a painting) is further reinforced by the suggestion that Neher's scenography is a device or machine for engaging the imagination of the audience.

Robert Edmond Jones (1887–1954)

Robert Edmond Jones is considered here not so much as a visionary of the theatre, although he did possess clear vision as a stage designer, but as an interpreter of the influences of change in the American theatre of the first half of the twentieth century. He was not driven by the fundamental concerns of theatre as might be seen in the thinking and work of Appia, Craig or Schlemmer, but he did bring a romantic imagination to the creation of theatre

13. Robert Edmond Jones, *Macbeth*, by Shakespeare. Director
A. Hopkins, Apollo Theater, New York, 1921

and he looked forward to a kind of theatre where the imagination could be set
free and where realism was abandoned.

His 1921 designs for *Macbeth* featured three enormous masks which 'con-
cretized the evil spirits of the play' and hung above the stage, dominating the
human performers. It was a scenic world 'visualized through the minds of the
tormented protagonists'.[155] (Figure 13.) The triangular shapes of the masks
were reflected by masks worn by the witches and in the stylised arches of the
sparse elements which created the setting for Lady Macbeth's sleepwalking
scene. His sketches for the production show that the intention of his lighting
was to activate the dynamics of the stage by working with diagonal lines and
steep angles to maintain a sense of terrible fate as it unfolded.[156]

Much of what Jones stood for in terms of his sought-after theatre has
become absorbed into the values, vocabulary and ways of working for the set
designer in the second half of the twentieth century. For instance, he considered that the 'set' was not an end in itself; it could only find its completion
through the life created by the actor. Thus he decried audience responses to
'clapping the set'. He required that the actor's style should be in complete
harmony with the set (and vice versa). John Marion Brown, in his Introduction
to Jones' *The Dramatic Imagination*, refers to two approaches to the theatre:

one, 'the cathedral' and two, 'the Broadway'.[157] He regarded Jones as more concerned with 'the cathedral' approach. Though these terms are not explained, the reader is left to deduce that 'the cathedral' approach seeks to produce theatre of purity and high ascetic value, whereas 'the Broadway' approach is governed by commercial criteria.

Jones identified what he referred to as 'A New Kind of Drama' in his *The Dramatic Imagination*. This new kind of drama was governed by:

> the exploration of man's inner life, in the unexpressed and hitherto inexpressible depths of the self. Modern psychology has made us all familiar with the idea of the Unconscious. We have learned that beneath the surface of an ordinary everyday normal casual conscious existence there lies a vast dynamic world of impulse and dream, a hinterland of energy which has an independent existence of its own and laws of its own: laws which motivate all our thoughts and our actions. This energy expresses itself to us in our conscious life in a never-ending stream of images, running incessantly through our minds from the cradle to the grave, and perhaps beyond. The concept of the Unconscious has profoundly influenced the intellectual life of our day.[158]

Although Jones was aware that playwrights produced work that explored this sort of territory, he similarly thought that there was a more important medium through which to explore man's unconscious life.

In his lecture tours of the 1940s he imagined that the theatre of the future would incorporate filmed images. The medium of film, he recognised, was able to provide different kinds of images from the physical stage; ones that created essentially subjective 'images of life'. He drew a distinction between a given actor appearing on the stage and also on screen: 'Each self has its own reality, but the one is objective and the other is subjective.' He imagined that the theatre of the future would involve the co-presence of live actors and screened images in a 'simultaneous expression of the two sides of our nature'.[159] The live element would provide an objective, outer expression of the action; the screen images would show their inner life or their dreams. Although Jones did not put any of his ideas into action, his writing on the potential of combining the media of film and theatre constitutes some of the earliest theorisation of multi-media theatre.[160]

Just as Craig's and Appia's respective visions embraced the notion of the actor and the setting as fused elements of production, so too did Jones further this sort of thinking in terms of the setting becoming an 'environment' in which the actor operated. It needs to be appreciated that Jones' concern for the setting as an environment in which the actor 'lived' existed long before other concerns for environmental theatre and in advance of social and political concerns for the environment. Conceptually speaking, Jones' vision that 'Players act in a setting, not against it' provided a formalisation that was to become highly significant in the creative endeavours of scenic designers.

> 9   One thing that is wrong, so far as you and I are concerned, is that we think of the various branches of the theatre as separate entities. We think of a play as a manuscript and not as theatre. Yes, we do! We think of a stage setting as a set and not as theatre. We think of lighting in terms of a remarkable electric console and not in terms of theatre. We cannot seem to grasp the conception that all these departments, perhaps I should have said compartments, of the theatre are organic parts of an organic whole, not a set of commissions efficiently carried out; but a nervous, temperamental, vibrating, living whole.
> Robert Edmond Jones in Delbert Unruh (ed.), *Towards a New Theatre: The Lectures of Robert Edmond Jones*, p. 42

Jones made a number of emotional and subjective observations about his expectations of theatre. One such consideration was 'When I go to the theatre, I want to get an eyeful. Why not? I do not want to have a look at one of the so-called "suggestive" settings, in which a single Gothic column is made to do duty for a cathedral.'[161] Effectively, Jones wanted to create, or have created for him, a feast for the eyes. But in requiring this he wanted the feast to stimulate the imagination and not simply to contextualise it. Although the 'suggestive' setting is capable of stimulating audience response, such representation was not enough for Jones.

Another simple yet profound observation is summed up by the following statement: 'as far as I am concerned … I have come to the theatre to see a play, not to see the work done on a play'.[162] This statement registers a clear imaginative difference between the two possibilities. He wanted to see the setting prepared exclusively for the audience's imagination and then be completed by it. He did not want to see the mechanism by which the setting was created or presented. Jones' careful and accurate use of language was very important in communicating the kinds of distinctions that he made. Another important difference concerned what was seen by the audience. Jones required that the audience should see an image and not a picture. By this distinction he alludes to the difference between active and passive content. In Jones' terms the former was active by virtue of its capacity to convey a feeling or an evocation. On the other hand, he considered the picture to be static and fixed. Again, in Jones' terms it was the actor who promoted appropriate kinetic qualities that took over from the designer: 'The sole aim of the arts of scene designing [is to] enhance the natural powers of the actor.'[163]

So many of Jones' observations, requirements and stipulations have found their way into the scenic designer's practice that they now seem commonplace and taken for granted. One of the most telling observations by Jones on the state of theatre during his time, and for that matter, any time, is the notion that theatre had become 'harmless'. Could there be a more powerful indictment of the failings of theatre?

Despite the clarity with which Jones expressed his views and ambitions for the theatre, his historical assumptions were often misguided in the way that he romanticised an imagined historical world.

Jo Mielziner (1901–1976)

The majority of practitioners who have been identified here as pioneers of scenography have worked outside the mainstream of conventional theatre. They have experimented with and proposed new hybrid forms of theatre, often within the context of laboratory-type conditions. Economic pressures placed upon commercial theatre have frequently stifled developments in scenography. Although commercial theatre has sometimes relied on the spectacular developments of design and technology, this has rarely led to any reappraisal of the role and impact of scenography. However, Jo Mielziner was an extremely successful and highly regarded designer in the commercial theatre of America, both before and after the Second World War, and his work was a significant influence in its contribution to an understanding of scenography.

He was committed to the idea that design should arise not only from understanding the play but also from an understanding of performance and the means of production surrounding that performance. He was able to establish that stage design was part of the performance and that it not only translated the play into a visual language, but that it also offered a complementary perspective. In comparison with other pioneers featured here his work was modest and subtle, yet it revealed the potential for design to penetrate a theatrical text and produce a scenographic dramaturgy which was as potent as the script.

10 I confess my unbounded delight in my early days at seeing my settings revealed by glamorous stage lighting after they were completed at dress-rehearsal time. I almost resented the prospect of the actors standing between my picture and the admiring audience! I eventually overcame … this childish blindness to the true values of the theatre; I finally recognized that in a collaborative art each part is dependent on the whole. As an artist painting my first sketch for a setting, I am master of that expression, but its value to the final result comes form submitting myself and my talents to the collaborative effort.
Jo Mielziner, *Designing for the Theatre*, pp. 6–7

14. Jo Mielziner, *Winterset*, by Maxwell Anderson. Director G. McClintic, Martin Beck Theater, New York, 1935

Mielziner's design for the opening scene of *Winterset* (1935), which was set underneath the Brooklyn Bridge, offered an impression of the towering supports of the bridge and the night sky beyond. This has been described as a metaphor for hope and faith. Mielziner described it in this way: 'The backdrop showing the thrust of the bridge span disappearing into the murk of the river mist was designed to suggest a promise of something dramatic to come – abstracted enough to be provocative, realistic enough to provide immediate recognition of the locale.'[164] (Figure 14.) For some, the poetic realism of the setting was more effective than the play. The original stage directions had stipulated a realistic setting of the river bank and the shabbiness and paraphernalia that went with it, but Mielziner created 'a setting of great majesty and beauty that is full of strength and alive with a poetry of its own. It is as simple, direct and impressive as one wishes the play were.'[165]

However, his work with Tennessee Williams represented a more productive exchange of scenographic vision and dramaturgical intention. His design for *The Glass Menagerie* used gauze (scrim) walls to dissolve one location into another and to suggest movement between reality and memory, dream and illusion. Mielziner's impulse was to 'design with an eraser'[166] and the more overt visual imagery which Williams had envisaged was omitted, leaving a more subtle and eloquent scenography:

For perhaps the first time Mielziner is able to fully demonstrate scenography as the expression of a psychological construct which, whilst quoting extant architectural forms renders those forms mutable and ambiguous. Mielziner presents permanence and solidity as temporary and illusionistic, as unstable as the psychology of Williams' characters.[167]

In response to Williams' text of *A Streetcar Named Desire*, Mielziner envisaged a combination of realistic elements and expressionistic images to reflect the perspectives of the key protagonists, Stanley and Blanche. Williams was, in turn, influenced by Mielziner's early sketches for the design in his development of the final version of the text. In the 1947 premiere, a key image was a dilapidated iron spiral staircase, which acted not only as a reference to the New Orleans apartment location and Stella's 'tenuous and temporary escape' but also as a suggestive metaphor for Blanche's descent into madness.[168] The gauze walls painted with distorted architectural detail of the Kowalski apartment could dissolve, through changes in lighting, to reveal other present and past locations of the play. The combination of real objects (worn rugs, a broken armchair, a battered fridge) and suggestive, evocative surroundings was considered to be sordid, ugly, dreamlike and glorious.[169] Lighting changes permitted fluid shifts from everyday reality to memory and nightmare. Mielziner described the effect of the scenography by saying:

> Throughout the play the brooding atmosphere is like an impressionistic X-ray. We are always conscious of the skeleton of this house of terror, even though we have peripheral impressions … This kind of designing is the most fascinating of all designing for the theatre. It deals in form that is transparent, in space that is limited but has the illusion of infinity, in light that is ever changing in quality and in color.[170]

Mielziner's designs also became part of the visual dramaturgy of Arthur Miller's *Death of a Salesman*. His setting fused with the text. The stage directions in the published text, derived from Mielziner's designs for the original 1949 production, marked the scenographical and dramaturgical intersection of their collaboration. The opening directions functioned as 'a kind of prose-poem',[171] and showed how the scenography was the result of a dynamic relationship between word and image.[172]

11   I prepared about twenty sketches for *Death of a Salesman*. I decided to dispense with color at this time because it was more important to get the mood – the light and dark – and the feeling of isolation that lighting only a small segment of the setting would evoke … I was careful to start each sketch with the figures of Willy Loman, the Salesman, or his sons, or his wife, not only to intensify the dramatic

mood of the sketch, but to control the interrelation of all the elements of the stage picture including the all-important human figure.
Jo Mielziner, *Designing for the Theatre*, p. 31

Mielziner used a skeletal Loman house hemmed in by impressionistic render-ings of apartments and buildings as the central image. But this image frequently dissolved into one of the house as it existed in Willy Loman's memory. The house was surrounded by trees and bathed in sunlight. Combination of light and gauze walls once again provided a means of shifting from the present to the past and back again. The mixture of real objects and the fluid nature of the surroundings embodied one of the central concerns of the play: the tension between reality and dream.[173] Lighting facilitated spatial fluidity and also worked through immediate sensory experience by using soft amber light to suggest the idealism of the past and a reddish orange glow to infiltrate scenes set in the present. Such lighting gradations permitted spatial, temporal, and the-matic statements to occupy the stage simultaneously. This approach also permitted the creation of inner visions of the characters.[174] Mielziner himself recognised the influence of Freudian thinking on that of modernist playwrights in their depiction of inner human characteristics and saw this as a challenge to designers to create stage worlds of many dimensions.[175]

Tadeusz Kantor (1915–1990)

The scenography of Tadeusz Kantor was part of a lifelong project in attempts to reconcile reality and art through theatre. He studied painting and stage design in the 1930s in Krakow, Poland, and his art work, which included paintings, drawings, collages, emballages and happenings, was exhibited widely in Europe.[176] But as well as establishing himself as an artist he also worked as a theatre designer. Although he worked on the conventional stage, it is his work with his own company, Cricot 2, where he was designer, director and performer, that best demonstrates his potential for scenography. This work represents the development of new thinking about theatre form. His approach to theatre, as a visual artist, focused on the environment of performance, that is, the organisation of space and the nature of things within space. This concern determined the foundation of Kantor's theatrical principles. Such principles were articulated through performances by Cricot 2, who performed from 1955 to 1990, and through Kantor's own essays and manifestos. He considered it was the duty of all committed artists to keep records of their processes of develop-ment. The notes, essays and manifestos which he produced reflect his own continuous modifications and reshaped theories. These notes are often written in a form that approaches poetry, and that conveys a vivid sense of the realisation of his ideas. His practice was to make notes as he worked. The work itself was often intuitive and open to chance or coincidence. In an interview in 1985 he said that it was only with the passing of time and through receiving meaningful feedback that he understood what he had created.[177] From the start, he was drawn to ideas which challenged or dismantled naturalist traditions of presentation in theatre. He characterises contemporary mainstream theatre thus:

> A plain wall extends behind the blue sky. Ropes, cables, lights, lifts, and iron platforms 'operate' above the green crown of trees and behind the marble walls of the palaces. The whole of this inferno of machinery, worked by the hands of the theatrical proletariat, moves the wheels of the stage, which creates the thin veil of illusion that is cast on the audience's eyes.[178]

This suggests a rejection of the practice of naturalism on political as well as aesthetic grounds, and it reflects a line of thought which connects with the approach of Meyerhold and other examples of Constructivist staging in Soviet Russia. There are also connections to Brecht's ideas about the need for aesthetic distance. When viewed from backstage, the 'mirages' of the stage were seen to be artificial, insubstantial and made of flimsy materials such as papier-mâché.[179] Kantor, most importantly, was driven to find forms of theatre that were expressions of the essence of reality and not imitations.

His early work was created against a background of the aftermath of the Second World War and Stalinist control of Poland. The oppositional and experimental nature of his theatre meant that he came into conflict with the authorities. His 1944 production of *The Return of Odysseus*, which he designed and directed, used the ancient Greek myth of Odysseus as a metaphor for the war and occupation of Poland by the Nazis. It was performed despite a ban on clandestine theatre. Kantor recalled 'The situation was one of encirclement. The Germans could enter at any moment and the audience was mad with anxiety.'[180] In 1949 his professorship at the Academy of Fine Arts in Krakow was revoked and for several years his paintings could only be exhibited in secret.[181] Later, when he was permitted to travel, exhibit and perform more freely, he saw himself as having something approaching outlaw status. He was the autonomous artist whose self-identified role was to challenge the establishment and its conventional practices of theatre.[182]

Although the influence of Russian Constructivism on the stage and the work of the Bauhaus excited him, his experience of the Second World War and the conditions of the German occupation of Poland drove him to reconsider appropriate modes of artistic expression. In his early work, he had, like Kasimir Malevich, Wassily Kandinsky and Oskar Schlemmer, experimented with pure, abstract form as a means of transcending everyday reality and revealing under-lying or universal truths.[183] But while working on *The Return of Odysseus* he came to realise that the aesthetic principles of modernist art and abstraction were not adequate as a means of expressing the true horror of war. Later he explained that 'Bestiality, brought to the fore by this war, was too alien to this pure idea … Realness was stronger.'[184] Kantor began to work towards a philosophy of theatre which embraced the most prosaic, useless objects, actions and situations as a means of releasing the imagination and trans-forming audience perceptions. *The Return of Odysseus* was staged not in a theatre, but in a room of a bombed-out building. Kantor's own description of this room and the performance which took place demonstrates how he con-ceived the room, and the things within it. The room was a most powerful means of connecting the mythological Odysseus with contemporary reality. Kantor imagined Odysseus as a German soldier in a waiting room at Krakow station:

> The room was destroyed. There was war and there were thousands of such rooms. They looked alike: bare bricks stared from behind a coat of paint, plaster was hanging from the ceiling, boards were missing in the floor, abandoned parcels were covered with dust (they would be used as the auditorium), debris was scattered around, plain boards reminiscent of the deck of a sailing ship were discarded at the horizon of this decayed décor, a gun barrel was resting on a heap of iron scrap, a military loudspeaker was hanging from a rusty metal rope. The bent figure of a helmeted soldier wearing a faded overcoat stood against the wall. On this day, June 6, 1944, he became a part of this room.[185]

The objects in the room were found by Kantor and the cast. They also included a wheel smeared with mud, a rotten plank and a kitchen chair. The act of finding, choosing and bringing these discarded and worthless chunks of reality to the room was considered to be an important part of the process of the production.[186] Items with little obvious value or purpose or things consid-ered to be rubbish in everyday life can, in theatre, become the means by which the imagination of the audience is activated. For Kantor, 'the Reality of the Lowest Rank' was that the more despised or contemptible the object, the greater the potential for it to transcend its everyday status and reflect the essence of life rather than a stylised, aestheticised version of reality often found in the theatre.[187]

In the Cricot 2 productions, Kantor used discarded objects and put them to new uses. In the first production, *The Cuttlefish* (1956), a hospital stretcher stood in for a comfortable couch, and a musty coffin was used as a conference table at the meeting of high-ranking officials who congregated to pass judgement on the fates of art and culture. In *The Country House* (1961) costumes were created by 'tearing apart, pulling apart, sewing, mending, burning, bleaching, soiling, smearing, wearing out, fading' in order to move beyond the decorative function of clothes and expose underlying conditions.[188]

Kantor found the term 'prop' (or stage property) offensive, as it suggested a position subordinate to the actor. He accorded objects the same potential power to communicate as actors. Objects were intended to resonate with or compete with the other objects and performers in the imagination of audience members. The concept of the 'object-actor' or the 'bio-object' was developed in performance through objects which were a physical extension of the actor. Actors performed with objects which both defined the character or situation and conditioned what the actor did. For example, in *Dainty Shapes and Hairy Apes* (1973) bio-objects included a Hanged Man with his gallows and a Bigot with her church pew and rosary.[189] Actors performed within the confines of or in spite of the objects. His description of another character from the same production conveys the sense of image as a confrontation between the actor and the object:

> *A man with a wooden board on his back*
> who is on the verge of insanity
> is
> an unusual case of absurd anatomy:
> being completely focused within
> the objectlike growth
> on his body,
> he is like a martyr crucified
> on himself.[190]

The concept of the 'bio-object' and the tension which was set up between actor and object has been likened to conventions of circus where there is often a symbiotic relationship between performers and objects. Without actors those objects would be incapable of doing anything. The symbiosis meant that the actors were 'conditioned' by the objects and in turn 'their roles and activities derived from them'.[191] (Figure 15.)

The Dead Class (1975) drew on Kantor's memories of childhood. In a performance space consisting of worn school benches, the pupils were 'old people', who represented the dead 'come to life' as if from an old photograph. They carried mannequins on their backs. These wax figures of children represented memories of childhood. The multiple images of death and memory which these 'bio-objects' created enabled Kantor to conceive of the performance

15. Tadeusz Kantor, a 'bio-object' from *Wielopole, Wielopole*, Cricot 2
Theatre, 1980

as a kind of séance where ghosts and memories from different times and
dimensions were encountered.[192] (Figure 16.)

Kantor disregarded illusion in the theatre. He also jettisoned naturalism as
delivered by the actor. He viewed it as 'naïve pretence' and 'exulted manner-
ism'.[193] Rather than embodying characters with apparent psychological depth
and interpretive nuances, Kantor's actors were required to be present as
themselves on stage, performing within the constraints of other elements

16. Tadeusz Kantor, *The Dead Class*, Krzysztofory Gallery, Krakow, 1975

which might include objects or the text. Acting was to be surreptitious and economic. His performers, who were not usually trained actors, often performed under duress, constrained by setting and objects within it. In *The Madman and the Nun* (1963) a 'death machine' made of folding chairs upset and disrupted the action. The actors were made to fight for stage space as the 'machine' pushed and threatened them. It was made physically impossible for the actors to employ illusionistic means to present lines and characters since most of their energy was diverted into action with the machine. Lines of text were interrupted and/or repeated. Physically and emotionally actors were increasingly unable to mask their real personalities, their frustration, their exhaustion and their neurosis.[194] The 1961 Cricot 2 production of Witkiewicz's *The Country House* used a wardrobe in place of the country house setting that the stage directions required. The decrepit wardrobe was surrounded by chaotically scattered stools, parcels and desks.[195] At the beginning of the performance the doors of the wardrobe burst open and actors and more parcels fell out. The wardrobe had a womb-like function and from within its 'suffocating and humid atmosphere, the dreams are unfolded, the nightmares are born'.[196] Kantor describes action from Act Three:

> The wardrobe is open.
> The husband and two lovers, the Steward of the estate and the Poet, of the deceased wife

are hanging in the wardrobe like clothes on hangers.
They are swinging, losing balance,
and bouncing into one another.
They are reading the diaries of the Deceased.
The revealed information, the most intimate details,
makes the three rivals
euphoric,
satisfied, desperate,
and furious.
These emotions are manifested
openly
with an increasing excitement.
The lovers, who are imprisoned in the wardrobe,
hanging on the hangers, are
spinning around,
bumping into each other,
and hanging motionless.[197]

Kantor's consideration of space as an active and influential force lay at the centre of his work. In both his painting and his theatre, space was seen as a dynamic agent giving birth to forms. Rather than considering space as a passive receptacle, Kantor saw the tension between objects and the space in which they were held. Space, charged with energy, moulds the objects within it. As a painter, Kantor understood that the act of creating images on canvas was as much about the space between forms as it was about the forms themselves. This principle was applied to his theatre and explains, in part, why actors and objects are conceived as being equals or competitors within space. In Kantor's own words:

I can feel its pulsating rhythm.
Space,
which does not have an exit or boundary;
which is receding, disappearing,
or approaching omnidirectionally with changing velocity;
it is dispersed in all directions: to the sides, to the middle;
it ascends, caves in,
spins on the vertical, horizontal, diagonal axis ....
It is not afraid to burst into an enclosed shape,
defuse it with a sudden jerking movement,
deform its shape ....
Figures and objects become the function of space
and its mutability.[198]

Josef Svoboda (1920–2002)

Although Svoboda did not invent the word 'scenography' he did conceptualise the term to refer to the means by which three-dimensional actualisation of theatre in performance is achieved. Svoboda's notions of scenography have provided a basis upon which other scenographers, designers, directors and performers have been able to build. His thinking and vision for the theatre were every bit as dynamic as Craig's and Appia's. Such dynamism arose out of the development of working principles in the course of production. He did not deliver his conclusions as a theorist; his extensive and widely acclaimed practice has served to demonstrate his ideas and further the development of scenography perhaps more than any other of the pioneers represented here.

Svoboda can be seen to have taken on several of the concepts articulated by earlier pioneers and realised them more fully. Through his willingness to experiment with a wide range of materials and technologies, Svoboda was able to extend Appia's notion of expressive light and realise Craig's vision of a plastic, kinetic stage space. His work also reflects Schlemmer's concern for precision and control of the use of space.[199] But Svoboda's notions of space did not simply embrace the stage space; they also included audience space in his creative calculations. He says: 'scenography also implies a handling of total production space, which means not only the space of the stage but also the auditorium in terms of the demands of a given production'.[200] So, it is within the three-dimensional context that Svoboda's theatrical vision existed. He was not concerned with 'decorating' the stage but with creating a three-dimensional context in which the agreed concept of the work could be synthesised and communicated.

Anything and everything was useful in building towards synthesis of intention and realisation. In 1947 he wrote: 'We don't promote any artistic discipline, that is painting, architecture, sculpture, as the central one. We synthesize – that is, we choose the artistic principle that corresponds to our theatrical concept … Priority on the stage belongs to the theatrician and only then to the designer or director.'[201] In prioritising the theatrical event over traditional expectations of production roles, he was prepared to start from the empty theatre space and introduce only what was necessary for the particular production. A concept for a production of *Faust*, for example, might spring from the impetus to distinguish between the dual identity of Faust's servant and Mephistopheles and suggest a huge, empty room and 'a floor designed to produce either a heavy hollow sound of steps or else absolutely no noise'. Svoboda imagined the theatrical effect: 'The servant walks to the door, and we hear the hollow sound of his steps in the vast room. He turns just as he reaches the door, and starts back – and suddenly – silence! – and we know, instantly, that this is the devil.'[202] Often, what was remarkable in Svoboda's scenography was the use of light. Lighting was a critical element used by Svoboda to create kinetic dynamism in otherwise static contexts. Light was not simply used to illuminate the scene but to condition it and provide energy to its dynamic unfolding. Similarly, lighting was not intended to supplant scenery: 'But we want to attempt composing individual, separate, and distinctive visual perceptions into a new total-image according to a given theme: to convey a given intention by a composition of images, their inter-relationship, their temporal and spatial rhythm.'[203]

Perhaps the most important and distinctive form of lighting developed by Svoboda was that produced by low-voltage lighting units. These units produce beams of near-parallel white light that are more intense and manipulable than those produced by conventional lanterns. Placed in strips or battens, these lanterns could create 'curtains' of light which defined and brought atmosphere to the stage space. In *The Seagull* (1960) these lighting strips, placed behind fragments of tree branches, evoked the feeling of light and heat in a summer garden.[204] Spatial dimension was achieved by placing the lighting units in different positions of three-dimensional depth. The effect of 'light-as-substance'[205] came about as the light beams picked up dust and other impurities in the atmosphere of the theatre. In other later productions, Svoboda also sprayed ionised droplets of water into the stage atmosphere to create a thicker haze against which the light beams could be seen as an 'insubstantial solidity'. This technique was memorably seen in *Tristan und Isolde* (1967) where a hollow column of light was achieved.[206] (Figure 17.)

Some of the most striking visual conditions to be achieved through low-voltage lighting were created for the 1969 Hamburg production of *Sicilian Vespers*. By this time, low-voltage techniques had improved and their effect upon a stage environment reminiscent of those sloping planes of stairs created by Craig and Appia were reworked to produce a new scenographic dimension:

> The scenography of the production was an example of pure architecture: flights of steps that are divided into sections that move laterally, supplemented by circular walls that rotate into the scenic area along with the movement of the stairs. But the main element was the diffuse light that created a kind of foggy ambience for the steamy Sicilian scene, the broiling sun and sweltering climate. The effect was that of light as substance, light materialized, resulting from the special new lighting instruments that we designed. I think that we achieved a new level of

17. Josef Svoboda, *Tristan und Isolde*, by Richard Wagner. Director C. H. Drese, Hesse State Theatre, Wiesbaden, 1967

lighting technique. And I think that Appia and Craig, especially, would have marvelled at the outcome.[207]

These lighting innovations enabled Svoboda to use light as though it were a plastic material; stage space could be demarcated and divided by light but in a way which was much more agile and subtle than more resistant materials. In light, seemingly solid forms could be created and then dissolved. In 1962 Svoboda worked on a production of a play by Milan Kundera, *Majitelé Klíčů* (Owner of the Keys) with the director Otomar Krejča. The action of the play required two separate interiors and the physicalisation of a number of visions perceived by the principal protagonist. The two interior locations and their scenes were played on and around two silently moveable platforms and the space in which the visions were presented was explained by Krejča:

> We became especially attracted to the idea of a hollow pyramid. Its base, formed by the portal of the stage, would face the audience, and its peak would be at some infinite point. But in the Tyl theatre the 'infinite' is a few meters from the curtain line. And what would the hollow pyramid be made of? ... And so we arrived at a pyramid that, according to need, would or wouldn't exist. It would be made of *light* ... like living matter,

which can be born before our eyes ... in which everything will seem more real than reality.'[208]

Upon withdrawal from view of the two platforms the whole stage space became useable for the demarcations of the visions. Light from units placed above the proscenium arch fell onto mirrors. The effect was to intensify the whole arrangement with rebounding 'threads' of light: 'The result is the impenetrably bordered, sharply defined, unreal space of a pyramid created by light.'[209] Here, Svoboda's concern was to bind scenography to the unfolding dramatic action. The combination of moving platforms and light allowed the spectator to experience the materialisation and subsequent fading away of spaces to achieve 'a sense of their diminution and enlargement, not only for the sake of the vision interludes but primarily for the sake of the interrelation of the action transpiring on both acting platforms'.[210]

Svoboda's capacity for experimentation with light was aided by his work on national exhibitions, particularly the World Exposition of 1958 in Brussels where Svoboda designed the presentation in the Czechoslovakian pavilion. The funding for these projects was far more generous than any theatre production and provided the opportunity for Svoboda to experiment with techniques which were later to be adapted for the stage. Despite the banal theme of Expo 58 (one day in Czechoslovakia), Svoboda used innovative projection techniques to present 'polyphonic composition of multiple images and high-fidelity sound'.[211] He called this technique 'Polyekran'.

The technique consists of projected images that exist as self-contained images; they do not interact with other live features. They do, however, form a composition where individually projected images are shaped, organised and timed in space in order to interrelate to produce a visual theatrical statement. Although the content of the projected images may be of people or objects, the relationships that may be developed need not be concrete ones. The technique creates an opportunity to make statements that may be reinforced by other images or juxtaposed to produce contrast, irony or surrealism. The scenographer is able to use such techniques with simplicity or complexity according to the desired theatrical statement. The Brussels event made use of eight differently sized screens suspended at angles to the viewer. Eight slide and film projectors were controlled and synchronised by tape on which was recorded stereophonic sound. For Expo 67 in Montreal, Svoboda developed 'Polyvison' and 'Diapolyekran'. Both techniques were developments from the Brussels experience. Polyvision made use of a variety of surfaces, such as rotating cubes and prisms, onto which images could be projected. Mirrors were incorporated to heighten the kinetic effect. Diapolyekran used 'a mosaic wall' of 112 cubes

18. Josef Svoboda, *The Birth of the World: Diapolyekran*. Director Emil
Radok, Expo 67, Montreal, 1967

which could receive projection. The flat surface of the wall was able to be
broken up by individual cubes moving forwards or backwards.[212] (Figure 18.)
Thus, the overall screen could become more three-dimensional. This capacity
was further developed by varying the content of each projection. These experiments with multiple and simultaneous projections, projection surfaces, mirrors
and kinetic effects all found their way into subsequent scenographies. On
the stage, these techniques were harnessed to the dramatic impetus of the
production. Svoboda used them to considerable organic purpose in a production of Josef Topol's *Their Day* in October 1959. The application of these
techniques in this production may serve as a representative example of the
way that such processes have been used. The play was concerned with the
hopes and disillusion of contemporary Czechoslovakian youth and was
episodic in its nature. Thus, these techniques were highly suitable in promot-
ing the purpose of the work. Here, nine moveable screens that were angled
to the viewer and came and went in timed sequence were projected upon
by eighteen slide projectors and three film projectors. The combination
of angled screens, timed and static images, filmed projections, lighting

and action by performers conditioned the dynamic of the production. Svoboda, in translation, says: 'here we wanted changes in the dimensions of space as well as rapid shifts of scene. Because we could project various images at various angles, we could create space and spatial relations at will.'[213] He further described development of the work that indicated its kinetic value:

> we projected whole sections of the city the full width of the stage, onto the black velour that enclosed the stage, the images thereby being invisible. But then a traveling screen picks up different parts of the projected image as a character walks along, for instance a row of billboards as he paces back and forth while waiting for someone. The technique is the obverse of film panning; it is as if you were looking through a window at part of your environment, and then the window frame started to move laterally, revealing new surroundings. In another scene, a juxtaposition of projected images creates a special emotive composition. We could use all the screens or only one, not merely to describe a locale, but to establish different relations. The result is tremendous selectivity that becomes poetic. Interiors, for example, had typical domestic details projected, but in fragmented, distorted perspectives, to eliminate any merely naturalistic illustration. Actors were seen in one perspective, projections frequently in another. Or these scenes could also disappear and suddenly we'd have night, moon, and clouds; that is, the stage would be empty except for two people and one screen. The result is real psycho-plastic space created by transforming the dimensions of space in response to the nature of the scene.[214]

At Expo 58, Svoboda was also co-creator of 'Laterna Magika'. This technique of combining live action with projected filmed material proved hugely popular and Svoboda founded the Laterna Magika Theatre in Prague in 1973 where he was Artistic Director until 2002.[215]

Here projected images are deliberately conceived to interact, promote, define or qualify motion/movement from actors or other environmental features. With this sort of technique it is possible to film the action and re-present it in different time, space and scale. It is possible for an actor to lead or initiate that which happens on the screen(s) and the reverse initiative is also possible. Equally, reinforcement or development of statement is possible through simultaneous 'real' and 'projected' action. Such interplay may be used to create and develop kinetic properties of a scene and further produce a dynamically living environment. Thus, it may be seen that this sort of technique represents a means of creating scenographic synthesis of a kind to which allusion has already been made. However, part of the resultant dynamic is created by the fact that the filmed subject matter needs to be filmed in advance of the performance. Filming the work prior to performance 'fixes' it in such a way

19. Josef Svoboda, *The Last Ones*, by Maxim Gorky. Director Alfréd Radok, Tyl National Theatre, Prague, 1966

that whatever the performer is able to do in respect of live performance must always relate to the fixed entity of the film. This relationship conditions the nature of the dynamic that may emerge and defines the hybrid relationship and its development as theatrical statement. In *The Last Ones* (1966), Svoboda used 'Laterna Magika' techniques to juxtapose projected images with live performers (in scale and in content) to achieve moments of 'symbolic parallel'. The material was deliberately unsettling, for example, while a performer's naked back was gently stroked with birch twigs a large image of a prisoner being whipped was projected. The aim was to set up 'a confrontation between the spectator's experience at the moment of performance with his experiences in the past, now awakened by the performance'.[216] (Figure 19.)

Alongside Svoboda's experimentation with light and projection, his concern for the kinetic qualities of the stage needs to be recognised. Several of the examples already discussed demonstrate Svoboda's concern for the evolution of scenography over the duration of the production. Such development was seen to be responsive to the dramatic action and was itself expressive. Many of Svoboda's designs incorporated mobile elements. For example, *Dalibor* (1964) used two massive rectangular towers placed off-centre on revolving platforms to provide an apparently infinite variety of spatial relationships. These changes in scene were often made to coincide with musical shifts and this, together with the scale of the setting, 'contributed to the power and magnitude of Smetana's music and the romantic tragedy of the libretto'.[217] However, Bablet points out that Svoboda over the course of his career became as interested in 'internal kinetics' as in physical movement of the stage.[218] Clearly use of light plays an important role here, as do materials which respond to light, such as mirrors and transparent and semi-transparent surfaces. The kinetic stage does not rely on machinery and obvious technology. Svoboda, writing in 1998, reflected that his 1968 production of *The Wedding* could not have been achieved with stage machinery. To accomplish the dreamlike distortion he required, he used glass walls placed diagonally on the stage. Depending on the light or on use of projection, these walls could function as mirrors, as screens or be rendered transparent. The interplay of these states was sufficient to create the fictional space of the play and the dramatic journey of the characters.[219] A key goal for Svoboda was to realise a 'psycho-plastic space', that is, a dramatic space which Svoboda described as 'elastic in its scope and alterable in its quality. It is a space only when it needs to be a space. It is a cheerful space if it needs to be cheerful.'[220] Despite Svoboda's reputation for extravagant and spectacular use of technology his aim was always to use the means at his disposal in order to achieve a 'transformable space that is maximally responsive to the ebb and flow, the psychic pulse of the dramatic action'.[221]

It has often been observed that the director's working problems are derived from the same root as those of the designer in that they both work from and to the same stimulus, namely, the play and its stated requirements; it is the expression and realisation of the potential solutions that exist in different forms – albeit ones that seek synthesis with each other. Thus, Svoboda was concerned to promote a symbiotic relationship between the work of the director and the designer: 'A good director is one who understands design, and a good scenographer can only be one who is also a director, at least in terms of his knowing the principles of blocking, movement, rhythms, and the expressive forces of the actor.'[222] This desired prerequisite embodies both conceptual and practical requirements. Clearly, realisation of the conceptual vision depends upon an understanding that drives the working relationship of the designer and director. Svoboda, however, understood the need for flexibility in attempts to mesh his thinking and interpretation with that of the director. He says: 'But I'm open to persuasion and ready to accept the director's interpretation as better than my own – or else to go along with a director who wants to play it by ear – but I must be able to *accept* it and *make it my own*, very much like an actor and the interpretation of his role, in relation to the director.'[223] It is perhaps because of Svoboda's relative success that he gained an unwarranted reputation for taking over the director's role and vision. Such aspersions are unfortunate for they inevitably misunderstand the conceptual vision of the total theatrical experience which was the central force driving Svoboda's thinking. The kind of vision sought by him transcended that to which a conventional theatre designer might aspire. In order to conceptually express this kind of vision he is quoted as saying: 'The scenographer must be in command of the theatre, its master.'[224] This kind of statement, often taken out of context, implies to some that he attempted to take over the role of the director. But here, the fundamental point may be missed; Svoboda was concerned with the total theatre experience and not simply its design.

His experience was mainly in creating scenographies for proscenium stages and he considered this 'the most theatrical space available'.[225] Unlike other pioneers he embraced the possibilities offered by this particular spatial arrangement: 'I never forget that a proscenium stage has a floor, a portal (that is, a proscenium arch), and ceiling, and these are its only real elements – this is also why I always use them as my starting point. In the understanding of these three realities lies the secret of dramatic and production space.'[226] He also embraced the division that it represented between 'those who watch' and 'those who perform'. Although he described an ideal 'atelier-theatre' which would be 'architectonically neutral' and permit new spatial relationships between audience and performers for each new production, he did not feel that he had exhausted the possibilities of stage formation. He was continually drawn to the challenge of the empty space of the stage.[227]

Robert Wilson (1941–)

Robert Wilson is an artist and director. His influence on the theatre has changed understanding of what contemporary theatre might be.[228] His theatre is one in which the visual and spatial elements are the primary text:

> Usually in the theatre the visual repeats the verbal. The visual takes second place to language. I don't think that way. For me the visual is not an afterthought, not an illustration of the text. It has equal importance. If it tells the same story as the words, why look? The visual must be so compelling that a deaf man would sit through the performance fascinated. Once in a while I let the visual align with the verbal, but usually not. Most directors begin by analyzing a text, and the visual follows from that interpretation. This naïve use of the visual code bores me. I always start with a visual form. In most theatre the eye is irrelevant. Not in mine. I think with my eyes.[229]

His interest in the articulation of space as an alternative mode of communication to the spoken text can be traced to his work of the 1960s when he taught children with special educational needs. He found that artistic expression and movement gave a voice to children who struggled to communicate in more conventional ways.

Wilson's friendship with Raymond Andrews, a deaf person, encouraged Wilson to think about two levels of perception: the exterior and the interior.[230] Wilson regarded the 'exterior screen' as the means of dealing with sensory information from the world around, while the 'interior screen' reflected dreams, imagination and intuition. Andrews' vivid drawings, his main means of communication, suggested that his perception of the outside world was filtered through this interior mode of seeing. His subtle and sophisticated body language led Wilson to conclude that he thought in visual signs and not in words.[231] *Deafman Glance* (1970) was based on Andrews' drawings with no spoken text. A monochrome prologue in which a mother-figure in a high-necked, black Victorian dress slowly and repeatedly performed a ritual of first feeding and then killing her children, gave way to a *trompe-l'oeil* 'magic forest' of tall slender birch trees which included a pink angel, a giant frog in a velvet smoking jacket and George Washington. The stagecraft was based on nineteenth-century painted flat canvases, but the imagery was a strange and surreal conglomeration of dreamlike visions which represented a child's attempts to come to terms with life and death. It is often said that Wilson's theatre is one consisting of images, but it is equally important to note how, over time, these images operate in relation to one another. Settings, lighting, costumes and objects do not provide a coherent or homogeneous environment for the performers. Instead, they offer a series of visual experiences which make it possible for meaningful images to coalesce. Hans-Thies Lehmann says that, in the place of dramatic action, Wilson has created a 'theatre of metamorphoses':

> He leads the viewer into the dreamland of transitions, ambiguities, and correspondences: a column of smoke may be the image of a continent; trees turn first into Corinthian columns, then columns turn into factory smoke-stacks. Triangles mutate into sails, then tents or mountains. Anything can change its size, as in Lewis Carroll's *Alice in Wonderland*, of which Wilson's theatre is often reminiscent.[232]

Christopher Knowles, born with severe brain damage and diagnosed as autistic, was also influential in developing Wilson's understanding of communication and perception. Knowles' approach to language was principally visual; he was interested in the structure, sound and materiality of language as much as its semantic value. The elaborate patterns and structures he created in his

20. Robert Wilson, *A Letter for Queen Victoria*. Director Robert Wilson, 1974

poetry formed the basis of *A Letter for Queen Victoria* (1974). The production deconstructed language in order to stretch and mould it, so that it became abstract, spatial and scenographic. Knowles' text was both spoken by performers and represented visually in the performance space.[233] (Figure 20.)

In more recent work with classic texts such as *Hamlet*, *King Lear*, *A Dream Play* and *Woyzeck*, Wilson has treated language as part of the composition of the scenographic whole, cutting or moving scenes, creating simultaneity, reassigning speeches and repeating sequences. Wilson's working method in the development and realisation of his theatre is based around the creation of visual storyboards which chart the way the stage space can shift and change through performance. These storyboards are a kind of script; but instead of dialogue, they describe shifts in terms of architectural space and structure.[234] Wilson explains it like this: 'When I make a play, I start with a form, even before I know the subject matter. I start with a visual structure, and in the form I know the content. The form tells me what to do. I begin to fill in the form. I can diagram all my plays.'[235] The Byrd Hoffman School of Byrds, established in 1968, consisted of a group of non-professional performers. These were Wilson's friends and associates and they were interested in trying to understand different forms of perception and communication.[236] Wilson had noticed, particularly through observing Raymond Andrews, that, alongside drawings, movement and body language were important modes of communication. The Byrds work-shops explored movements, gestures, sounds and articulation of space. They did this by focusing on the body in relation to other bodies through an intense awareness of movement and the body in space. The workshops 'put you in tune with your body, being conscious of your body and being conscious of other people without having any physical contact with them'.[237]

Wilson's scenography brings about a sensitivity to space and shifts in space for the audience by extending or slowing down action. This aims to 'induce a trance-like or hallucinatory state in the spectators so that they would begin to intermix interior and exterior perception'.[238] *The Life and Times of Sigmund Freud* (1969) lasted for four hours and consisted largely of non-verbal tableaux, inducing 'a new means of watching' which 'required a different sort of con-centration'. The movement was extremely slow, but Wilson insisted this was 'natural' time and not 'accelerated' time as is usually the case in theatre.

> 12   Time in the theatre is special. Time is plastic. We can stretch it out on stage until it becomes the time of the mind, the time of a pine tree moving gently in the wind or a cloud floating across the sky and slowly becoming a camel, then a bird. I'm the slowest director in the world. You must always give the audience space to see and time to think. The time of my theatre is the time of interior reflection.
> Robert Wilson in Arthur Holmberg, *The Theatre of Robert Wilson*, p. 162

It has been pointed out that Wilson's work is non-linear but not non-narrative.[239] Numerous fragments of narratives are present in layered and juxtaposed images and in temporal and spatial patterns of performances where carefully organised images interrogate and celebrate themselves. *Einstein on the Beach* (1976), an opera which was the result of collaboration with composer Philip Glass, is structured around permutations of the number 'three'. There were three main visual motifs for the nine main scenes – the train, the trial and the spaceship – and each was repeated three times from different perspectives and in different combinations. Images of human interaction with technology were juxtaposed, layered and repeated, creating 'a poetic meditation on Einstein' which culminated in a nuclear explosion.[240]

In *A Letter for Queen Victoria* it is the design itself which provides the structure of the performance. Wilson used vertical, horizontal and diagonal lines from the back of an envelope to establish the visual and spatial organ-isation of the performance. The performers were assisted by the clean and stiffened lines of their costumes and operated as elements of the scenographic composition rather than characters. The visual composition of the stage unfolded through movement, effecting gradual transformations of stage space, set, actors and objects. In *La Maladie de la Mort* (1991) (Figure 21),

21. Robert Wilson, *La Maladie de la Mort*, by Marguerite Dumas. Director Robert Wilson, Lausanne, 1996

Lucinda Childs appeared in a white column dress. As she moved slowly across the stage the white fabric of the dress stretched out behind her and divided the stage space with a narrow white triangle.

Wilson's images are symbolic but they also operate phenomenologically. Some of the visual references are to well-known images from history, art and popular culture. In the Cologne section of *the CIVIL warS* (1984), spectators were able to see Frederick the Great on his horse, a spaceship, Abraham Lincoln, two bears and Confederate soldiers preparing for battle. In some measure, the juxtaposition of these images brings about speculation on the part of the audience, but equally, meaning may be evoked through the materiality of the stage itself and the shifting emphasis and weight of abstract form. Richard Foreman draws attention to the 'sweet and powerful "placing" of various found and invented stage objects and actions' in Wilson's theatre.[241] It is not simply the selection of images and objects that is noteworthy, but the way they are made to interact through the stage composition. This composition is often informed by the use of organising principles which offer contrast and tension between the vertical and horizontal, light and dark, abstraction and detail. The composition and transformations that occur within it generate meaning but they also operate on the level of 'pure sensory pleasure'.[242]

Manipulation of light is central to Wilson's scenography. He says 'light is the most important part of theatre … how it reveals objects, how objects change when light changes, how light creates space, how space changes when light changes … I paint, I build, I compose with light. Light is a magic wand.'[243]

Light is used to shape and transform dramatic space and to pick out actors and objects with intensity. Wilson's orientation is that of a painter using light to focus attention upon details such as face, hand gestures and objects: 'The performers in Wilson's landscapes often seem to glow as if they had somehow absorbed the light into their bodies; the human figure itself becomes a luminous object.'[244] Light activates the stage space, rendering it expressive and dynamic. In *Orlando* (1989) the stage was divided horizontally into two zones through blue light and a black cloth. Orlando was 'recumbent on stage in a narrow horizontal band of blue light … The weight of the blackness pushes down on the narrow band of space … The colored planes are the forms that convey the expression of the images … Wilson plays with how viewers understand space as a communicating medium, to convey something about the character of the idea contained therein.'[245]

Wilson also uses light to create scenic elements and objects. The space ship in *Einstein on the Beach* used a wall of bars and circles of light against which the operatives were silhouetted, and in *When We Dead Awaken* the river was rendered as a 'ribbon of bright blue fluorescent light, cutting the stage diagonally'.[246]

Interaction and arrangement of all elements of the stage create a complex whole where a combination of performers, objects, light, sound and text or any one of these single elements might become significant. Wilson tells an actor to 'think of your body as a piece of living sculpture … The line you're drawing in space is not functional. It's formal … Think of your body as a spotlight. That light can be beamed in any direction.'[247] Stephen Di Benedetto compares Wilson to Tadeusz Kantor and his concept of the 'bio-object', where actors are considered to be objects and part of the visual and kinetic composition of the whole stage. An object, animated through light, can become a 'biological entity' and can itself perform.[248] In Kantor's case, scenographic objects often work in opposition to the performers, as they tend to do in Wilson's work. Wilson's use of performers can also be compared to Craig's ideas about the Über-marionette in the way that they are often subsumed under the overall composition of the stage and required to subordinate their movement and expression to it.

Viewers and critics have sometimes found Wilson's work frustrating. Irrational combinations of images, such as a scene in *Death Destruction & Detroit II* which features 'a Medieval knight, a blond woman in [a] red evening gown playing with a puppet, a black panther at large, an old man locked up in a steel cage', provoke interest and imagination in the viewer.[249] Such combinations can be troubling yet humorous, apparently arbitrary yet clearly presented within a highly controlled frame. Elements of production also operate independently from one another and, as in the Brechtian tradition, comment on one another, disrupt and open up gaps between each other. Sound, for example, does not illustrate the image, but is deliberately discordant. For the entrance of the two Irenes in *When We Dead Awaken*, the sound is that of 'a spoon squeaking against a coffee cup and the heaving of a pneumatic pump'.[250] In his work with composer and sound designer Hans Peter Kuhn, Wilson has explored the possibility of creating 'an acoustical space that can displace and subvert not only the image, but also the speaking subject'.[251] Microphones allow separation of voice from body so that it can then be manipulated and played back from different parts of the auditorium, layering live, recorded and manipulated sound and rendering the human voice as an autonomous object.[252] Kuhn says that the intention is to 'wake people up who spend their lives sleepwalking in a perceptual fog'.[253] As with the device of slowing down movement, the use of striking and apparently non-rational combinations of visual and acoustical images is intended to reawaken audience imagination.

Part 2

Processes of scenography

Chapter 3

Text as conditioner of image

The relationship between text and image in performance has been central to scenographic practice in the twentieth century. Although several pioneers actively resisted the play text as the leading component, others, such as Appia, Neher, Mielziner and Svoboda, explored ways in which scenography and text could be interdependent. This chapter sets out some of the ways in which this interdependence can be conceptualised. It is important to draw upon wider historical and contemporary examples to identify key conceptual frames which chart connections between play text and scenographic image in order to put some of the pioneering work into context.

Mielziner's collaborative work with playwrights Arthur Miller and Tennessee Williams involved close working relationships in which practical staging solutions and evocative scenographic environments emerged from the themes and images of the play text in such a way as to allow the words to resonate and take on additional layers of meaning. However, collaboration between designer and playwright does not always lead to aesthetic fusion; it may lead to a different kind of interaction. For instance, Caspar Neher worked closely with Brecht as the play text and scenography developed simultaneously. However, Neher's scenography developed in parallel with the text and was designed to comment on it. Text and scenography were required to share the political purpose of Brecht's productions and yet develop distinct and independent means of fusing their contribution.

Playwrights have also engaged with the stage image. Some have seized on the increasing capability of the stage to represent 'real' places whilst others have recognised the potential of strange and arresting images which work in more poetic ways. The work of Samuel Beckett is particularly relevant in this context because of the way in which his texts define the scenographic nature of his plays.

However, production methods typically separate the work of the playwright from the actual production of the play text. Classic and revived texts are often mounted in the light of prevailing staging conventions and with available technologies which are quite different from those originally envisaged by the playwright. Craig and Svoboda both explored the potential of stage technology to create spaces and images which arose from the play text but in many cases moved beyond the playwright's intentions or expectations. In some cases, scenography and its contribution to the resultant performance can be used to radically revise a text. Meyerhold's production of *The Magnanimous Cuckold* and Kantor's *The Return of Odysseus* both used scenographic means to prompt a reappraisal of older texts in the light of contemporary conditions, bringing new social and political insights through the scenographic environment.

Pioneers of scenography who have been considered so far have emerged from a background of practice dominated by three key concerns. In the first place, there is, in Western theatre, a longstanding distrust of the visual in relation to the text. Such scepticism can be traced back to Aristotle and implies that theatre images are only concerned with technical prowess and/or craft, and thus incapable of communicating dramaturgically or poetically. Secondly, the search for theatrical languages and modes of presentation which are both a reflection of and a provocation to the experience of daily life has led to the practical exploration of the relationship between text and image. Here, theatrical manifestations of both naturalism and expressionism have been particularly important. Thirdly, the continuing interest in restaging classic texts has placed a new emphasis on scenography as a means of interpretation and renewal.

Tension between the play text and the scenographic image

Perspectives contained in the histories of Western theatre staging have influenced the way scenography has been represented. The predominantly literary orientation towards theatre history has contributed to the visual aspect of theatre being overlooked and often denigrated.[1] Aristotle, for example, considered that the texts of ancient Greek theatre carried more artistic merit than their visual elements and claimed 'spectacle is attractive, but is very inartistic and is least germane to the art of poetry'. He clearly valued the text of the play over the performance of it and thought that 'the effect of tragedy is not dependent on performance and actors'.[2] Until the 1960s theatre scholarship concentrated on the literary text as an object of study. Although much more attention is now given to the performance of theatre and the analysis of the theatrical event, impact of visual and spatial elements at the point of performance has been given relatively little attention.[3] At the same time, studies of stage design have tended to concentrate on technological and aesthetic developments in isolation from performance as a whole.[4] Furthermore, there have been recurrent concerns over the artistic merit of scenographic intervention. As well as the sense that visual and technological aspects of performance may be less important than the text, there is a suggestion that they present a challenge or even a threat to both text and actor. The spectacular effects which scenography can produce might captivate and engage but they might also be seen as redolent of extravagance and waste: 'spectacle is also associated with cheap thrills, visual indulgence and the commercial pandering to an audience who were supposedly too unlettered to follow or understand fine dramatic poetry and diction'.[5]

Concerns such as these can be traced back to the quarrel between the poet Ben Jonson and the architect and designer Inigo Jones in seventeenth-century England. Jonson was contemptuous of claims that Jones' designs for the court masques upon which they collaborated were the artistic equal to Jonson's text. Jones had travelled to Italy and had become familiar with staging techniques of the Italian Renaissance stage. He used new techniques of scene painting, stage machinery and elaborate costumes to create visually extravagant productions which he felt did not merely illustrate the text but actually embodied and expressed the theme of the masque in visual form. He saw his designs as not merely a decorative addition to, or illustration of, Jonson's texts, but as capable of elevating the spectator's thoughts towards moral virtue; the aesthetic qualities of the design could lead to philosophical contemplation of beauty and virtue.[6]

Simultaneously, Jonson argued that the design was merely the 'body' of the masque, a transient stimulation of the senses, whereas his poetry was the 'soul', and the appeal to the intellect which would last long after the sensation of the performance had faded. He mocked the suggestion that painting and carpentry, the products of manual skills, could convey ideas of equal weight to those expressed in the text.[7]

In many ways, development of scenography has been motivated by an exploration of the relationships between the visual and the textual. In avant-garde work the text has been rejected altogether. Artaud and Schlemmer both imagined a concrete language of the stage where bodies, objects, sounds and costumes and their articulation in space replaced the conventional idea of a play text. In mainstream settings, explorations and developments have been more subtle and have often been enabled by technological innovations.

In European theatre, important changes gradually took place through the eighteenth and nineteenth centuries to provide catalysts for many experiments in and manifestos on scenographic practices in the twentieth century.

These developments can be seen largely as part of a concern to ensure that the stage provided an illusion of reality. Changes in design and technological function of theatre buildings and auditoria meant that the stage became increasingly separated from the auditorium and the audience. During the nineteenth century, the proscenium arch came to be widely used as a frame or opening to the world of the stage. Audiences were invited to view actors in scenes which strove to achieve the illusion of another world. These scenes were intended to be believable in their attention to detail and their fusion of all available scenographic means with the text and style of acting.[8] Rather than making use of stock scenery which showed generic settings, sets were designed specifically for individual productions and were often modelled on actual locations which incorporated authentic details through props and costumes. In the 1870s and 1880s, the Duke of Saxe-Meiningen's theatre company was renowned throughout Europe for productions which attempted to recreate historically accurate settings and costumes, through painstaking research and carefully orchestrated crowd scenes.[9] Increasingly, sophisticated lighting equipment meant that control, direction and intensity of light also helped to achieve lighting states which reflected the way natural light behaved and completed fusion of visual aspects of the stage. But maintaining a productive relationship between the visual and the textual was problematic. Henry Irving, actor, director and manager, was inspired by a pictorial approach to scenography. He was concerned less with historical accuracy and archaeological detail and more with the creation of scenographic environments which opened up the scope for actors. He also understood how lighting could be used in conjunction with three-dimensional pieces and painted cloths to create the effect of a three-dimensional painting. Although electric lighting had been introduced to English theatres by the time Irving became manager of the Lyceum Theatre in London (1878),[10] he continued to use gaslight for he considered it to be softer and more evocative than early forms of electric light. This softer light was capable of relatively crude dimming. It was also effective at blending three-dimensional structures with painted shadows on canvas backdrops and could be used to offer completion to pictorial compositions.[11] Such elaborate settings often demanded frequent pauses with interruption of perceived natural rhythms and pace of texts. The flow of action of texts, such as those of Shakespeare in performance, was thus compromised. Irving was prepared to cut lines to make the play fit the scenography. In the tomb scene of his 1882 production *of Romeo and Juliet* where Shakespeare's words indicate a seamless shift from outside the tomb to inside, he featured two separate and entire sets, one for the churchyard and another for inside the tomb:

> The first part ended after the death of Paris with Romeo breaking open
> the door of Capulet's vault, showing a flight of steps leading down.
> Then the curtain dropped and the spectators waited. When it rose again
> they saw one of the most formidable accomplishments of pictorial design
> yet created, Romeo now coming through the door he had broken open,
> but far upstage, at the top of a massive flight of steps leading down to
> Juliet's tomb.[12]

This monumental setting remained in place until the end and not only
dominated the physical space but reinterpreted the ending of the play. The
deaths of the two lovers became a more important statement than the effect of
their deaths on the rival families. This was the lasting image and Irving cut
most of the lines after the deaths in order to maintain integrity of the scene over
that of the text.

Scenographic implications in the play text

It is important to distinguish between the play text – the words to be spoken
and stage directions concerning action – and the performed text that includes
character, words spoken, space and action. Combinations of dialogue and
explicit stage directions in the play text indicate particular conditions for the
performed text. Play texts often require or imply locations, atmospheres and
arrangements of the stage space, and dictate use of specific objects or effects.
The social, psychological and emotional standing of the play's characters and
the nature of their relationships are determined by the play text. This information may be executed in developing ideas for costume, setting, lighting and
sound as part of the performed text.[13]

Explicit stage directions can give an insight into the playwright's ideas for the
performed text and can also reveal dominant staging conventions of the time
when the play was written. Additionally, plays are often not published until they
have been produced and then they reflect the scenography that was employed at
the first production of the play, as in the case of Miller's *Death of a Salesman*.

Extremely detailed stage directions and notes on characters can appear to
offer readymade scenographic solutions. Sam Shepard's plays, for example,
give instructions for all aspects of the scenography. In stage directions for *True
West* (1981) he has a precise idea of the location of the play: 'about forty miles
east of Los Angeles'. He includes details of the exact layout, style and content of
the kitchen setting. Costumes include: 'dark blue baggy suit pants from the
Salvation Army, pink suede belt, pointed black forties dress-shoes scuffed up'
and the precise nature of sound. He also notes that:

> The set should be constructed realistically with no attempt to distort its dimensions, shapes, objects, or colors. No objects should be introduced which might draw special attention to themselves other than the props demanded by the script. If a stylistic 'concept' is grafted onto the set design it will only serve to confuse the evolution of the characters' situation, which is the most important focus of the play.[14]

Other playwrights include scenographic requirements as part of the play text. Caryl Churchill's *Far Away* (2000) offers a dystopian view of a world where brutality and division is expressed through seemingly benign acts: two hat makers construct strange and exotic hats in grim and repressive conditions for an unseen and cruel regime. The full impact of the hats is revealed in a parade where brutalised prisoners wear the hats on the way to their execution. Each new hat is more insanely decorative and preposterous than the one before. The audience watches as the crafting of beautiful materials is subverted into things that are unbalanced and ugly. The hats make palpable the full extent of the collapse of social order in a way that is truly shocking. Una Chaudhuri's review of the 2002 production by the New York Theatre Workshop, designed by Ian MacNeil, describes it like this:

> The hats of *Far Away* manage to be, grimly, both dislocational and marvelous … Colossal creations of grotesque proportions, bizarre shapes and riotous colors, they silently scream out the horror that results when aesthetics loses all concern for the material reality from which it works. As the two characters work steadily and diligently, assembling their wild concoctions, the seduction of pure form is palpable, distracting us from the bleak sweat-shop they work in, just as their preoccupation with the particulars of their employment seems to distract them from the brutality of the system they serve. There could hardly be a more graphic rendering of a social contract in tatters, a world where art and labor have been turned into weapons of domination and alienation.[15]

Perhaps the most scenographically inventive playwright, Samuel Beckett has concerned himself with space and image to the extent that words and scenography are inextricably intertwined from the start of the play. Beckett's concern is with staging plays and not just the text on the page. The operation of scenographic elements, particularly spatial ones, is deliberately mobilised by Beckett's texts. Stage directions and descriptions of the settings of his plays are precise and the objects on the stage are seen to be as fundamental to the text as the words given to the characters. For him, use of stage space is a primary element in dramatic construction.[16] In *Endgame* (1958), the particular arrangement of two small high windows is an essential part of the whole.

Clov's repeated struggle to report on the world outside by means of a ladder and a telescope provides the audience not with any pictorial sense of that world but with the relationship between Clov and the other inhabitants of the 'bare interior'.[17] The stage space is regarded as the only real space. The way space, objects and text are orchestrated contributes to the dramatic structure of the performance. In *Happy Days* Winnie sits, half buried, at the centre of a mound of scorched grass in blazing light. 'Another heavenly day' she declares, where she is at once elevated and imprisoned in a landscape that presents both a vision of limitless horizon and purgatory.[18] Here the image contradicts the words and establishes a productive tension.

In *Waiting for Godot*, first performed in 1953, the setting is described as 'A country road. A tree. Evening'.[19] This apparently sketchy direction belies the importance of the tree, both as a symbolic object and a pivotal structure around which the action of the play is planned. The tree, which is at first bare and then acquires four or five leaves between Act 1 and Act 2, appears to be both a symbol of life and a symbol of death. The tree as a symbol of life is both artificial and ironic for now that 'it's covered in leaves … it must be spring'. Equally, the tree may be seen as a symbol of death when Estragon and Vladimir consider hanging themselves on it. The simple visual image carries worlds of complex thoughts.[20]

Notes from Beckett's own 1975 production make it clear that he associated characters with objects on stage. Vladimir belongs to the tree and is associated with light and orientated towards the sky, Estragon belongs to the earth, whilst the Boy is associated with the moon. Beckett's notes for this production show that he may have been influenced in this by Caspar David Friedrich's painting *Two Men Observing the Moon* (1819) which depicts travellers, a bare tree and a deserted, moonlit landscape.

Beckett disapproved of productions which deviated too far from his directions. One such example was Josef Svoboda's production of *Waiting for Godot* (1970) which employed a detailed baroque set implying bourgeois decadence.[21] However, for the first production of *Happy Days* (1961) Beckett conceded that his desire for 'maximum symmetry' and his requirement to place Winnie in the centre of the stage restricted depiction of the relationship between Winnie and her husband, Willie. Thus, Winnie was required to move 'slightly to stage left'.[22]

Naturalism as the catalyst for scenography

At the end of the nineteenth century attempts to render more life-like scenes were to be witnessed through the harmonious development of theatrical naturalism. This came about through the efforts of playwrights and designers. Naturalism became a shared impetus for the play and the scenography. Raymond Williams observed that a common understanding of the term 'naturalism' referred to life-like reproduction and methods to achieve it. However, in a philosophical sense, 'naturalism' emphasised the contrast between the natural and the supernatural, or a distinction between 'revealed (divine) and observed (human) knowledge'. Naturalistic drama combines these two senses resulting in theatre where 'the method of accurate production and the specific philosophical position are intended to be organically fused'.[23] Émile Zola's 1867 novel, *Thérèse Raquin*, was staged as a play in 1873. It is the story of the murder of a sickly husband by his adulterous wife and her eventual guilt-driven suicide. The story is infused with the sense of the grim surroundings of working-class Paris. There is a causal link implied between the characters and their environment. 'Zola believed that art and literature should serve the inquiring mind, investigating, analysing and reporting on man and society, seeking the facts and the logic behind human life.'[24] Naturalistic theatre emerged from a desire to come to terms with a world which no longer trusted implicitly in the reassurances and explanations of religion or the designation of fate. Instead, such theatre drew inspiration from new ideas of the natural world. Darwinian ideas of the natural and inevitable evolution of species chimed with Freud's exposure of mechanisms of our inner selves and offered explanation of the world based on observation of nature involving heredity, environment and psychology. August Strindberg's preface to *Miss Julie* (1888) makes it clear that he tried to create 'modern characters, living in an age of transition'. The rigidity of dominant, class-based structures of society, reinforced by religion, were exposed and opened up for possible change. Strindberg's characters were motivated by complex social and psychological influences and he saw the environment of the stage as contributing to the drama. He called for environments which allowed the characters to 'accustom themselves to their *milieu*'[25] and to be seen within a setting which was both a result of their lives and which also affected them. So the stage design here is more than an exercise in historical, geographical or pictorial reconstruction which operates separately from the text; it is an active constituent of the drama. The locations of dramatic naturalism are agents in the drama and 'the rooms are not there to define the people but to define what they seem to be, what they cannot accept they are'.[26] They establish the particular environment of the characters and show the action of that environment on them. For example, in the stage directions of *A Doll's House* (1879), Ibsen describes the specific layout of a particular room so that it is possible to imagine the layout of the whole of Nora and Helmer's apartment. It facilitates the coming and going of characters to reinforce Ibsen's plot. Descriptions of the objects in the room help to establish the social standing of the couple. But the living room also resonates with Ibsen's text at a deeper level. The room, located in an apartment, emphasises Nora's predicament of being trapped in a situation where she is the centre of attention with no immediate access to the outside world.

Although Chekhov cannot be characterised simply as a naturalist playwright, the first productions of his work which Stanislavsky directed and which Viktor Simov designed have come to represent naturalist practice. These productions with their carefully sourced furnishings and their insistence on a welter of authentic details were criticised, not least by Chekhov himself, for trivialising the text.[27] However, the attempt to integrate the design as part of a complete and sympathetic reading of the text needs to be recognised. Stanislavsky's preparation for productions involved consideration of the relationship between the physical and the psychological. In his work with actors the interrelatedness of body and mind was central to an ability to create not so much the imitation of reality, but an embodiment of reality.[28] Likewise, Simov's designs appeared to reference both the objects and materials of the real world and the underlying psychic charge they carried. Stanislavky and Simov made extensive journeys together to gather items for their productions and also to steep themselves in the atmosphere of the place. Vera Gottlieb considers that Simov's design for *The Three Sisters* made its own scenographic statement about the small provincial town where the sisters lived.[29] The subtle but recognisable contrast between the former social standing of the family and its current accommodation underlines its financial situation and the sisters' desire to return to Moscow. Simov described the provincial context as one where 'colours fade, thoughts become debased, energy gets smothered in a dressing-gown, ardour is stifled by a housecoat, talent dries up like a plant without water'.[30] The designs were not only accurate and recognisable environments which spoke directly to their audiences, they also suggested a sense of place which was rooted in the psychological and social dynamics of the play:

> In high naturalism the lives of the characters have soaked into their environment. Its detailed presentation, production, is thus an additional dramatic dimension, often a common dimension within which they are to an important extent defined. Moreover, the environment has soaked into the lives. The relations between men and things are at a deep level interactive, because what is there physically, as a space or a means for living, is a whole shaped and shaping social history.[31]

Strindberg, too, was not motivated by verisimilitude for its own sake. When he railed against painted shelves and painted saucepans, he was mainly concerned that this theatrical convention had outlived its purpose and had become a barrier to audience engagement with production. He was not concerned that the stage should replicate an actual kitchen, but that it should engage the audience in the construction of the illusion:

> As regards the décor, I have borrowed from the impressionist painters asymmetry and suggestion (i.e., the part rather than the whole), believing that I have thereby helped to further my illusion. The fact that one does not see the whole room and all the furniture leaves room for surmise – in other words, the audience's imagination is set in motion and completes its own picture.[32]

However, the pursuit of naturalist stage design proved illusive. The influence of pictorialism and a painstaking, but ultimately self-defeating, approach to detail often threatened to overwhelm the fragile balance between the suggestiveness of text and the solid reality of the stage. As is evident from the earlier chapter on pioneers, reactions against naturalist stage design provided the catalyst for several practitioners in the twentieth century to re-examine the role of design in relation to the text and resulted in new perspectives on the role of scenography.

Expressionist scenography and the inner dimension

Expressionism was particularly influential during and shortly after the First World War in Germany. Like naturalism, it was a movement that influenced both literature and art. On the stage, it was particularly influential for the development of scenography. Expressionism concentrated on the inner dimension of human experience, the subjective, visceral and embodied aspects of existence and its contention with an external reality. Paintings such as Ludwig Kirchner's *Self-portrait as a Soldier* (1914) and Max Beckmann's *The Night* (1918) made use of distorted perspectives, angular lines and striking contrasts of colour in order to present, from an entirely subjective viewpoint, the anguish and struggle of the individual in the time of war and its aftermath. Films of the time also explored expressionism as a means of representation. *The Cabinet of Dr Caligari* (1919), directed by Robert Wiene, portrayed madness and murder and made exclusive use of studio sets composed of harsh angles and exaggerated proportions. Further contrast was achieved through lighting which was intended to create shadows of nightmarish proportions. Expressionist scenography embraced these influences so that 'the scenic place became the focal point of dramatic tensions that permeated the entire stage space' and created an 'expressive trampoline' for the actor.[33] The spatial concerns of Appia and Craig were exploited further to enable scenography to produce powerful and resonant symbols for a contemporary audience. Director Leopold Jessner and designer Emil Pirchan developed an approach which made use of pared-down space that activated the dynamic potential of the stage as a means of setting up underlying tensions and symbolic action. Platforms and steps provided the basic grammar of the scenographic space. In a 1921 production of *Othello*, Pirchan focused the viewers' attention by making use of concentric platforms which created steps and focused action in relation to the centre of the stage. Desdemona was murdered in an immense white bed with towering curtains placed alone in the centre of the stage. In the design for a 1920 production of Shakespeare's *Richard III*:

> there wasn't the slightest historical indication of place; only a platform raised below a greyish-green wall that represented the menace threatening everyone, the ever-present Tower of London, symbol of the reign of terror in England. Periodically, a monumental staircase leading to the platform was incorporated into the action. This red staircase, red for the royal mantle and the blood of many victims, presented a spatial description of the rise and fall of Richard.[34]

The simple, yet potent, arrangement of the stage space and the carefully controlled and forceful use of colour were given additional impact by use of light. High contrast was achieved through selective lighting of the actors' expressions in key 'ecstatic moments' and through creation of enormous shadows of characters across a grey wall. These devices accentuated the actor's presence by enlarging and exaggerating the image. Lighting was also used, in conjunction with the rhythmic space of the stage, to achieve fluid changes of scene, to underscore the relationships between characters and to engulf the audience with its 'magical fluctuations'.[35]

Expressionist scenography like this sought to achieve effects that were visceral and shocking. Bold spatial arrangements and symbolic use of colour, light and shadow were meant to be stirring and intense. Images of spiritual isolation of the individual, common in much expressionist art, were used here to underline Richard's evil persona and to permit contemporary German audiences to make links between Richard and the autocratic Kaiser Wilhelm II who had led Germany into the First World War.[36] This distillation of evil power was graphically and emotively manipulated by Pirchan's scenography. On the other hand some critics found Jessner's approach heavy-handed and over-simplistic. Notably, Robert Edmond Jones and Kenneth MacGowan found the symbolism striking but rather obvious: 'Richard begins the play in black against a black curtain ... Richmond ends it in white against a white curtain ... This is symbolism in baby-talk, presentational production in kindergarten terms.'[37] Jones' own version of expressionism was more suggestive. Coincidentally, his own designs for *Richard III*, completed in 1920, before he saw Pirchan and Jessner's version, also made use of enormous walls and a swathe of red sky in the final scene. In addition he introduced symbolic elements in each scene, including a prison cell with gibbet or gallows which 'contextualized Richard's death with the murders he has caused'.[38] What is important about the influence of expressionist theatre is that, as with naturalism, scenographic means were integral to the meaning and impact of the production.

These explorations of ways of conveying truth of human experience on stage, whilst clearly influenced by movements in literature and art, cannot be neatly compartmentalised into various movements, styles and ensuing sets of theatrical conventions. Although naturalism and expressionism were undoubtedly central to the development of scenography, it is not necessarily helpful to view these two approaches as oppositional or contradictory. It might be more productive to trace the connections and developments between naturalism, expressionism and the varieties of representation that emerge from them. Expressionism is in some ways an extension of, rather than a break with, naturalism. What unites both approaches is a direct appeal to the audience in the recognition of their own lives: 'What the spectator was seeing was his own rooms or the inside of his own head.'[39] Raymond Williams points out that well beyond the alleged break with naturalism at the end of the nineteenth century, the idea of the creation of a real experience within the artifice of theatre was far from exhausted and that 'the trap of a room, of a street, from which a man looks at a world that at once determines and is beyond him' could be replayed but newly experienced throughout the twentieth century.[40] Or as Bert States puts it: 'Expressionism was an inside job in the sense that it was prepared from naturalism's principle that drama arises from the conflict of individuals and institutions. Expressionism did not in the least kill off naturalism ... it made it possible for naturalism to remain alive ... while it reconstructed itself.'[41] Much twentieth- and twenty-first-century scenographic practice demonstrates a negotiation or dialogue between the perspectives of the outward and the inward, the objective and the subjective, the rational and the emotional. Viktor Simov's designs for *Hedda Gabler*, directed by Meyerhold, retained a sense of Hedda's milieu, her place in society, but at the same time the designs attempted to present the essence of her character and the way in which other characters operated in relation to her. Robert Edmond Jones' later ideas on combining filmed action and live action stem from an interest in revealing the inner dimension of a character through contrast with the external presentation of that character. Robert Wilson uses a jumble of references to the external world in order to access what he calls the 'interior screen'. Caspar Neher's designs insisted on a reflection of the real without resorting to illusionism, yet their potency was often contingent upon some revelation of Neher's own sensibility and experience. For example, the slides for *Fear and Misery of the Third Reich* were drawn from his own experience of the First World War.

Metonymic and metaphoric images

Another way in which modes of scenographic representation have been considered is in relation to its metonymic or mimetic properties and its metaphoric or poetic qualities. The metonymic approach is based on likenesses or 'the contiguity of the presence on stage to the absence it represents'.[42] Conventions of theatre allow such approaches to operate selectively. For instance, single objects such as a sturdy wooden table or a red velour chaise longue or an item of clothing such as a floor-length fur coat or a leather biker jacket can instantly evoke a wealth of references and associations drawn from audience knowledge of the external world. Historical, geographical, sociological and political implications can be inferred from the selection of objects on stage which provide a kind of visual shorthand within which the text can be located. Use of metaphors in scenography relies on more complex interaction between text and image as means of exploring possible meaning or significance of text. This often demands more time or more conscious effort on the part of the spectator to register the full significance of image in relation to text. Svoboda's 1963 design for *Oedipus Rex* centred upon a flight of steps which occupied the full width of the stage and covered the orchestra pit at the bottom. The top seemed to disappear in the flies.[43] As the tragedy unfolded, the staircase revealed itself as a metaphor for Oedipus and his doomed struggle against his fate. In 1992, George Typsin made use of the same text and designed a set which was a giant eye rendered in strips of bent wood with a reflective mobile disc at its centre. This structure sat above a black 'lake'. The set was intended as a portent of the climax of the play where Oedipus is blinded, but also suggested to Typsin 'a mythic bird or a strange spider-like animal … The place seemed mysterious, sick and cursed.'[44]

Often the metonymic and the metaphoric operate simultaneously. José Carlos Serroni used a 'forest' which consisted of slim, straight trunks of real eucalyptus trees over 8 metres high (the full height of the stage) for his designs for *Salvation Path* staged in São Paulo, Brazil in 1993. The play dealt with religious fanaticism and the massacre of religious followers by the police. The forest was the location of this massacre, but the trees achieved another level of significance when the performance happened in and through these vertical lines. A year before the production, a real massacre had been carried out by the military police. Following a riot, one hundred and eleven inmates were shot in a São Paulo prison. Against this background, the image of the forest, dominating and constraining the performers, described the plight of the characters. This setting suggested barriers, entrapment and prison bars of 'people [who] were caged up in their nearly paranoid world of abandonment'. Despite the subject matter, Serroni considered that it was a poetic and subtle play, and his abstract use of natural materials allowed the production to have 'impact without being blunt or crass'.[45]

In *What Is Scenography?* (2002) Pamela Howard describes a contemporary scenographer's approach to theatrical texts and the way scenography develops. Like Serroni, her way of working moves subtly between mimesis and metaphor. The aim is to create visual images which resonate with texts and are suggestive rather than illustrative of the words.[46] A design for *Macbeth* was triggered by watching coverage of the burial of a contemporary political leader on a tiny Scottish island. A television image of 'the elliptical outline of Iona silhouetted against a luminous sky' and the words of the officiating priest who described Iona as 'a very thin place where only a tissue paper separates the material from the spiritual world' stimulated Howard to envisage 'a fragile thin curved shell-shaped stage' that could be lit from underneath to suggest visual proximity of the natural and supernatural in *Macbeth*.[47] Here, Howard's aim was enhancement and revelation of the text.[48] The scenography is bound up with the text and operates in close dramaturgical relationship to it in order to extend and illuminate aspects of the original text. She sees her role as that of a 'visual detective', mapping and investigating the play text in terms of space, movement, colour, texture. She makes connections between the world of the play and her own experience. Howard describes a period of her design process which involves intuitively experimenting with paintings and sketches that relate to specific moments of the play.[49] At such times the sound of words can suggest colours. Rhythms and patterns of speech can indicate particular proxemic and spatial placements. Further investigation may reveal chance connections between objects or images and the text which can further enhance meaning.[50]

Fusion and separation

Another consideration in tracing the relationship of image to text is the extent to which images work in fusion with or in separation from text and performers. This is an issue concerning the operation and impact of scenography in relation to other elements of the stage. As noted earlier, the importance of fidelity to Wagner's notion of *Gesamtkunstwerk*, where the arts of music, painting and drama worked in fusion towards a single theatrical entity, was an inspiration for Appia. Although he needed to rethink Wagner's ideas, which were based on mid nineteenth-century techniques of staging, he worked towards a harmonious synthesis of sound, movement, space and light as a means of furthering theatrical intention and its realisation. For Appia, the musical score was the determinant of this fusion. Expressiveness of the performer, settings and lighting were guided and determined by music. Jaques-Dalcroze's work revealed the musical discipline of the body in relation to external space and the potential of light. He regarded the power of music as fundamental to the revelation of the inner essence of all vision and transcendent aesthetic truth.[51]

Craig, too, was captivated by the idea of theatrical fusion or harmony. This could lead the viewer through an appeal to beauty and an abstract universal language of the stage towards revelation. His infinite range of ideas for a single setting through use of mobile elements and their interplay with light and figure freed the stage from mimcry and impersonation. Through the unity of architecture, light and movement, abstract form might be seen to perfom:

> There are no definite forms. Nothing seems to bound the horizon, the ground is invisible, overhead is a void. Soon, in the centre, a single form stirs and slowly rises, like the beginning of a dream; and then a second and a third. And now, on the right, something is unfolding, without haste. Forms descend, mysteriously. The whole space is in motion, stirred by the inner life it receives from the light.[52]

Notions of separation or estrangement have had just as much influence on scenography as the concepts of fusion and harmony. Viktor Shklovsky, one of the group of literary theorists known as the Russian Formalists, made this statement in 1917:

> Art exists that one may recover the sensation of life; it exists to make one feel things, to make the stone *stony*. The purpose of art is to impart the sensation of things as they are perceived and not as they are known. The technique of art is to make objects 'unfamiliar', to make forms difficult, to increase the difficulty and length of perception because the process of perception is an aesthetic end in itself and must be prolonged.[53]

This analysis of the way art works highlights separation and strangeness as opposed to aesthetic unity. And this way of thinking about scenography can be traced in much pioneering work. For Neher and Brecht the effect of making the familiar strange was a device to provoke a more conscious, intellectual and social engagement with what was being presented on stage.

---

13   If you place a baroque candelabra on a baroque table, both get lost. You can't see either. If you place the candelabra on a rock in the ocean, you begin to see what it is. Usually in the theatre the visual repeats the verbal. The visual takes second place to language. I don't think that way. For me the visual is not an afterthought, not an illustration of the text. It has equal importance. If it tells the same story as the words, why look? The visual must be so compelling that a deaf man would sit through the performance fascinated. Once in a while I let the visual align with the verbal, but usually not. Most directors begin by analyzing a text, and the visual follows from that interpretation. This naïve use of the visual code bores me. I always start with a visual form. In most theatre the eye is irrelevant. Not in mine. I think with my eyes.
    Robert Wilson in Arthur Holmberg, *The Theatre of Robert Wilson*, p. 53

Their rejection of the *Gesamtkunstwerk* was a political act as well as an aesthetic one. It led to a model where the scenography worked in parallel with, but separate from, the actor, text and music. Caspar Neher's scenography was conceived as a comment on the text, not an illustration of it. Neher's scenography ran counter to the text, offering a response to or intervention in the text. Describing Neher's designs, Brecht said, in translation, that they 'display a lovely mixture of his [Neher's] own handwriting and that of the playwright'.[54] Brecht admired Neher as 'an ingenious storyteller'[55] able to use carefully chosen images to add another dimension to text. In his designs for *Macbeth*, Act One, Scene Four, where Duncan and Banquo praise Macbeth's castle, Brecht describes how 'Neher insisted on having a semi-dilapidated grey keep of striking poverty. The guests' words of praise were merely compliments. He saw the Macbeths as petty Scottish nobility, and neurotically ambitious.'[56] Here, dislocation between words and setting induced a train of thought which invited the viewer to consider text in the light of image. A productive gap was created between text and image that afforded an active involvement on the part of the audience.

Shklovsky's observation also refers to the role of art in imparting the sensation of things, which suggests a more phenomenological or visceral experience than Brecht seems to have envisaged. Use of text and image by the British performance group, Forced Entertainment, presents another orientation to the idea of making familiar relationships seem strange in the theatre. In *The World in Pictures* (2006) they attempted to tell the 'Story of Mankind' in a performance environment cluttered with what appeared to be discarded matter of the consumer society.[57]

Cheap fancy dress costumes, tinsel, theatrical snow, fake grass and 1970s pop music played at full volume. The scenography is an assault on the senses. At the same time, the text explored the behaviour of contemporary humans in confronting or avoiding the world – in attempts to make sense of individual daily lives in the face of history and world events. Often the welter of stuff on stage seemed to overwhelm anything else that was happening but there was ironic humour in the cheapness and clichéd nature of the materials used by the company, and in combination with the text, the chaotic accumulation of clutter seemed unexpectedly touching and poignant.

Scenography and contemporary approaches to classic texts

New productions of classic and revived texts often begin with the expectation that scenography need not reflect wishes of playwrights and that it is by means of scenography, in particular, that new insights may be brought to bear on old texts. This is partly because theatrical conventions of previous generations often lose their power to speak to current ones. Although conventions most frequently arise from deep-rooted desires on the part of theatre makers to reflect truthful and meaningful responses to life, they need to be continually reviewed and challenged in the light of shifts in experience and understanding and consequently in ways of explaining the world, if they are not simply to become outmoded or irrelevant theatrical devices. For instance, an approach to a twenty-first-century production of *A Doll's House* may well be concerned with viewing Ibsen's original stage directions in the light of current staging practices and the particular context of the intended production. This may bring a fresh vision to the performed play text. Thomas Ostermeier's 2002 production of *A Doll's House – Nora* reinterpreted the living room by using a set designed by Jan Pappelbaum which was influenced by contemporary consumer culture.[58] The setting featured cream leather sofas, abstract paintings and a large glass aquarium. Strobe lighting and loud music underscored the unravelling of Nora's psychological state. Mabou Mines' *Dollhouse* (2003), directed by Lee Breuer and designed by Narelle Sissons, took a more symbolic approach to examining power relationships between men and women.[59] The set was a doll's house with child-sized furniture. The male actors, all around four feet tall, were more at home on the set than the tall performers cast to play the women.[60] Their size in this particular setting rendered them less powerful in this particular environment. The performance began with a bare stage and the usual theatrical apparatus was visible to the audience. But, then, a red velvet curtain appeared which covered the bare walls, wires and cables. Finally, flats lying on the stage floor were pulled up to create a room in miniature. The scale of the set underscored the balance of power between the genders and set up a particular frame in which the performance could take shape. Elinor Fuchs' review of the production points out that this treatment was not inconsistent with Ibsen's text, even if it ignored his stage directions:

> In three moves, before a line was uttered, Breuer had signalled a dense theatricality; he would keep before our eyes the drawing-room play of a century ago, shift its scale to frame it in a ferocious commentary, yet remind us that behind the stage illusion (and its dissolution) lies the impassive machinery of theatrical artifice. The layering of metatheatre is of course licensed in the text, whose centerpiece is Nora's performance of the notorious tarantella.[61]

Notions of fidelity to the text are relative, broad and shifting; adherence to the dramatist's intention is not the only purpose of performance. Fidelity to a text from the past might be achieved by ignoring the stage directions in order to create 'visual environments that make the strangeness of the plays seem right or comfortable or arresting in the present'.[62] Shakespeare's texts, in particular, have been seen as receptive to such approaches. The familiarity of his plays and their apparent universality of themes provide room for specific interpretation. Original sixteenth- and seventeenth-century productions operated within a convention of 'architectural scenography' where the architecture of the theatre building and its stage determined fixed but versatile elements such as walls, doors, columns and upper levels.[63] Stage technology such as trapdoors, winches and curtained recesses facilitated 'discovery', or revelation scenes.[64] Such architectural elements enabled fluid movement from one scene to another, allowing performers to exploit the full dimensions of stage space and their proximity to the audience in the performance of plays. Props and small pieces of set were important, but imagery was derived in the main from words spoken by characters. Conventions of presentation with which Shakespeare and his contemporaries were familiar relied on the imagination of the audience and engagement with words. A clear example of this relationship may be seen in the prologue of Shakespeare's *Henry V*:

> And let us, ciphers to this great accompt,
> On your imaginary forces work.
> Suppose within the girdle of these walls
> Are now confin'd two mighty monarchies,
> Whose high upreared and abutting fronts
> The perilous narrow ocean parts asunder.[65]

Beyond Shakespeare's own time changes in theatre architecture, acting style and scenographic approach have afforded new ways of presenting and performing his plays. Furthermore, increasing distance between Shakespeare's language, his references and his modes of theatrical presentation mean that any visual assumptions about the performance of the texts need to be reconsidered.[66] At the beginning of the twentieth century, Edward Gordon Craig advocated abstraction and suggestion in attempts to reveal cosmic dimensions in Shakespeare's texts. He responded not to the geographical and historical dimensions of the plays, but to poetic aspects, atmosphere, emotions and human relationships to each other and the world. In his account of 'The Artists of the Theatre and of the Future' he offers advice to would-be designers:

> Although you know that I have parted company with popular belief that the *written* play is of any deep and lasting value to the Art of the Theatre, we are not going so far as to dispense with it here. We are to accept it that the play still retains some value for us, and we are not going to waste that; our aim is to increase it. Therefore it is, as I say, the production of general and broad effects appealing to the eye which will add a value to that which has already been made valuable by the great poet.[67]

He advocated working with the text in order to make an intuitive aesthetic connection. His concern was with the way the designer responded as an artist to the work of the poet and not as a technician. Play texts were the source of Craig's inspiration: 'What are the colours that Shakespeare has indicated for us? Do not first look at Nature, but look in the play of the poet.'[68] Craig laid emphasis on the process of designing as one of seeking a deep connection with the heart of the play, leading to the 'creation of another beauty'. He continues: 'I let my scenes grow out of not merely the play, but from broad sweeps of thought which the play has conjured up in me, or even other plays by the same author have conjured up.'[69] In the 1912 production of *Hamlet*, Craig responded to the play from the perspective of Hamlet himself. When he described a preliminary sketch of the second scene, he saw 'Hamlet, fallen as it were, into a dream, on the other side you see his dream. You see it, as it were, through the mind's eye of Hamlet.'[70] Hamlet sat downstage to one side slumped in the shadows. Behind him, the court was represented by Gertrude and Claudius, resplendent in huge golden costumes with cloaks which appeared to engulf the mass of courtiers looking up from below. Actors playing courtiers were required to stand still for most of the scene in order to maintain this image. It suggested both Hamlet's dislocation from the court and Claudius' tyrannical authority over it. Craig's vision of Shakespeare's text was all-encompassing and demanded a total realisation through the entire production.

All stage means, including setting, light, costume and actors, were intended to work towards the single over-riding expression of the stage and its contents as a complete entity.

Many productions have sought to bring contemporary meaning by relocating the action of Shakespeare's texts. References through costumes and settings have been used to draw parallels between themes in plays and contemporary events and characters. In 1937 Orson Welles used scenographic statements to relocate *Julius Caesar* to Fascist Italy. The costumes resembled Italian and German military uniforms of the time and the lead actor looked like Mussolini. The designer, Samuel Leve, set simple steps and platforms across the floor and contrasted this with a blood-red brick wall running the width of the stage. However, the boldest scenographic statement came from lighting. Jean Rosenthal used lighting angles and intensities that were intended to evoke the Nuremberg rallies.[71] Strong 'up-lights' projected expressionistic images onto the back wall of the stage and pools and beams of light isolated individuals, leaving the audience to imagine what might lurk in the shadows.

Jan Kott's book, *Shakespeare Our Contemporary* (1965), was influential in developing the notion that Shakespeare's plays could speak as well, if not better, to modern audiences as they did to original ones. Kott not only advocated the need to find visual correlations between the contemporary world and the text but he also focused on the timelessness and essential cruelty of texts like *King Lear* and the emotional effect they could have on an audience.[72] Influenced by Kott, directors such as Giorgio Strehler have achieved contemporary resonances with Shakespeare through their use of ambiguous and layered imagery. Strehler's *King Lear* (1972), designed by Ezio Frigerio, made use of the concept of a 'cosmic circus'. A semicircular cyclorama was stretched and attached to the floor which was covered with sand in order to suggest a circus tent. Lear and his family appeared wearing glittering and gaudy, but faded and worn, theatrical garments which looked as though they had been pulled from an old costume hamper. Kent wore a decorative breastplate, and Lear appeared to be wearing a cardboard crown. The Fool, who doubled as Cordelia, wore traces of clown make-up, a battered top hat and an ill-fitting ringmaster's jacket. Other costumes were cut like Renaissance breeches and jackets but made up in black biker leathers. When mad Lear and blinded Gloucester appeared in Act Four in theatrical rags, 'it seemed as if two naked old men were being tamed in a circus ring by animal trainers, or that a motorcycle gang was taunting and torturing them'.[73]

It is now commonplace to witness productions of Shakespeare that take this eclectic approach to references in setting and costume. Mixing potent visual elements from different times and places establishes a new visual vocabulary and a new frame of reference which provides potential to reinvigorate familiar texts. There is of course a great deal of subjectivity in judgements about whether a production has been successful in re-presenting Shakespeare whilst maintaining the integrity of the text. In the English-speaking world, in particular, there is often a concern that Shakespeare's words might be misrepresented or distorted by their visual representation. But, at the same time, theatre makers are interested in using scenographic means to test the limits of these texts. Romeo Castellucci, whose company Socìetas Raffaello Sanzio has staged *Julius Caesar* and *Hamlet*, says:

> Work with the classics demands that we confront the traditional, but that is precisely why the work can surpass the traditional, but never in a literary way. Therefore one mustn't tackle these classical texts as a superstitious person who believes the classics to be safe; quite the opposite. One must make an effort to put them to the test of fire, in order to better determine their supportive structure, which leads exactly to the revelation that they speak to everyone, to the frail and private nature of every individual. And the book, as object, is no more.[74]

Castellucci uses powerful visual and sonic images and experiments with ways to present text in order to open up the reach and impact of that text. He is interested in how the presence of actors, their individual appearance and their physical idiosyncrasies become inseparable parts of theatrical presentation. He uses performers who have an extreme variety of body shapes and range of physical abilities, including people who appear anorexic and/or obese and performers with disabilities. In placing them within striking visual and sonic environments, Castellucci attempts to create a theatre which, in prioritising the scenographic, challenges normal perspectives. The 1997 production of *Julius Caesar* explored ways in which performers' bodies evoked visual and sound images as a means of embodying text. In *Julius Caesar* he used casting to make physical and emotional connections between performers' bodies and oratorical displays by their characters in a deconstruction of rhetoric and power. The performer who played Mark Antony had no vocal chords and had to use a throat microphone so that 'a new voice that came from the viscera, from deep down inside' could 'make the speech truthful, outrageous, and moving'.[75] At the same time Brutus used helium gas to distort his voice. On the stage a clean space became a rendition of 'the burnt-out remnants of a cinema or theatre' and evoked 'ruin and apocalypse'. Through the soot, detritus and rubble the painfully thin figures of Brutus and Cassius (played by a woman) emerged 'like survivors from the death camps'.[76] In this version of *Julius Caesar* the text was processed through action and arresting images so that the physical language of the stage acts became the prime means of expression.

Chapter 4

Recognising and realising space

Configuration and manipulation of space in relation to the performance event is the key element in determining the nature of scenography. Why is this? In the first instance, it is because of what happens within the confines of the theatre stage. The special characteristic of the stage space is that anything that happens in it is offered for the attention, reception and consideration of the audience and is presumed to have some kind of intended effect or meaning. Take, for example, the placement of a chair on stage. This chair 'is first and foremost *onstage*, and before it conveys any information about the fictional world or the real world outside the theatre it presents itself to the spectators as a theatrical chair'.[1] The framing nature of stage space and its contained objects suggests and stimulates expectations of the action that is about to take place. Those particular qualities of a given stage space, as defined through the setting, objects within the setting, lighting, costumes and sound, also have a tangible and concrete influence upon the performed action.

The way space is determined and organised brings about different possibilities with regard to the functions of space in performance. Attempts have been made to clarify spatial function in the theatre in ways that distinguish between 'stage space', 'presentational space' and 'fictional space'.[2] Distinction may be made between the basic stage itself which possesses its own particular characteristics such as width, height and depth, and the way it is organised in relation to occupation by the audience and provision of access to and from this space. Following McAuley, 'presentational space' refers to the use of 'stage space' in a particular production or performance. It covers and addresses the space occupied by actors, scenery and objects. 'Fictional space' is the imaginatively conceived space in which action occurs. This takes place in the presentational space. Locations determined by the play text are presented, represented or evoked in this space. These locations are often named in the text. Play texts locate different orders of places, some of which are directly presented to the audience and others implied. For example, in *The Cherry Orchard* (1904) Chekhov places most of the play in Ranyevskaya's country house. In the interior scenes, the main spaces consist of the former nursery and the drawing room. These are connected to other spaces which border the stage but are not fully seen. In the nursery, doors lead to Anya's room, the hallway and outside. In Act Three, the half-seen ballroom and the sound of an orchestra extends the drawing room and the sound of a billiards game locates a further adjoining room. The only exterior scene is, in contrast, an open, empty space, defined principally by a line of telegraph poles. Moscow, Kharkov and particularly Paris feature as places that are not connected to the stage but are nonetheless part of the dramatic map of the action.[3] The cherry orchard itself is referred to in the dialogue but is not a physical location in the play, and although its presence is central to the narrative and is often, in production, implied in the presentational space, it does not have a clearly defined physical relationship to the other locations. It is an evocation of the past as much as it is a real location.

The fictional space is only partly determined by the text. The presentational space, or the way any given production occupies and interacts with the physical stage space also evokes fictional space. This chapter discusses ways in which this occurs.

Architectural space

In addition to the spatial classifications already considered, 'architectural space' shapes the fundamental proposition of theatre, that is, the space where someone watches and hears someone else performing. Spatial arrangements define acts of theatre because they establish the essential relationship between performer and audience, even when this relationship does not take place in an enclosed structure.[4] Performers and audience imaginatively engage each other from their respective spaces. This inevitable spatial dynamic is in a constant state of flux irrespective of the nature of the occupied space.[5]

Several forms of Western theatre buildings incorporate stages where permanent architectural features determine the nature of the scenography and the mode of viewing the performance. Furthermore, these spatial arrangements constitute a 'frontier zone', where presentational and audience space meet, and reflect wider cultural norms and behaviour in the society from which they arise.[6]

The architecture of Greek theatre reflected the social hierarchy of the time which underscored the dramaturgical impact of plays. The chorus used the same entrances as the audience and was restricted to the playing area (the 'orchestra') between the audience and the 'skene' which reinforced its role as one of embodying the views and experiences of the citizens.[7] Only principal characters such as royalty, heroes and gods made use of the 'skene' and the area

immediately in front of it (the 'proskene').[8] Violent deeds and murders happened out of sight of the audience although resultant dead bodies were sometimes revealed on a wheeled cart, pushed through the central doors in the
'skene' wall. Gods and divine messengers were further delineated by their
descent from the roof of the skene by means of winch or crane.[9] The use of
presentational space made physical the social structures and beliefs of ancient
Greece. The relationship of auditorium to stage also reflected development of
theatre as a democratic forum. Although there appear to have been areas of
seating reserved in the front row and centrally for officials and favoured
guests,[10] for the majority of the audience, the experience of the performance
was one held in common. Furthermore, the sweep of seating, which almost
encircled the main playing area, presumably permitted clear views for performers and audience of each other. The architecture determines the relationship between the viewers and the performance and establishes scenographic
conventions for the presentational space. In doing so it provides a frame for the
experience of performance which resonates beyond the theatre event itself.

In contrast, most European theatre buildings from the Renaissance onwards
were designed to offer a privileged point of view situated centrally in the
auditorium and elevated above the rest of the audience. Stage designs of the
seventeenth century, such as those recorded by Sebastiano Serlio, were organised around a single-point perspective which was ideally viewed from this place
of privilege.[11] Allocation of seating in the auditorium reflected contemporary
social distinctions along the lines of gender and class.[12] The view of the stage
was determined by the social standing of the audience and controlled by the
dominant use of perspective scenery.

Theatre auditoria in eighteenth-century England also reflected divisions
within society. Seating boxes at the front and sides were provided for the
privileged enabling good views of the stage and the rest of the auditorium. In
the middle gallery one might have seen trades-people and in the upper gallery 'a
motley assemblage embracing all ranks from servants to impecunious profes-
sionals'.[13] But the relationship between the auditorium and the stage afforded a
viewing experience very different from that of Renaissance stages. A deep
forestage projected well into the auditorium. A scenic stage, where painted
scenery and effects were employed, was located up stage behind the forestage
but very little action occurred here. Instead, the actors operated on the forestage,
midway between the scenic stage and the audience, using doors onto the
forestage in a highly conventionalised but flexible way. Two very different scenic
approaches were employed simultaneously, giving audiences two contrasting
modes of presentation. Use of the doors signified changes in location, both
interior and exterior, and facilitated farcical situations whereby characters were

enabled to narrowly miss each other or overhear others.[14] Successful incorporation of doors relied on the physical dexterity of actors and audience acceptance of the convention. This theatrical use of architectural features signified (rather than represented) locations in the same way that Shakespeare's company at the Globe had done. At the same time, however, the scenic stage provided a separate pictorial, decorative rendition of the fictional location.[15]

In the nineteenth century, the nature of scenic presentation expanded to encompass the actor. But here in its eighteenth-century incarnation, it existed at some distance from both performers and audience and was somewhat at odds with the rest of the performance which centred on the exchange between audience and performers. The forestage effectively placed the actors in the same room as the audience. Both forestage and auditorium were constantly lit by chandeliers. In contrast to the illustrative scenic stage in the background, the mode of performance on the forestage was overtly theatrical and in direct contact with the audience. The positioning of some side boxes actually on the stage itself, together with the general level of rowdiness in eighteenth-century theatres, meant that actors were frequently interrupted and disturbed. Performers were often seen to step out of character and address the audience as themselves.[16] This arrangement was a very different proposition from late nineteenth-century practice where audiences sat in a darkened auditorium looking through the frame of the proscenium at a more brightly lit stage where actors appeared to be in a separate world. The proscenium-arch theatre of the nineteenth century provided a particular kind of relationship between audience, performers and scenic devices. Benjamin Wyatt, architect of the 1812 version of the Theatre Royal, Drury Lane, London conceived of the proscenium as a 'picture frame' for the actors and the scene and thus rejected use of stage doors and boxes at the side of the stage. Actors were discouraged or even forbidden to step out of the 'picture frame'.[17] This restriction brought about a conceptual separation between the real world of the auditorium and the fictional world of the actor. At Bayreuth Richard Wagner and Otto Bruckwald designed the Festspielhaus (1876), an opera house specifically for the presentation of Wagner's operas where a double proscenium was used to frame the illusionistic stage. The orchestra area was partly sunk beneath the stage so as to prioritise vision of the stage. The audience was seated in a single, fan-shaped sweep of seating extending to the full width of the auditorium while boxes were situated at the back of the auditorium. All the audience faced in the same direction with an unrestricted view.[18] The effect achieved was that of an audience united in the darkened auditorium in its contemplation of Wagner's vision and subdued in its concentration on a stage picture which totally enveloped the performers.[19]

In consideration of the intersection of the spatial arrangement of theatre buildings and the social dimension provided by the audience, McAuley refers to the 'play of looks' that spatial arrangements of a theatre auditorium can provide.[20] The 'Spectator/Actor look' refers to the basic requirement of theatre whereby the performers require the attention of the audience. The 'Actor/Spectator look' acknowledges that actors need to be acutely aware of the way a particular audience responds to their performance. Between these two 'looks' there is potential for an exchange of energy.[21] Such dynamism was clearly evident in the design of eighteenth-century theatres where reciprocal exchanges of energy were inescapable because actors and audience effectively shared the same space. In the nineteenth century this exchange of energy became more subtle. Architectural prioritisation of the stage and the technological capability of darkening an auditorium cast the audience into potentially passive observational roles. The conditions of the darkened auditorium worked to dampen the energy exchange between performer and audience and this tended to bring about less demonstrative audience responses.[22]

The importance of two-way relationships is further explored by Iain Mackintosh when he refers to the potential of a two-way 'channel of energy' between stage and contemporary auditorium: 'Although this energy flows chiefly from performer to audience the performer is rendered impotent unless he or she receives in return a charge from the audience.'[23] Theatre architecture, he claims, can engender 'a system of dynamic spatial harmony'.[24] This is far from being an exact science, but tracing the interior dimensions and organisation of successful theatres leads Mackintosh to speculate about effective interior proportions of theatre auditoria. He is particularly concerned with the density and distribution of an audience in relation to the performers. And the vertical relationship, he believes, is as important as the horizontal. Ideally, audience members need to be situated both above and below the performers' eyeline.[25] This was achieved in many eighteenth- and nineteenth-century theatres by the rake of the stage. This tipped the stage floor towards the audience which was positioned below the stage in the front stalls and above it in the circle and galleries. In designing contemporary theatres, Mackintosh says, architects need to balance consideration for comfort and good sightlines with an attempt to provide a channel for energy.[26] A single sweep of seating may appear fair to all in that it gives each member of the audience the same unrestricted view but there may be good reason to change such an arrangement to one engendered by asymmetry or disorder. Seating that wraps around the stage rather than facing square onto it allows performers 'to feel' the audience and the audience 'to see' one another. Thrust stages such as Tyrone Guthrie's theatre at Stratford, Ontario and arena or in-the-round stages such as the Royal

Exchange Theatre, Manchester afford simultaneous views of performance and audience. But even in theatres where the audience faces the same direction, the proximity of other audience members permits them to sense reactions and energy exchange which might occur between stage and auditorium.

Conceptually and practically this is a different kind of experience to that of viewing cinema. This is mainly because the nature of live theatre is more appropriately identified as a spatial experience as much as a visual one. The spatial dimension accounts for the experience of 'being there'. Even when audience members choose to concentrate on particular visual details on stage such as an actor's face, a pair of shoes or a shadow, they do so in the conscious-ness of the rest of the space.

Architecture as scenography

Craig recognised the potential of architectural space and attempted, in differ-ent ways, to replace the 'Pictorial Scene' with an 'Architectonic Scene'.[27] Craig experimented with the expressive potential of architectonic space in *The Steps* (1905) where he designed a single scene or place to present what he called a 'silent drama'. His sketches show a flight of steps stretched across the width of the stage between two high walls. Four designs show this same place animated in four successive 'moods' by the placement of human figures and by four distinct states of lighting (Figures 22a, 22b, 22c, 22d). In the first mood children play games bathed in soft light, in the final mood a lone figure leans against a wall surrounded by shadows. But perhaps the central focus of the scene is the flight of steps itself. Craig described the steps themselves as 'trembling with a great life'. The human figures might temporarily dominate but 'the steps are for all time'.[28]

14   And among all the dreams that the architect has laid upon the earth, I know of no more lovely things than his flight of steps leading up and leading down, and of this feeling about architecture in my art I have often thought how one could give life (not a voice) to these places, using them to a dramatic end. When this desire came to me I was continually designing dramas wherein the place was architectural and lent itself to my desire. And so I began with a drama called 'The Steps'.
Edward Gordon Craig in J. Michael Walton (ed.), *Craig on Theatre*, p. 108

The potential of steps and flights of stairs as a scenographic metaphor has since been explored by many different productions, not least by those of Svoboda. His designs for *Oedipus* at the National Theatre in Prague (1963) (Figure 23), as referred to earlier, used a giant staircase which filled the entire width of the

22a. Edward Gordon Craig, *The Steps, First Mood*, *c.*1905, published in Craig, *Towards a New Theatre*, London, 1913

stage and stretched from deep within the orchestra pit seemingly without end up into the flies intending to suggest Oedipus' doomed struggle against the inevitability of fate.[29]

15   The end of *Oedipus* always frightened me. Where does Oedipus go? Abandoned by everyone, he goes in search of truth, even though he knows it will destroy him. He wants to do good, though he now realizes the futility of battling fate. In spite of everything, he goes, bent over dragging himself up the stairs. The audience can read his back and sense his misery. Only stairs can express all this to me.

   Josef Svoboda in Jarka Burian (ed.), *The Secret of Theatrical Space: The Memoirs of Josef Svoboda*, p. 61

Svoboda made much scenographic use of steps in other productions. For example, they may be seen in *Hamlet* (1959), *Prometheus* (1968) and *Sicilian Vespers* (1974). Svoboda, like Craig, was drawn to the power and mystery of steps: 'They'll never stop exciting me, any more than I'll one day become bored

22b. Edward Gordon Craig, *The Steps, Second Mood*, *c.*1905, published in Craig, *Towards a New Theatre*, London, 1913

with Jacob's ladder or Icarus's wings.'[30] Their use is characteristic of Svoboda's approach to scenography and his desire to create a 'psycho-plastic space' where three-dimensional space can 'relate with the psychological realities both of the dramatic action and of the audience'.[31] Craig's 'The Thousand Scenes in One Scene' was a forerunner of this idea in that they were intended to create three-dimensional performance space to convey moods and expressions rather than any external location. They were designed to be used to present a single scene within which many more scenes or moods could be created:

> Any space and any atmosphere could be suggested by an appropriate arrangement of the screens. If the angle of a screen were altered, the appearance of the stage would change at once. This was, therefore, a single scene, which could take on many different aspects. Craig compares his device to the human face. A face consists of two eyes, a forehead, a nose, a chin, a mouth and two cheeks, which add up to a definite pattern;

22c. Edward Gordon Craig, *The Steps, Third Mood, c.*1905, published
in Craig, *Towards a New Theatre*, London, 1913

> but its expression alters with any change in one of its features. It is the
> same with Craig's scene which is not a series of separate pictures, but a
> series of different expressions passing over the same structure.[32]

What is clear in the above account by Bablet is the importance of movement.
These scenes were not to be presented as a succession of static images, but as an
'architectonic construction with a life of its own'; a mobile entity which was
responsive to the actor's movements and changed as the audience watched.
And the change in scenic expression was achieved through spatial arrangements of screens in relation to each other and the action of lighting in order to
'attain its full expressive power' through colour, intensity and direction of light.

Svoboda was able to take the idea of kinetic scenery much further than Craig.
His access to and interest in more advanced technologies and new materials
allowed him to explore the properties of light in combination with solid objects
to produce space-altering effects. *Romeo and Juliet* (Prague, 1963) used architectural components which could move independently from each other and
form new configurations of the presentational space for each scene. The pieces,

22d. Edward Gordon Craig, *The Steps, Fourth Mood*, c.1905, published in Craig, *Towards a New Theatre*, London, 1913

like beautifully constructed building blocks, moved in different planes; a large trap rose and sank to provide a bed or a catafalque; wall units slid in and out from the wings and a 'graceful Renaissance arcade' moved up and down stage, appearing to float ten or twelve feet above the stage floor. The design achieved far more than a simple and elegant practical solution to a fluid staging of the play. Design and manipulation of the presentational space took on its own qualities of drama. Orchestrated movements of various pieces, seen by the audience 'rising, sinking, advancing, retreating or moving laterally', provided a 'dramatic counterpoint' to the action of the performers while 'the mobile architectural scenography created a paradoxical impression of lyric grace and menace'. This embodied one of the central tensions of the play: the hope of the young lovers set against the brooding conflict of their two families.[33] Svoboda also used light, projected images and reflection to achieve three-dimensional space which was 'maximally responsive to the ebb and flow, the psychic pulse of the dramatic action'.[34] In *Hamlet* (Brussels, 1965) the kinetic scenery was

23. Josef Svoboda, *Oedipus Rex*, by Sophocles. Director M. Macháček, Smetana National Theatre, Prague, 1963

achieved in the main through use of 'a massive wall of intermeshing elements'. Rectilinear architectural units fitted together like a monumental three-dimensional puzzle. Some of the blocks housed stairs and voids. These units slid forwards from the main wall to create spaces of different dimensions and dynamics. But the key element in this production was the inclusion of a mirror, suspended above the stage at a forty-five degree angle, reflecting the stage and the performers below. Initially, the mirror provided a solution to creation of the ghost of Hamlet's dead father, but Svoboda saw how it also contributed to the presentation of the entire world of the play.[35] Working with the scale model of the set to explore various combinations of the staging, Svoboda noted:

I pushed one piece and suddenly saw the reflection of the movement in the mirror. And suddenly I saw Elsinore as a certain spiritual world, a microcosm of Hamlet's world, one which must change psycho-plastically along with the development of the action. It became a world that grinds and weighs on man; it suggested the atmosphere of the Middle Ages, a castle without feeling, anti-human. Obviously we had models enough for this: the Nazi occupation as well as the Stalin era. In other words, Elsinore was represented ultra-flexibly, plastically.[36]

Mirrors, like stairs, were for Svoboda another potent means of expressing ideas in space. Their reflective quality was capable of providing the effect of extended and multiplied spaces. They could be used to summon up simultaneous orders of reality, as in *The Wedding* (Berlin, 1968) where a semi-transparent mirror allowed the main character, a soldier fighting at the front, to experience visions of the past, 'from reality to dream and back again'.[37] Mirrors can also be used to bring spaces that are in reality adjacent and make them appear as though they are in the same space. In *The Magic Flute* (Prague, 1961) a series of large triangular mirrors at different angles created a space which comprised fragmented reflections of the stage, the wing space and the auditorium. This use of mirrors was profoundly theatrical in that it pointed to the essential craft and artificiality of stage space. Delight was also offered through the created illusion of an impossible space. The effect consisted of a collage of spaces which summoned forth a new and imaginary space.

Although scenographers have generally sought to shape existing and purpose-built theatre space, many have also explored the dramatic possibilities of alternative spaces. Perhaps Craig's most ambitious project to envisage architecture as scenography was expressed through his designs for Bach's *St Matthew Passion*. Craig's idea was that a church should be specially modified and kept solely for the performance of this piece 'given under my direction' each Easter.[38] Although the project was never realised, photographs of the original model, which was twelve feet tall, show how Craig intended to create a space which reflected the structure and impact of the music. Using a modified church based on a church he had seen in Giornico, Switzerland allowed him to exploit the dramatic potential of church architecture and bring together the audience and the scenic space. Craig developed a series of spaces for the different aspects of *St Matthew Passion*: 'a high and distant eternity; smaller intimate spaces for human interaction; platforms for declaration and more intimate interaction with an audience; and an interior basement "cellarage" of mystery and atmosphere'. Spaces were linked with flights of steps and animated by the quality, colour and movement of light. This meant that within a permanent setting spaces could be created which were 'simultaneously neutral and eternal, but might also become as particular and intimate as the garden of Gethsemane'.[39] Craig's intention was for architectural space to be harnessed to make a key contribution to the dramatic action in such a way that the audience would be enfolded and thoroughly implicated in the experience.

Space as a means of manipulating audience experience

The implied involvement of an audience has been a recurrent point of focus in most forms of aesthetic performance. Theatre practitioners, particularly in the twentieth century, have attempted to find ways to create an experience of theatre which involves audiences on bodily, visceral and intellectual terms. Use of alternative theatre forms, and experiments with physical relationships between audience and performance, have been developed by many to effect new and more engaging experiences of theatre. Thrust, arena, theatre-in-the-round and promenade stage performances have brought more of the audience into direct contact with the stage than have proscenium and other end-on arrangements. Flexible stages such as the National Theatre's Cottesloe space in London and the Schaubühne am Halleschen Ufer in Berlin have permitted different physical relationships between audience and stage.[40] Such relationships determine viewing positions for productions and influence ways in which productions are experienced. Svoboda writes about his ideal 'atelier-theatre'. This is conceived as an architectonically neutral space and capable of making possible 'a different relationship between audience and stage for every production'.[41] He envisaged galleries on several levels with the capacity to support technical operations involving lighting, projection, actors' entrances and spectators. The proportions of the basic rectangular space could be altered by moving these galleries. The audience could also occupy mobile units which allowed the seating to be adjusted, even during the course of a performance, in order to respond to particular production demands. Artaud imagined a theatre space in which the audience would be surrounded and overwhelmed by extravagantly costumed performers, giant puppets and masks, strange sounds and disorientating light. Kantor frequently worked on the outside of theatre buildings, enjoying the juxtaposition of theatre and real life and the blurring of audience and performer space. Meyerhold worked with El Lissitsky on plans for a production of *I Want A Baby* (1926). Here the idea was that the whole theatre, stage and auditorium, would be designed to involve the audience, a kind of machine for engagement of the audience in active debate.

Sergei Tretyakov's *I Want a Baby* tells the story of a Latvian Party worker called Milda who wants to help towards the revolution by bearing a child.

However, she has no desire to be married. The play shows harsh details of life in an overcrowded block of flats where drug addiction, corruption, violence and squalor threaten to thwart Milda's dreams of creating a healthy baby and a symbol of the future. Tretyakov explained that the construction of the play was 'deliberately problematic' in order to 'demonstrate possible variants, which might provoke the healthy discussion which society needs on the serious and important questions which are touched on in the play'.[42] The projected production by Meyerhold and Lissitsky was intended to highlight the role of the audience in this discussion:

> The setting for *I Want A Baby* was to be a sort of 'Milda-machine', a complete environment, using the theatre's galleries and gangways for 'stage' action, seating the audience around the whole interior, and providing spectators with the means to take part in what was happening. Lissitsky 'fused architectural and theatrical elements to create a new concept of the theatrical stage and the theatrical interior'.[43]

Although this production was never staged, it is nonetheless a striking instance of revolutionary theatre. Leach points out that revolutionary theatre was 'typically created equally by writer, designer and director' and that in the particular case of *I Want A Baby* 'the democratic collaboration was extended to include the actors and the audience also'.[44] (Figure 24.)

Jerzy Grotowski and his scenographer Jerzy Gurawski were particuarly interested in manipulating the actor–audience relationship through use of space so that the audience might be implicated as part of the performance. The aim was to create a specific and appropriate relationship for each new production. 'The scenographer's function was no longer to create a scenic place, but a specific physical rapport.'[45] In *Kordian* (1962), set in a mental asylum, the spectators were distributed on chairs around the whole perform-ance area and could also sit on the same beds which were used by the perform-ers.[46] In *The Constant Prince* (1965), the scenography separated the spectators from the actors by requiring them to view the performance 'by standing on benches and looking over a wooden partition like voyeurs'.[47] This gave a very different perspective from that afforded by the scenography in *Kordian*. Here the spectators could be made to feel like 'the public at a bull-fight, or medical students observing an operation'.[48]

More recently, theatre companies have used combinations of scenography and spaces which were not initially designed as theatre spaces in order to create a heightened experience for their audiences. Ariane Mnouchkine's company, Le Théâtre du Soleil, is based in La Cartoucherie de Vincennes, a vast building, formerly an armaments factory and army barracks, where there is scope to

24. E. Lissitsky, *I Want a Baby,* by Sergei Tretyakov. Director Vsevolod
Emilievich Meyerhold, 1926 (reconstructed model)

shape the audience's gradual immersion in the performance for each new
production. Audiences are brought through a succession of spaces in preparation for the performance. As there are no assigned seats, audiences arrive
early and can see displays and objects relating to the performance. This
approach may include an invitation to share food prepared and served by the
company. Before the performance has begun, the audience is being acclima-
tised to the colours and textures of the performance they are about to see. They
are also able to see actors making final preparations with 'exquisite costumes
and elaborate make-up' in their dressing rooms.[49] Audience members may
walk around the performance space itself and notice the way the space has been
designed. They may also choose where to sit. During the run of *The House of
Atreus Cycle* (1992–3) the audience walked over 'a huge excavated chasm in
which life-sized terra cotta figures, replicas of the choral members in
Agamemnon, marched in serried rows. When the chorus of actors entered
the playing space, it was as if the dream figures haunting the excavation site had
come to life.'[50] The audience went through a kind of induction, both into the
images and ideas of the performance and also, through exposure to backstage

preparations, into their particular role within the theatrical event. In *1789* (1971–2) spectators could choose whether to sit on bleachers looking down on the action from four separate platforms or stand within the performance space and become, 'within the logic of the production', spectators at an eighteenth-century fair watching scenes from the French Revolution, themselves being watched by those who had chosen to sit.[51]

For the Sòcietas Raffaello Sanzio the physical experience of the audience was a central concern when they staged their version of a children's fairy story, Tom Thumb, as *Buchettino* (2001). Audience members were invited into an environment that stimulated almost all their senses. Stephen Di Benedetto describes the experience:

> Enter the door of the building from out in the cold – the smell of cedar will envelop you as you stand there warming up. It is dark. As your eyes adjust you notice that the only light comes from the centre of the space, where a naked bulb hangs beneath a metal shade. Below it is a worn wooden stool, where a woman dressed in brown peasant clothes, holding a large red velvet book, ushers you inside and tells you to get into bed and go to sleep. In rows on either side of the stool are wooden beds, and bunk beds line the perimeter walls … The mattress is plush and you sink into it … As you curl up and pull the blanket over you, you notice that your head rests against the wooden headboard and your feet press against the footboard, but it does not matter because the blanket cocoons you and your head sinks down into the pillow. The cedar smell and the dim light are relaxing, your eyelids begin to droop, and the hustle of the outside world subsides. Then a soothing voice tells you a story.[52]

The nature of the space and the presence of an audience within it was such that senses of touch, sound, smell and physical proximity were, like sight, capable of influencing responses. As the performance unfolded, a kind of 'live radio play' heightened audience sensitivity and stimulated imagination: 'we could feel the vibrations from the axe chopping the wood, the bristles of the broom on the floor and the slamming and bolting of the window shutters. Our beds shook and trembled and gave substance and form to the environment of the woods-man's house.'[53]

Site-specific space

Of necessity, the architecture of theatre space embodies assumptions about the way in which theatre is viewed, and this has a direct bearing on the way scenography is constructed and communicated. Since the 1860s, theatre

makers and scenographers interested in exploring relationships between performance and audience have sought to move outside purpose-built theatre
spaces to challenge conventional practice. This practice has been linked to a
desire to speak to new and previously disenfranchised audiences or to reduce
the distance between theatre and real life. These concerns present implications
for the role of scenography. It has been asserted that working in non-theatre
spaces has challenged theatre designers to confront and rethink communica-
tive assumptions. One conclusion is that theatre design in alternative spaces is
centrally concerned with 'the necessity to both assert the dynamics of the stage
area, and to define the entire theatre space, its geometry and its relation to the
spectators'.[54] In non-theatre buildings the usual spatial relationships between
audience and performance can be explored and manipulated to create a more
intense engagement with performance.

As Le Théâtre du Soleil has shown, a large space gives scope to create spaces
where audiences can be literally immersed within the world of the play. In
Peter Stein's 1977 production of *As You Like It*, the Berliner Schaubühne
moved temporarily to film studios in Spandau. Here the set designer, Karl-
Ernst Herrmann, was able to create an extravagant scenographic experience for
the audience which allowed them, literally, to take the journey from Frederick's
court to the Forest of Arden. The opening scene was created in a pale blue
hallway with cool, concealed lighting which permitted the audience to feel as
though they were 'standing inside a glacier'.[55] The actors, dressed in dark, stiff
Elizabethan costumes designed by Moidele Bickel, occupied platforms and
walkways situated above the spectators' eyeline. Stein required the performers
to deliver lines from the opening scenes of the play which had been cut up,
interposed and delivered in a rather stilted manner. However, this unpromis-
ing and disorienting introduction gave way to a very different Forest of Arden
where the audience did not simply witness the characters' escape from the
austerity and hostility of the court, but were said to experience the release for
themselves. Audience members were led from the hall, in single file, through a
dimly lit passage which was overhung with creepers. Dripping water ran down
the walls. Eventually the audience emerged into a huge film studio dominated
by a huge live beech tree. A pool, a field of corn, the sound of bird song and
beautiful light contributed to the sense of idyllic woodland: 'The conception
was brilliant: to pass from the formality and brutality of the court through an
underground labyrinth to the freedom and innocence of the forest was like
being born anew.'[56]

The nature of architectural space which is initially non-theatrical in its
intention, or 'found space' as it is also termed, has become a key feature of
work designed for specific sites. Here, inherent qualities of particular places

have been used to striking effect where productive and imaginative associations between the nature and location of performance space and text are being performed.

In 2001 the Almeida Theatre, temporarily located in an old coach station at King's Cross in London, used the location to comment on the final scene of their production of Frank Wedekind's *Lulu*. Just the bare walls of the station and the murky glass window of the original office served to show how far Lulu had fallen in the final scene.[57] The connection was made between the exploitation of the fictional Lulu and the squalid reality of the evident trade in drugs and prostitution at King's Cross.

In some cases, the site itself is the starting point. Robert Wilson's 1995 installation *HG* was staged in the Clink St Vaults on the site of one of London's medieval prisons. In collaboration with sound designer Hans Peter Kuhn and film production designer Michael Howells, Wilson devised an event where the qualities and atmosphere of the subterranean site provided the raw material of the installation. The maze of tunnels and rooms provided different viewing points for the audience. The first room contained a sumptuous candlelit banquet, apparently abandoned with chairs overturned and meals left half-eaten. The audience was ushered through a door into corridors. Further spaces were embellished with an intriguing collection of objects and given further definition through light, music and sound:

> Round a corner, and a wide, low-ceilinged area opens, filled with row on row of hospital beds, each neatly made, each lit by a weak naked bulb. Move between them; shafts sunk in the floor hold buckets of gouty blood, and from traps in the roof, printed matter cascades down as if from some overflowing archive. Peer through a grille in the wall and you see far off, beyond another gloomy chamber, a luxuriant and leafy arbour, a, glade apparently growing greenly underground. Everywhere you look, it seems some tableau or vision is waiting, and always something more, just out of clear sight.[58]

The spaces offered a progressive series of tableaux, sometimes only glimpsed through peep holes, suggesting potential for various narratives but providing no clear line. The event, staged 100 years after the publication of H. G. Wells' *The Time Machine*, referred to periods from the intervening century through surreal juxtapositions and magical fantasies. Ultimately, as with all Wilson's work, the viewers were left to make up their own minds about the purpose of the work and their responses to it.

Cardboard Citizens is a company which works with homeless people and makes use of the kind of techniques embodied in Augusto Boal's 'forum theatre' as a vehicle for examining oppression and envisaging change. The company works with alternative sites where the scenography emerges from the nature and identity of the chosen building. *Mincemeat* (2001), performed in an old jam factory in Bermondsey, London, was concerned with homelessness and war. These themes were permitted to develop the revelation of sceno-graphic and performance possibilities steered by the nature of the building:

> *Mincemeat* was written alongside the negotiated possibilities and limitations that the available space could offer. The old Hartley's Jam Factory had all the necessary qualities of industrial Victorian architecture. A vast upstairs warehouse was destined to become both Heaven's waiting room and a Bomb site, and the discovery of a tiled room inspired the writing of the Mortuary scenes. Broad, subtle strokes were used to intervene and manipulate the spaces. Modification rather than absolute change was an important principle as the building had its own visual language which was harnessed in order to create meaning and develop the potential for the audience to 'read' the spaces.[59]

Interpretation of the nature and identity of spaces, or 'reading' spaces, partic-ularly in the context of site-specific performance, is complex and layered. Sites possess their own aesthetic qualities and their own histories and even though they may be adapted to accommodate specific performances, inherent charac-teristics remain.

In 1995, Brith Gof's *Tri Bywyd* (Three Rooms) bussed an audience to a location deep in a forest near Aberystwyth in Wales. On the site of a ruined farm, the designer Cliff McLucas devised a skeleton structure from two cubes of scaffolding and planks which provided a series of rooms on three levels running through the ruin. Audience seating created with similar materials wove through the trees. The moss which had taken over the farm building, after it was abandoned in the 1930s, enabled the performance to be viewed through a web of tree trunks.[60] The lives and deaths of the inhabitants of the farm and two other lives and deaths from different times and places in Wales were presented in interleaved fragments which thus invited the possibility of further resonances. McLucas described the site itself (the architecture) as the 'host' and the event that arose (the performance) as the 'ghost':

> The Host site is haunted for a brief time by a Ghost that the theatre makers create. Like all ghosts, it is transparent and Host can be seen through Ghost. Add into this a third term – the Witness – ie the audience, and we have a kind of Trinity that constitutes The Work. It is the mobilisation of this Trinity that is important – not simply the creation of the Ghost. All three are active components in the bid to make site-specific work. The Host, the Ghost and the Witness.[61]

These three components and their particular frames of reference opened up the possibility of generating further layers and connections between hosts, ghosts and witnesses. What McLucas proposes here is that the site, the performance and its witnesses were brought together for the duration of the event through which they retained their own identities and idiosyncrasies.

Gestural space

So far, consideration has been given to the impact of space on the creation and consumption of scenography. However, the spatial dimension is also crucial when considering the way scenography and performers interrelate. In gestural space, the two come together. Pavis has defined gestural space as 'the space created by the presence, stage position, and movements of the performers: a space "projected" and outlined by actors, induced through their corporeality, an evolving space that can be expanded or reduced'.[62] On the one hand it can be seen that scenographic space shapes the way performers physically inhabit the stage space and the way they negotiate it during the course of a performance. On the other hand, the way performers use space through their gestures, movements and physical actions is a fundamental consideration for scenographers and a constituent part of the creation of scenography.

Caspar Neher's approach when working with Brecht was to start from a close observation of the actors in rehearsal. He carefully noted their gestures and movements, isolating and recording those he found particularly productive from a scenographic point of view and made suggestions, in sketch form, as to how a hat, a chair of a certain height or a piece of scenery might comment on the performance. This process provided a dialogue between the actors and the evolving design which was rooted in the use of stage space.

Several commentators have sought to distinguish between the fundamental spatial properties of the stage and the particular uses made of them in performance. Schlemmer embodied this concern in his *Gesture Dance* where the dancers were encouraged to take on motion specifically suggested by carefully selected objects and to let the inherent aspects of their identity condition the nature of the dancer's movement.[63] Such movement inscribes and prescribes definition of space which overlays stage space. Movements of performers leave a 'trail' in their wake which cuts through the stage space.[64]

For Robert Wilson, manipulation of gestural space is one of the principal means by which performers in his productions present themselves and their characters. In rehearsals for *King Lear*, Wilson used the entrances of the three daughters to explore their characters. He drew the walks as lines: a strong straight arrow for Goneril, zig zags for Regan and a graceful curve for Cordelia.[65] What Pavis calls the 'kinaesthetic experience' of actors when they move on stage is made up of their sense of movement, weight, balance, rhythm and tempo, and although this experience resides in the actor, these qualities are transmitted unconsciously to the spectators. These gestures can also underscore the trajectory of interaction with other characters. Patterns of movement provide actors with 'reference points and orientation in space' and provide spectators with a sense of the development of a character or itinerary of a performer which is 'inscribed in space as much as space is inscribed in them'.[66]

Also included in this definition of gestural space are the proxemical relations between performers. 'Proxemics' describe the codes at work through negotiation of different kinds of space and the comfortable distances between individuals.[67] The distance between performers, or the way they approach one another, might convey something of the understanding between them. Scenography shapes proxemical relations on stage. In Craig's scenography for the 1912 Moscow *Hamlet*, the King and Queen were placed in a position which dominated the court but were held at a distance from Hamlet who observed their influence but was not subject to it.

Space as a creative and active force

Behind much of the work that represents developments in scenographic thinking is the concept of space as a dynamic and creative force and the reciprocal action between stage space and performing bodies and stage space and the objects contained within it.

Much of Oskar Schlemmer's practice was motivated by his interest in the way the performing body relates to the space; the way it shapes and is shaped by space: 'Let us now observe the appearance of the human figure as an event and recognize that from the very moment at which it becomes part of the stage, it also becomes a 'space bewitched' creature, so to speak. Automatically and predictably, each gesture or motion is translated in meaningful terms into a unique sphere of activity.'[68] This sense of active space also comes through in Kantor's writing. Space, he says, is the main object of creation. It is charged with energy, it shrinks and expands. 'It is space that conditions the network of relations and tensions between objects.'[69] Space is also an agent in the creation of multiple realities.

16   I am a visual artist, I think spatially ... I have no sense of direction until I have a sense of space. Architectural structure is crucial in my work. If I don't know where

I'm going, I can't get there. The crown was the visual key that unlocked the play for me. It became a tiny wall in this enormous space, and I started thinking of the stage as a dialog between empty space and walls that fly in from time to time to change the space.

Robert Wilson in Arthur Holmberg, *The Theatre of Robert Wilson*, p. 77

In Kantor's later works, such as *Wielopole, Wielopole* (1980) and *The Dead Class* (1975) which are largely autobiographical, the performance space becomes a kind of portal through which Kantor can reflect on the past and the present simultaneously, moving beyond the physical aspects of the stage towards the metaphysical.[70] The set for *Wielopole, Wielopole* was an attempt to remember his childhood, conscious that memory is illusive and constantly reconstructing itself:

> It is difficult to define the spatial dimension of memory.
> Here, this is the room of my childhood,
> with all its inhabitants.
> This is the room which I keep reconstructing again and again
> and that keeps dying again and again.[71]

Kantor appeared in these productions as himself, often interrupting, redirecting the action and walking around the space 'as if trying to find the traces of his life'.[72] Kantor's stage became a mutable, multi-layered space where his 'immaterial memories' were located in 'a three-dimensional heterotopic performance space'.[73] It is interesting to compare these accounts of Kantor's space with discussions of multi-media and digital theatre where it is often claimed that new technologies have afforded ways of presenting time and space which escape the conventions of the physical stage.

Chapter 5

Technology as performance

Throughout the history of Western theatrical presentation, technology has been used to captivate and astound audiences. Early theatre such as that of the Greeks and Romans made use of available technology in order to produce visual transformations, interventions and spectacle. Although later European medieval theatre put stress on the need for audiences to hear and listen to plays, there was also considerable emphasis on the spectacular in performance. For example, staging features such as the medieval device known as Hell Mouth, in which devils and damned souls could appear and disappear through the gaping jaws of a bear's or bull's head, made use of opening and closing doors, lifted jaws or curtains to cover the opening of the mouth. Devils appeared to be consumed by flame.[1]

A powerful example of the way in which aspects of early technology coalesced, and still do so in performances today, is the *Misteri d'Elx* which began in the fifteenth century and is still performed on 15 August every year at Elche, Spain. Here, in the Basilica de Santa Maria, community actors and singers perform a representation of *The Assumption of the Virgin*[2] where scenography provides a key visual focus and simple technology transforms the basilica. Three skeletal metal frames suspended on three thick hemp ropes are separately lowered and raised through a trap door in the dome of the basilica. From here to ground level is some 130 feet. One of the frames is known as the *mangrana*, or the 'pomegranate'. This frame is encased by lightly constructed wooden segments of a shape like that of an orange after it has been peeled. The eight segments of the *mangrana* are connected to thin ropes at their lowest points and thus pulled upwards and outwards to reveal the Angel of the Annunciation inside the device. A second gilded metal frame, known as the *araceli*, is constructed to accommodate five figures of which four are angels who surround the Son on his descent. He is replaced by an artificial representation of the Virgin on the return journey to heaven. The third frame contains three places for the Trinity. When ascending and descending, the three frames on their respective ropes are kept apart by the strength of men lying on their stomachs above the trap door in the dome of the basilica.

126

Needless to say, these operators are secretly anchored in their positions as indeed are the figures on the lowered frames.

The technology employed at Elche has been part of the performance for almost six centuries. The only concession to modern technology occurs towards the end of the event when thousands of pieces of gold-coloured tinsel are showered down upon the audience/congregation through a wide pipe from the dome of the basilica. This action is driven by an electric fan. This modest technology produces wonderful effects which can only be properly appreciated in the context of this liturgical performance. In the *Misteri d'Elx*, technology is used to demonstrate, in scenographic mode, the miracle of the Assumption. It is in this way that strong theatrical power is brought about and communicated by technology.

Despite such traditional and integrated use of technology in the service of early theatre, there is a pervasive and implicit criticism which regards technology as a force for detracting from communication of the narrative or poetic value of the text. As noted earlier, use of technology is sometimes criticised for being costly and indulgent, pandering to the superficial thrill provided by spectacle and nothing more.

> 17   Whether or not technology belongs in the theatre isn't an issue at all – there can be no doubt that it does – but what function does it have in it, and how can it function in the dramatic work? And you can't answer that with a formula.
> Josef Svoboda in Jarka Burian (ed.), *The Secret of Theatrical Space: The Memoirs of Josef Svoboda*, p. 17

Scenographers such as Appia, however, have looked to lighting technology to facilitate a meaningful fusion of the actor, the space and the text. Svoboda has demonstrated how new technology can be exploited and integrated as part of the overall theatrical statement. It should be remembered, too, that technology does not only refer to sound and lighting, but to all the devices and materials of the stage. What is of interest here is not the technologies in themselves, but to what end they can be used, or the extent to which they can be made to perform. Various ways in which theatre technology performs and the means by which technology can provide new ways of re-presenting the world are considered in this chapter.

The craft of technology

On occasions where technology performs supporting roles, there are subtle pleasures in witnessing skilfully timed lighting cues or well-choreographed changes of scenery. The Slottsteater at Drottningholm in Sweden, originally built in 1766 and restored in the 1920s, shows how various pieces of eighteenth-century stage machinery work together as a harmonious whole to create scenic transformations through use of winged chariots, sky borders and back cloths in conjunction with horizontal 'barley sugar' waves, cloud machines and mechanised trapdoors. These devices are controlled through a system of rollers in the roof and below the stage floor.[3] Similarly, satisfaction may be derived from observing the craft of well-built scenery, the attention to detail given to painting or its finish, or the elegance or inventiveness of a solution to a particular staging challenge. These might be said to be occasions through which well-established technological and scenographic conventions service productions without drawing attention to themselves and yet are not entirely invisible. Here, technology performs within the boundaries of expectations; skill and its execution is admired and enjoyed. Elsewhere, use of technology might be seen to offer meaningful experience in and of itself.

Development of scenography has been bound up with the gradual and continual incorporation of materials and technologies as they have become available. New technologies encourage new possibilities of presentation and expression which are not only central to development of scenography but are also intertwined with performance as a whole, the performance register of actors, themes, genre of texts and ways in which audience members experience performance. For example, through the nineteenth century new forms of lighting such as gaslight, limelight and, later, electric light contributed to major changes in European theatrical practice.[4] In scenography, new lighting methods paved the way for gradual development of scenic techniques which aspired to create the illusion of reality on stage. With the development of more powerful and more easily controlled light it was also possible for the auditorium to be made darker than the stage. Thus, it was further possible for that which appeared on stage to be conceived of as another world. Such 'other-worldliness' could be achieved through the depiction of convincing detail brought about by combinations of skilfully painted scenery and coloured light. Completion of this 'world' came about through performers seemingly inhabiting, rather than representing, characters of the play.

Adoption of new technologies is not of itself likely to bring about developments in scenographic representation. Use of video projections as part of scenography is now commonplace, but such an application does not necessarily lead to new scenographic principles. Greg Giesekam suggests that it is possible to achieve a level of realisation through video and computer-generated imagery which 'achieves the dynamic effect of cinematic dissolves'.[5] The illusion of three-dimensional reality and fluid movement from scene to scene is now seen in mainstream theatre. In the London West End musical *The*

Woman in White (2004), computer-generated projection was used to move between locations which included stately homes, London streets, Cumbrian hills and a lunatic asylum.[6] Additionally, production techniques such as panning and tracking, derived from cinema, may be seen through projected animations as aiding transitions between scenes. However, as Giesekam points out, although the production was technologically complex, the scenographic principle behind it harked back to the traditional role of scene design in providing a series of locations in the same way as painted back cloths have done for centuries, and 'there is little challenge to the ideological assumptions which underpin dominant representational conventions'.[7]

Elsewhere, attempts have been made to harness technology in the creation of new forms of scenography. Audiences of the opera *Monsters of Grace* by Robert Wilson and Philip Glass, first staged in 1998, were fascinated by computer-generated stereoscopic imagery which created the appearance of enormous three-dimensional animations such as a sleeping polar bear and an unfurling hand being sliced by a scalpel. Each of these compositions hovered above the spectators, between auditorium and stage. Wilson and Glass described the piece as 'a digital opera in three dimensions' where staged scenes, live music and singing and three-dimensional projections explored intersections between grace, or a divine state, and the human condition (monsters). Projections, directed by Diana Walczak and Jeff Kleiser, demonstrated a novel use of theatre space where life-like images and 'synthespians' (computer-generated characters) could appear to be within an arm's reach of each spectator. They occurred at intervals between Wilson's familiar use of stage modes where lighting operated poetically in relation to human performers in a spare and elegant space. These two kinds of images were held in relation to each other by the Glass score and libretto. Wilson aims to create an experience which audience members can give themselves up to while beginning to make their own associations and connections. In the programme he wrote 'I am not giving you puzzles to solve, only pictures to hear … you go to our opera like you go to a museum. You appreciate the colour of the apple, the line of the dress, the glow of the light.'[8] In the opening twenty minutes the only movement came from light as it gradually flooded and changed the audience's view of the cyclorama which created vistas of coloured space. It acted as a kind of decompression chamber, preparing the audience for a slower, more open and associative mode of viewing. However, technical aspects of the scenography posed some problems for the viewer. Audience members needed to break off from their contemplation of the stage in order to put on 3D glasses to enable them to see the projections. Consequently, the reverie induced by the action on stage was interrupted as the audience was required to physically shift its attention to the stereoscopic images in the auditorium. There was a thrill in experiencing effects which were unfamiliar, at least in the theatre, and unfathomable for most people in terms of the means by which they were created. Scenographically, these animations effectively extended the usual dimension of Wilson's theatrical space, bringing it to within what seemed like an arm's reach of the spectators. But the expectation of the projections and their realisation also dominated the event, making it difficult to maintain the audience immersion required by the production.

The practice of enticing audiences through the promise of new technological innovations has long been part of the process of theatre. Productions of *Miss Saigon* in the 1980s were often promoted using images which referred to the famous scene of the helicopter taking off from the roof of the American Embassy in much the same way that nineteenth-century theatre posters made explicit reference to new scenery and machinery in order to attract audiences. Isolating effects in this way and, effectively, using technology as a gimmick or marketing tool seems to undermine claims for the dramaturgical and poetic capabilities of scenography. Yet the incorporation of these effects may also be proof that the theatre responds to the apparatus of the changing world, appropriating, and misappropriating, technologies as they become available. It may not have succeeded entirely, but *Monsters of Grace* was an attempt to find a new scenographic form for opera in a digital age.

Structure of feeling and the drive for new means of representation

Clearly, technical innovations and the availability of new materials afford new developments in scenography. But developments in dramatic/theatrical form also influence shifts and developments in stage technology. In his study *Drama from Ibsen to Brecht*, Raymond Williams traces experimentation in theatrical form from the late nineteenth century to the mid twentieth century. He notes the way theatrical conventions are challenged and superseded by new practices and how images, both metaphorical and actual, achieve theatrical potency. At around the same time that theatre lighting became sophisticated enough for the stage to present a three-dimensional illusion of reality, Ibsen, Chekhov and Strindberg were writing plays where the domestic room became a highly charged symbol of bourgeois life. These were 'traps of rooms'[9] that illustrated the gap between the apparent comfort of the home and the unsettling societal and emotional shifts at work, unseen 'beyond the door'. Williams is careful to stress that these experiments and innovations were not simply a case of overturning what had gone before, for the sake of style or novelty, but part of a more deep-rooted endeavour in the use of art and cultural objects to find effective ways to reflect a contemporary view and experience of the world. Development of new ideas and new ways of representing the world happens through what Williams calls a 'structure of feeling' which emerges from the 'deepest and often least tangible elements of our experience'.[10] Throughout the history of scenography, experiments with the materials and mechanisms of the stage have led to new ways of representing the world. Genuinely new perspectives often seem strange and isolated at first, but when they begin to find common ground in the work of other artists and find acceptance with a wider public, these innovations start to gain recognition as part of mainstream culture. With their gradual absorption into dominant cultures, formerly challenging yet truthful representations become widely accepted conventions and, with time, lose their initial potency.

18   The theatre, the world of appearances, is digging its own grave when it tries for verisimilitude; the same applies to the mime, who forgets that his chief characteristic is his artificiality. The medium of every art is artificial, and every art gains from recognition and acceptance of its medium.
> Oskar Schlemmer in Tut Schlemmer (ed.), *The Letters and Diaries of Oskar Schlemmer*, p. 126

In Europe during the 1920s, social upheaval and technological innovations created opportunities for the re-evaluation of theatrical form and scenography. In Germany, Piscator embraced the use of projected images alongside live action to produce powerful theatrical spectacle which sought to achieve authentic representations of the world. In Russia, Constructivist stage ideas attempted to produce a new theatrical vocabulary for scenography which embraced the way the Revolution had thrown aside previous conventions. The machine became a powerful symbol of the intended Soviet future and the Constructivist set was conceived as a kinetic and interactive environment for performers. Italian Futurists considered the stage as a mechanical device which offered abstract images for sensuous contemplation. New forms which were prompted by these technological innovations can be seen to have had lasting influence on contemporary uses of technology and on the nature of its performance on stage. Steve Dixon has traced practices in avant-garde theatre in the early twentieth century which have paved the way for contemporary work of a kind which he describes as 'digital performance'; that is, where computer technologies take a key role in the content, techniques and aesthetic forms of theatre and performance.[11] Forerunners to digital performance can be identified in uses of technology in early twentieth-century European avant-garde theatre which have influenced the development of scenography. Three modes of operation of technology emerge: scenic representation; interaction between scenic devices and performers; and the capability of scenic objects and materials to 'perform' independently of a theatrical text.

Scenic representation: immersion and distance

A combination of technological and political developments informed the emergence of new scenographic forms in the 1920s. In Germany, Erwin Piscator's dialectical approach to theatre, which aimed to raise the political consciousness of the working class, was influenced by his commitment to communism and, in addition, his allegiance to the Dada movement. He used technological means to establish a new form of theatre which communicated through collages of projected images, recorded sound and live action. His productions aimed at an immediate, authentic and spectacular impact. Still and moving projected images which mixed documentary film footage, newspaper cuttings and statistics with specially shot sequences and hand-drawn caricatures gave the productions an epic scope, underscoring and contextualising actors' performances. Edward Braun refers to these techniques as ones which occasionally overshadowed the players.[12] *Hoppla, wir leben!* (1927) was designed by Traugott Müller and featured a multi-storeyed structure constructed of gas-piping to encompass various scenes of the play and to demonstrate the structure of society in cross-section. Screens permitted both front and back projection. Archive film conveying the immediate historical and political context of the central character's situation was used to 'intercut' filmed sequences which conveyed key themes and events in the story of the play. Piscator saw film as 'living scenery' and the means of creating the 'motive force' of story.[13] That is to say, it went beyond the simple establishment of location or suitable backgrounds and became a key component in the construction of visual argument. Piscator understood the potential of well-chosen images from his association with John Heartfield, an artist who pioneered the technique of photomontage, reusing and manipulating photographic material to create loaded and powerful political statements.[14] In *The Good Soldier Schwejk* (1928) (Figure 25), George Grosz, an artist and savage caricaturist, created animated cartoons which combined with film footage projected over the actor (Max Pallenberg) who walked on the spot on a conveyor belt. This was intended to establish Schwejk's journey to the eastern front during the First World War. In execution, Piscator's complex productions could be chaotic and the technology intrusive and noisy.[15] Piscator's influence on Brecht's staging

25. G. Grosz, *The Good Soldier Schwejk*, by J. Hacek. Director Erwin Piscator, Piscator Theater, Berlin, 1928

has been widely acknowledged, especially in relation to use of 'revolves' and projection. Although use of technology may have been similar, the outcome was quite different. For Piscator technology allowed the audience to become immersed in a collage of images aimed at conveying political reality. Use of levels, revolves and conveyor belts allowed a fast-moving presentation which merged the way film was conceived and edited with live theatre. The film itself was seen to be a crucial part of the performance; the 'photographic image' was seen by Piscator as capable of conducting the dramatic action and became the 'motive force, a piece of living scenery'.[16] The aim here was to draw in the audience by means of technology and thus immerse its members. Brecht, on the other hand, used technology 'as a means of breaking the audience's involvement and recalling to it the critical attitude at which he aimed'.[17] Caspar Neher's projections for the Bertolt Brecht–Kurt Weill opera, *Rise and Fall of the City of Mahagonny*, provided a visual counterpart to music and text, with each element standing in dialogic relation to the others. These projections were intended to help the audience achieve critical distance, rather than be unthinkingly absorbed by the spectacle.

In a contemporary context, Dixon has written about use of projected images by The Builders Association as a post-Brechtian dramaturgical intervention in the live action rather than as a device of representation. *Alladeen* (2003), a multi-media production which addressed technological globalisation, used screens situated above, before and behind live performers. The material shown on them made use of an aesthetic vocabulary from computer games and computer interfaces. This was considered as important as the live action.[18]

Conscious use of projection as a separate element from performers echoes Caspar Neher's use of projection as a means of commenting on live action. For example, in The Builders Association production of *Jump Cut* (1997–98) 'the live action and the projections are dialectical: they undertake an intellectual dialogue, making mutual connections and commentaries between and about one another'.[19] Dixon contrasts this work with uses of projection that aim at a *Gesamtkunstwerk* which is visceral, sensory and immersive, as seen in the work of George Coates. His company uses 'ingenious stepped, receding screen systems which combine with matched projections beamed directly onto a pivoting, bowl-shaped curved stage, to create an illusion of live actors inhabiting immersive three dimensional settings with an acute sense of realistic, vanishing perspective'.[20] Notions of 'distance' and 'immersion' can be useful in describing ways in which scenographic environments are intended to work with performers who inhabit them and the ways they are to be viewed. Some scenography manages to move between both modes of audience engagement. Svoboda's work shows that incorporation of projection can shift effectively between visceral and emotive images, which offer captivating associations between performer and environment, and images which offer visual and spatial intervention.

Svoboda believed that adoption of new technologies and new materials was inevitable and necessary if theatre was to reflect its own time. At the same time, he was keen to point out that it was not technology itself which was important but the way that it was intended to work and the dramaturgical impact it was calculated to effect. Svoboda's interest in and willingness to experiment with the ways in which technology could be harnessed for dramatic purposes drove him to believe that it was knowledge of the technical which made for creativity.

Experiments with projection and performing bodies through 'Laterna Magika' enabled Svoboda to develop techniques that could be used in his scenography for literary-based theatre. But such experiments also offered a new form of theatre. In this non-verbal, carefully synchronised combination of film and live performer, Svoboda saw the filmed material and the performers' actions as interdependent: 'One thing is not the background for the other; instead you have a simultaneity, a synthesis and fusion of actors and projection. Moreover, the same actors appear on screen and stage, and interact with each other. The film has a dramatic function.'[21] In *Wonderful Circus*, a performance that has been in the 'Laterna Magika' repertoire since 1977,[22] this sort of synthesis has been achieved technically through projection onto layered curtains devised to be easily pulled up or back, enabling performers to walk through or into a projected image. The particular themes and important reference points of this piece may well seem to a contemporary audience to be firmly fixed in the Czech cultural past, but the way in which the projected material was intended to relate to live performers continues to demonstrate the principle of technology as a dramatic device. The apparent simplicity of such techniques belies the potential richness of the effects. The combination of filmed images and live performance enables different perspectives to be shown simultaneously. Space and time in the theatre can be extended through augmentation with film. Footage of a road filmed from a moving vehicle allowed characters to 'travel' whilst standing still. This was more than just a storytelling device; the speed of the film and the obvious separation between performers and their fictional environment developed comedic and poignant nuances to the scene. Projected images of performers' faces, magnified several times beyond their normal size, set up a particular relationship between images on screens and live performers. The nature of filmed material is that it is, or appears to be, an authentic rendering of the real world. However, Svoboda did not use film to lend illusory realism to his stage. Instead, he played with selected references to the real world by bringing them into contact with the stylised and more abstract language of physical theatre and dance. Burian refers to Svoboda's use of technological instruments which become 'dramatically integral elements' whilst Svoboda himself said 'the technical is an organic, synthetic element; it acquires poetry and metaphoric power'.[23]

Director Robert Lepage has named his Quebec-based theatre company Ex Machina. He describes his work as being concerned with 'implicitly ascribing creative powers to technology itself'.[24] Lepage's work is the result of collaboration between actors, writers, set and lighting designers, video artists, puppeteers and composers. Kinetic constructions blend with filmed and live video projection and physical theatre to produce theatre which owes much to cinematic techniques of storytelling. This occurs through the way it uses visual and sound material to move fluidly between scenes as collages of non-linear images in order to establish different points of view, ideas, feelings and the passage of time:[25] 'The weight of communicating is thrown onto the non-verbal language of action, requiring imaginative participation by the audience to piece together a holistic interpretation.'[26] Innes describes a famous scene from *Needles and Opium* (1991) where Lepage used parallels and coincidental moments in the lives of American jazz trumpeter Miles Davis and the French poet Jean Cocteau to explore themes of drug addiction and artistic creation. Here Lepage, suspended on wires, became Cocteau:

> Lepage-as-Cocteau apparently floats upwards through the skyscrapers of Manhattan (as a physical rendition of Cocteau's proclamation of his own transcending genius in *Lettre aux Américains* – achieved by film of lighted windows and fire-escapes moving downwards behind Lepage's

suspended figure) then like Icarus tumbles down from the heights (running the film in reverse).[27]

In a radio interview (2006) Lepage explained his stance towards the synthesis of the technological and theatrical narrative: 'I think that the very technological allows me to invite film and/or television into the theatre and I think that's a very, very important step to take for theatre, because theatre cannot survive on itself if it doesn't take into account all the different narrative languages that are around.'[28] Although Lepage borrows cinematic techniques for use in the theatre, the scenography in his work is rarely confined to the pictorial. Even so, the technologies used by him are not all new. In *Needles and Opium*, for example, a screen shows abstract shapes in silhouette which are gradually assembled to reveal a trumpet: the representation of Miles Davis.[29] The technology here was based on the same principle as shadow puppetry and required no more than a translucent screen and a light source. What is noteworthy is the way that the images are incorporated into the rest of the production. Lepage thinks of his technique as multilingual:

> I have an idea, I say it in a language people don't understand so they are interested to know what it is all about. So I say it again, but in another language they don't understand … It's very active. It's like saying the same thing over and over again, but with different images. People associate words and senses and objects and imagery.[30]

Lepage's productions are characterised by the way stage images are established through interaction of technology and performer. A good example of this is Lepage's production of *Elsinore*, an adaptation of *Hamlet* which was presented almost entirely through one actor (Lepage) at the centre of a technological construction.

The structure, designed by Carl Fillion, contained a central platform which could rotate vertically and horizontally and which contained a trapdoor and further moving side panels. These neutral surfaces were given definition and purpose through projected graphic images and video to establish locations or to refract and multiply images of characters. Dexterity and seemingly infinite flexibility of the construction allowed Lepage to move fluidly from the presentation of one character to another. For example, 'Ophelia' was seen to drown by disappearing through the trapdoor and 'Hamlet' climbed out of the same opening to emerge on board the swaying deck of the ship that took him to England. Later 'Hamlet' was pushed through the same trapdoor and through white fabric which stretched it into a vast white dress which covered the stage and became 'Ophelia'. Such inventiveness goes beyond presenting clever solutions to staging problems; as Innes points out, the technology of the set is also a metaphor for Hamlet's inner psychological state.[31] Like Craig, Lepage explores the play from Hamlet's perspective. In *Elsinore*, Hamlet was trapped inside a machine or a kind of cat's cradle and the other characters were reflections of himself. The technology was both a facilitator of action and an essential element of the dramaturgy.

Scenography as an 'Acting Machine': interactivity

The Russian Revolution of 1917 prompted radical rethinking as to how the world should be portrayed through art. Many artists felt that their work needed to respond to and even encourage creation of a new Soviet society. The Constructivist movement, which included artists working in painting, sculpture, architecture and textiles, formulated approaches which were based on 'the effective organisation of material elements'.[32] The notion of artists motivated by aesthetic concerns delivered through their own individual expression was displaced by the model of an artist as a constructor or technician. These impulses were to find alignment in other forms of industry.[33] This was considered to be the only way in which art might be rendered purposeful and become an active agent in the transformation of society: 'We the Constructivists, renounce art because it is not useful. Art by its very nature is passive, it only reflects reality. Constructivism is active, it not only reflects reality but takes action itself.'[34] Mechanisation was intended to be the cornerstone of Soviet society; industrialisation was meant to be the means by which the economy developed, and Soviet citizens were supposed to work like cogs in a machine towards a common goal. Constructivism adopted an approach which was characterised by elimination of any superfluous or merely decorative elements. Geometric forms were broken down into their basic units with a focus on the utilitarian and on purposeful incorporation into everyday life. In this climate the challenge for the theatre was to overcome mistrust of the imaginary and illusionary. Drama and its staging were required to be drawn into line with an ideal where art was 'an instrument capable of transforming both man and society' through an appeal to the intellect. Ironically, claims Rudnitsky, theatre was the eventual means by which Constructivism realised large-scale ideas which had been restricted hitherto to models and manifestos.[35] Popova's designs for Meyerhold's production of *The Magnanimous Cuckold* can be seen as a realisation of 'the utopian notion of society as an engine'.[36]

The full effect of Popova's design can perhaps be best appreciated by focusing on the kinetic nature of the set and the way the movement of the performers was underlined and enhanced. The 'bio-mechanical' approach to gesture and movement which characterised the approach of Meyerhold's company enabled a physical embodiment of the actors' intelligence and expression. The basic techniques were 'designed to develop the ability to control one's body within the stage space in the most advantageous manner'[37] and Popova's design provided an ideal environment for the actors. 'Bio-mechanics' employed popular forms of performance movement, particularly those derived from Commedia dell'Arte and circus. Acrobatic sequences and rhythmic gestures were enhanced by steps, slides and levels of structures. Sets were considered to be like a piece of gymnastic apparatus on which trained performers could be tested in order to demonstrate their mastery. An eyewitness describes how the actor presenting Stella worked with the physical space:

> Her performance is based on rhythms, precise and economical like a construction. Not the rhythms of speech, of words and pauses. No, the rhythms of steps, surfaces and space. Few words to speak of. The part is built on movement … Her feet are trained not for the gentle rake of the ordinary stage, but for the dizzying cascades of steps, ramps, bridges and slopes.[38]

Several parts of the set were designed to move, at certain points in the action, like cogs in a wayward machine. When Bruno, in a rage of jealousy, slapped his wife's cousin, the wheels revolved almost as though they were laughing at him and commenting on his ridiculous behaviour. As the events in the play became more farcical and outrageous, the wheels turned faster and more frequently and thus underscored the action. Rudnitsky claims it was Meyerhold himself who operated the wheels.[39] Popova said of her design that she aimed first to organise 'the material elements … as an apparatus' and to prioritise function over form and then secondly to 'underline and intensify the kinetic value of each movement of the action'.[40] Some contemporary commentators were critical of the play because of its apparent lack of revolutionary content,[41] but for others it succeeded in achieving distance between the recent past and a bright new future:

> In revolutionary Russia, which had dispensed with privacy and the sexual monopoly of bourgeois marriage, Crommelynck's maniacal hero seemed genuinely magnanimous, donating his wife to the common good. The farce was now a fable about social lubrication. Popova illustrated this new and unexpected moral in a kinetic set which represented a windmill in cross-section, with grinding wheels and revolving sails, steep ladders, pulleys and delivery chutes: it made visible the motor of desire, but also displayed the economy in farcically furious, hyperefficient action. Actors scrambled over the bare frame, scampered along catwalks and slid down ramps, exemplifying the socialist transformation of work into fun.[42]

The set was actually a radical re-presentation of the play. The machine-like structure became not only an effective environment in which to demonstrate bio-mechanics; it also worked on a metaphorical level where it presented a new vision of Soviet society.

A more subtle kind of acting machine was provided by Sally Jacobs' set and costumes for Peter Brook's production of *A Midsummer Night's Dream* (1970) (Figure 26). It contained no reference to the historical past of the play and seemed to exist solely to generate a playing space for the performers. The single setting consisted of a three-sided white box. The mechanicals wore work clothes and the lovers simple cotton clothes reflecting the cut of clothes

26. Sally Jacobs, *A Midsummer Night's Dream*, by William Shakespeare. Director Peter Brook, Royal Shakespeare Theatre, Stratford, 1970

contemporary to the production. Oberon, Titania and Puck, dressed in bright satin costumes reminiscent of Chinese acrobats, descended from trapezes. A walkway ran around the top of the box walls where actors could look down on those performing. The spareness and strangeness of the setting worked to suggest several different spaces at once: 'a clinic, a scientific research station, an operating theatre, a gymnasium and a big top'.[43] Above all, it provided a dynamic space for performers, 'the visible puppets of the machine'.[44] The magic of the play was reinterpreted not as a supernatural force but as something that was located in the human world. The world of the court, in the shape of the blank box, never disappeared and served to undercut the magic and high spirits of the wood.[45]

The 'machines' of Popova and Jacobs produced reciprocal relationships between the performers and their environment. Such interaction worked simultaneously at technical and symbolic levels and maintained the 'liveness' and spontaneity of performance.

Introduction of pre-recorded projections has proved challenging to the fundamental concept of 'performer-centred', live theatre. Svoboda identified this problem with 'Laterna Magika' techniques. The success of this kind of approach depends on pre-recorded footage and well-rehearsed execution on the part of performers and theatre technicians. This may be seen to detract from the invention or spontaneity that are possible in the theatre. Pre-recorded footage can be made to appear interactive, but in actuality, performers have to follow the projections and time their performances to fit the film.

The appearance of interaction has been a feature of experiments which bring together digital scenography and dance. Choreographer Merce Cunningham's 1999 production *Biped* made use of stylised video animations which were projected onto a gauze. Created by Paul Kaiser and Shelley Eshkar, these animations were based on 'motion-capture' data of the dancers so that the stylised and abstracted forms nonetheless echoed the movement of the live dancers. However, the final choreography and the video animations were prepared separately. The same was the case with Gavin Bryars' score. As with previous works, Cunningham embraced 'chance' interactions between various elements, effectively inviting the audience to consider relationships between live performers and projections in order to make connections between them.[46]

The goal of genuine interaction between dance performer and technology has been pursued by companies such as Palindrome and Troika Ranch. In the production of *16 Revolutions* by Troika Ranch (2006) the real-time performance of the dancer affected the quality of the projected material and the sonic environment. Sensory systems allowed the path of the dancers' skeletons to be tracked as they performed. The quality of their movement, for example, slow, fast, lyrical, sharp, simple, complex, was detected and then reflected in the scenographic environment through sound and projected images. The timbre of the music shifted or the colour and composition of the image altered in response to changes in the movement so that the dancers were able to influence the composition of the scenography as they performed.[47]

Palindrome uses environmental and body sensors which track heart beat, brain activity, musculo-skeletal changes and touch in order to trigger outputs of sound, projected images and light. In *Digital Dreaming* (1999) a dancer is almost obliterated at times when she triggers digital 'rain'. The 'ones' and 'zeros' fall thicker and faster in response to the quality of her movement as they are projected over her body onto the floor and onto vertical screens.[48] In other pieces such as *Talking Bodies* (2005), the dancer has finer control over the visual and sonic environment. Here, fragments of recorded speech and pro-jected text can be summoned by the performer's movement, creating a scenog-raphy that is, like the performance, always unique.

Although he did not have access to the software that Troika Ranch and Palindrome have developed, Alwin Nikolais (1910–93), designer and choreo-grapher, was one of the first to explore interactivity between performers and scenography. His work serves to remind us that it is not only the new digital technologies that afford interactivity. He used fabric, materials and costumes to abstract the dancers' bodies and liberate dance from what he saw as an overly psychological approach.[49] *Tensile Involvement* (1953) used elastic ribbons which were attached to the dancers' hands and allowed their bodies to become part of a larger abstract environment which changed and developed with each movement. Also costumes which covered the body defamiliarised the human form, creating strange new shapes and possibilities.[50]

Nikolais' work is still interesting now for the way that it demonstrates a dialogic relationship between the bodies of performers and the scenographic environment. A delicate balance is explored between the scenographic materi-als and the dancer so that even when the performer's body is obscured, altered or made strange by the scenography, it never disappears.

Sometimes, the technological intervention which threatens to overwhelm the performer is taken as a stimulus. Choreographer Wayne McGregor used prosthetic extensions, designed by Jim Henson's Creature Shop, with his dancers in *Nemesis* (2002). The dancers' own limbs were augmented with animatronic extensions, doubling the reach of an arm, for example, or altering its inherent movement. The technology was grafted onto the body so that the dancers experienced a lack of control and, in doing so, discovered new vocabularies of movement which arose from a 'misbehaving body'; one that does not respond predictably.[51]

In echoes of the dispute between Jones and Jonson, the intersection of technology and human performer is often expressed in terms of relative control. On the one hand there are concerns that the performer will be reduced to the role of puppet by the use of technology, especially with pre-recorded technology which tends to set a pace to which the live performer must yield, or where complex technology is prone to break down and inhibit performance. Christopher Innes explores the implications of this idea in relation to Lepage, Craig and Wilson, but he concludes that 'Being a "puppet" offers in fact a liberation from gravity and time, expanding the conventional two-dimensional movement of performance into new spatial possibilities.'[52] On the other hand, performers' movements, physical states and dialogue can be made to trigger technology, giving the appearance of scenography which is responsive to the performer. In this case, the scenographic environment is controlled by the performer. What remains elusive in these new technological applications is a reciprocity between performers and scenography that has been achieved by more modest stage devices.

Technology performs

The Italian Futurist movement, led by Filippo Tommaso Marinetti, attempted to harness the power of art as an active social force. The work of the movement linked an aesthetic revolution to a revolution in society where art 'invaded society and stimulated active responses from the spectators'.[53] The concept of the machine as a model for realising the potential of humankind was central to the aesthetic of the movement. The merging of man and machine offered an 'interchange of intuition, rhythm, instinct, and metallic discipline' and a way for humankind to 'master and reign over space and time'.[54] Although Futurist art manifested itself in forms including painting, sculpture, literature and architecture, a central focus was on performance events which combined presentations of their manifestos with examples of work which arose from their theories.

Marinetti's concept of a 'synthetic' theatre centred on abstraction, improvisation and the use of elements such as gestures, words, sounds and lights which were considered to be autonomous and alogical and which came together to create 'stage ambiences where different actions, atmospheres and times can interpenetrate and unroll simultaneously'. Above all, it was 'directed at the audience's senses, not their intellect'.[55] The concept of a specifically Futurist scenography was further developed by Enrico Prampolini, whose 1915 manifesto *Futurist Scenography* envisaged 'colourless electro-mechanical architecture, powerfully vitalized by chromatic emanations from a luminous source, produced by electric reflectors with multi-coloured panes of glass, arranged, co-ordinated analogically with the psyche of each scenic action'.[56] That is to say, mobile three-dimensional elements animated by coloured light and coloured vapour were required to replace static painted sets. Furthermore, harnessing new technology in this way permitted scenography to go beyond the provision of backdrops for performers and thus become the focus and substance of the theatrical experience. Prampolini describes the effect of the abstracted shapes and the action of coloured light as a liminal and transcendent experience: 'With the luminous irradiations of these beams and planes of coloured lights, the dynamic combinations of these chromatic fugues will produce marvellous effects of interpenetration and intersection of lights and shadows, creating a space for abandonment or shapes of luminous and exulting quality.'[57] He envisaged that this approach to scenography could create 'new sensations and emotional values in the spectator' and do so quite independently from text or human actors.[58] Prampolini pursued these ideals in his own work, but it was another Futurist artist, Giacomo Balla, whose scenographic performance of Stravinsky's *Feu d'artifice*, produced by the Ballets Russes in Rome in 1917, provided perhaps the most striking attempt to realise Futurist scenography. In 1914, Stravinsky's composition had been interpreted through dance by Loïe Fuller.

As early as 1892, the American dancer Loïe Fuller performed what was known as her 'serpentine dance' in which fabric and light were as important and significant as the dance itself. She danced with voluminous silk skirts and veils which were fluidly manipulated with bamboo rods so that they swirled and undulated around her body. All this was illuminated with coloured light, which transformed the moving body and created ethereal, glowing and stylised natural forms which in turn fused and transformed images of a butterfly, a blooming flower, clouds and flames. She experimented with and developed new ways of creating and mixing colours in light and developed new angles from which to organise light through use of mirrors and lantern projectors. At the Paris International Exhibition of 1900 she performed on a glass stage which could be lit from beneath and in some instances signalled technicians to change the colour of the light as she responded to the music.[59]

Instead of using dance and human performers, Balla created a stage full of mobile abstract geometric shapes (prisms, curves and spirals) made of wooden frames and clad in a variety of materials, both opaque and reflective. They were further animated by coloured light, both emanating from within the forms and projected onto them, which was refracted by the incorporation of reflective surfaces. Balla plotted fifty cues in the five-minute performance.[60] He also directed light and shadow towards the audience, in order to implicate them in the event. The intention was to create 'a spectacle which evoked the sensations of cosmic life' and an impression of 'the futuristically reconstructed universe'.[61] The performance, however, was not recognised as an artistic breakthrough at the time. The critic from *La Tribuna* found the performance 'pleasant' but found that 'repetition of the same effects aroused a sense of boredom'.[62]

Although Futurist scenography may not have found immediate popular acceptance, the legacy of this approach can be seen in contemporary work. Certainly, Wilson and Lepage have embraced the idea of non-literary forms of theatre where ideas are communicated through associative imagery. Furthermore, possibilities presented by digital and computer technologies are allowing the properties and potentials of fundamental scenographic elements such as light to be reappraised.

Fabrizio Crisafulli is an Italian theatre director and a visual artist who uses projected light as a structural and poetic device in his performances and installations: 'I believe that light does not belong only to the technical or visual domain. Its fundamental functions are to shape time and space, to become a dramatic structure, and serve as a means of unfolding or producing "actions".'[63] Crisafulli works intently and sensitively with the relationships between light and the performer's body or, in the case of site-specific work, between light and the 'text' provided by existing architecture; that is, the space, texture and rhythm of the place. He aims for a 'reciprocal exchange between the projection and the object, between the digital realm and the material world'.[64] As discussed earlier, frequent concerns are expressed regarding effective interaction between technology and human performers, between the virtual and the real. Crisafulli addresses this delicate balance. His projections may be seen to make objects 'perform', but they are, at the same time, shaped to respond to the objects they illuminate. 'Such an encounter between digital image and matter opens up a new dimension – empty, mysterious, suspended – that is difficult to attribute to a solely digital sphere.'[65]

---

19   An actor is standing in the middle of a theatre space. He is motionless. The light moves around. The light is directed at him from various directions and heights. The shadow keeps changing. At one time it is very long and thin; at other times it is very short and obese. It shrinks or expands ….

The shadow is a l i v e !

   Tadeusz Kantor, A Journey through Other Spaces: Essays and Manifestos, 1944–1990, p. 219

Although new technologies do not necessarily produce new forms of scenography, they can call into question conventional use of technology and provoke a reappraisal of all the materials and technologies that scenography has at its disposal.[66] This may in turn lead to new 'architectures of performance'[67] where scenography shapes new modes of theatrical expression and new relationships between performance and spectator.

Technology and the postdramatic theatre

Hans-Thies Lehmann claims that the 'postdramatic theatre establishes the possibility of dissolving the logocentric hierarchy and assigning the dominant role to elements other than dramatic logos and language'. This opens up the possibility of a 'theatre of scenography' or 'visual dramaturgy'[68] where perception and meaning are communicated through optical and spatial data without being subordinated to the text. This, he suggests, leads to a different kind of logic where concepts from the world of visual art have been adopted by the theatre.[69] This applies even more to the visual than to the auditory dimension. In place of a dramaturgy regulated by the text one often finds a visual dramaturgy.

New technologies play an important role in postdramatic theatre because they lend themselves to the production of several of its characteristic traits. A non-hierarchical approach draws on all the elements of the stage, including the scenographic and the technological, as outlined here by Heiner Goebbels:

> I am interested in inventing a theatre where all the means that make up theatre do not just illustrate and duplicate each other but instead all maintain their own forces but act together, and where one does not just rely on the conventional hierarchy of means. That means, for example, where a light can be so strong that you suddenly only watch the light and forget the text, where a costume speaks its own language or where there is a distance between speaker and text and a tension between music and text.[70]

Technologies of the stage can 'speak' their own various languages while working 'alongside' rather than 'behind' the text. Additionally, technologies of recording, editing and replaying or projecting can be used to help create distance between the various elements. The Wooster Group have developed ways of using technology in conjunction with live performers in ways that echo but exceed Robert Edmond Jones' ideas. They use film (pre-recorded, live-feed, and 'found' clips from existing films) which is shown on multiple monitors placed in and around the performance space. Sound, too, is layered and fragmented in a similar way. Their postmodern approach is built around 'quotation, appropriation and displacement'.[71] *Frank Dell's The Temptation of St Antony* (1987), for example, drew on multiple and disparate texts, including Gustave Flaubert's *La Tentation de Sainte Antoine*, Ingmar Bergman's film *The Magician* and late-night cable TV, whilst the Frank Dell of the title refers to an alter ego of the comedian Lenny Bruce.[72] The collage of literary, visual and sonic texts that they use is distributed across the stage space via technology which is deliberately visible: screens and monitors, microphones, cameras and cables, and the tracks and scaffolding that they require. The film material they use comes from found clips from existing movies alongside pre-recorded footage and live-feed images of the performers. Just as Svoboda's experiments with 'Laterna Magika' have shown, the introduction of film technology can disrupt the usual expectations of space and time. Whereas Svoboda liked to conceal technological means, the Wooster Group's work brings it to the fore, 'moving technology to the center and the live performer to the periphery'.[73] The sets are 'often constructed like obstacle courses', which requires the actors to adopt 'active negotiation' in relation to the scenic environment.[74] This may suggest a displacement of the performer, but it is instead a reconfiguring of the stage. The Wooster Group's rehearsal process incorporates objects and technologies and develops the live and the mediated aspects of performance simultaneously so that 'microphones and video monitors' are like performers themselves.[75] The aesthetic of their work is informed firstly by a 'utilitarian, rather than a decorative, function' and the costumes, furniture and objects they use are often recycled from one performance to another and 'carry imprints of the everyday activities' of previous use.[76] But the compositional aesthetic of their work borrows from the technologies of audio recording and film. In *House/Lights* (1999) use is made of the 'structural language' of film (camera moves, close-ups, long shots) as a 'template' for the organisation of movement and space.[77]

Lehmann identifies the characteristic of postdramatic theatre as its affinity with performance art. Of particular interest is 'the physical, affective and spatial relationship between actors and spectators'.[78] This offers possibilities of participation and interaction and of redefining theatre as a process rather than a finished work, for example *Blast Theory* and *Desert Rain*.

Desert Rain was a performance installation which involved the audience of six as though they were in a computer game. Each participant had a 'target' to find which was associated with the Gulf War. The manner of the action was that of a Hollywood action drama. The participants progressed through virtual reality spaces such as an American motel room, underground bunkers and tunnels, together with real materials as a projection curtain of fine rain, a large heap of real sand and a real room which represented an English hotel. After all this, the audience was finally confronted by the targets recounting, via video, their experiences of the war. Each participant left with a small bag of sand which was concealed in the coat or bag they handed over at the start of the performance. This combination of the real and the imaginary is intended to provoke consideration of the way the war was reported and the real impact it had on actual people, and 'attempts to bring visitors to a new understanding of the ways in which the virtual and the real are blurred and, in particular, the role of the mass media in distorting our appraisal of the world beyond our own personal experience'.[79]

The scenography of *Desert Rain* brings about an immersion in the very ideas that the piece aims to explore; the participant's active experience of the war as a game offers a productive set of conditions from which to think about wider issues. In work like this, technological means offer new ways of approaching contemporary debates and concerns. As Baugh has observed: 'The contributions of computer-controlled technology and computer-created scenography offer metaphors of transience, instability, multiple framing and interactivity to a postdramatic world of performance.'[80]

Part 3

Realisation and reception

Chapter 6

Analysis of scenography

So far, this book has focused on the creation of scenography and key issues of its production. This has necessarily involved consideration of scenographic practitioners and the role of scenography in relation to processes of performance and their realisation in production. The following chapters consider ways in which scenography might be discussed from critical and academic viewpoints as central components to the experience of viewing or witnessing performance.

It is important to identify relevant approaches to the analysis of theatre performance in order to determine how they might assist specifically in the analysis of scenography. The dominant influence in this respect has been 'semiotics' and theories of the 'sign' as means of communication. Although there have been objections to the structuralist nature of semiotics and several post-structural and post-semiotic departures,[1] semiotics has had a widespread influence on the way the performance event is conceptualised and analysed. Bearing this in mind, it is important to examine concepts and approaches which have had particular impact on the way scenography can be considered as an object of study. Elaine Aston and George Savona state that the 'visual dimension of theatre is in general accorded a somewhat surprisingly low priority in critical and theoretical discussion'.[2] Their work on 'reading' the stage image goes some way towards addressing this concern by providing a semiotic account of the creation and analysis of scenography. Their work will be considered in further detail at a later stage.

Semiotics and scenography

First of all, it is important to consider the origins of semiotic analysis and the ways in which scenography operates as a sign system. Semiotics, or the theory and study of signs, originated in the study of linguistic communication, but has come to be applied to all manner of culturally produced objects and systems. Ferdinand de Saussure (1857–1913), a Swiss linguist, proposed that communication in language is made up of units of meaning or signs, each consisting of a 'signifier' and a 'signified'. The signifier is the sound-image, the concrete utterance, and the 'signified' is the concept for which the sound-image stands. There is generally no obvious connection between sounds of words and what they mean to those who hear them. These are links which have to be negotiated or learned. So, what a signifier produces in the way of a signified is therefore not fixed but a matter of agreement. Like two sides of a coin, the signifier and the signified are entirely dependent on one another for communication to occur and for meaning to be created. Saussure's model of the linguistic sign has been widely applied in the field of visual culture. Here the signifier is material and physical rather than a sound-image produced by speech:

> The signifier may be thought of as any physical object which has been
> given a meaning. The signifier may be thought of as the material or
> physical vehicle of meaning. Thought of in this way, it is the sign's image
> as we are able to perceive it visually; it could be gestured, drawn, painted,
> photographed, computer-generated and so on. The signified may be
> thought of as the meaning that is associated with, or given to, the signifier.
> It may be thought of as the mental concepts or thoughts that come into
> one's head on seeing (or hearing, etc.), the signifier.[3]

As Barnard suggests, the signifieds generated by these visual signifiers are not fixed. Although the meaning of a road sign ought to be grasped quickly, a painting might well be open to interpretation by the viewer. Semiotics is not concerned with specifying particular meanings; it deals with the study of processes of signification and the means by which 'meanings are generated and exchanged'.[4]

Application of these ideas to the study of theatre was first taken up in the 1930s and 1940s by theorists belonging to the Prague School where concepts with important implications for scenography were developed.[5] Firstly, the notion of a theatre production as a signifying entity allowed scenography, a part of that entity, to create meaning separately from the text. Secondly, it became necessary to 'view the performance not as a single sign but as a network of semiotic units belonging to different cooperative systems'.[6] The contribution of the Prague School showed the signifying potential of all things on stage and emphasised that this is something that happens at the point of performance. This challenged traditional academic approaches to the analysis of theatre which were based on literary criticism of the theatrical text. Previously, the stage spectacle was 'considered too ephemeral a phenomenon for systematic study'.[7] Jiří Veltruský's statement that 'all that is on the stage is a sign'[8] indicates that anything on stage, even things which are there to fulfil a largely functional role, are part of the network of signs and as such have the potential to carry dramatic meaning.

'All that is on the stage' incorporates all that is apparent to the audience, so that a particular lighting state or a costume might be seen to carry as much meaning as an exchange of dialogue or an actor's gesture. What is important here is the extent to which scenographic components might be viewed as participating in the action on equal terms with the other elements of theatre.

The signifying capability of all that is on stage, whether it is animate or inanimate, shifts and changes through the course of a performance 'so that even a lifeless object may be perceived as the performing subject, and a live human being may be perceived as an element completely without will'.[9] Veltruský traces a hierarchy of the various parts of a performance from actor to object, where the performer playing the central character attracts most attention and is the focus of the action. All the performers/characters form a cohesive whole in the unfolding dramatic action. This notion also applies to those in supporting roles whose actions might be seen to be increasingly schematic or limited as they move away from the 'lead' characters. Performers on stage may be seen to contribute to the action in varying degrees to the point where some figures, such as servants for example, operate more like props than performers. And beyond that point, figures such as soldiers standing on guard may become part of the set, and more like objects than human. Additionally, the set contributes towards action by defining space for performers which can convey action even when no performer is present. So, during the course of a performance there is a constant shift of attention between elements or objects. Veltruský calls this the 'action force' of an object and one which demonstrates that props are not passive entities that rely on a performer to animate them but things capable of signifying action by themselves. In turn, these features can provoke expectations of future action. An object might displace an actor in the fluid hierarchy of stage action. In semiotic analysis the human and the object are accorded the same signifying potential: 'It is therefore impossible to draw a line between subject and object, since each component is potentially either. We have seen various examples of how thing and man can change places, how a man can become a thing and a thing become a living being.'[10] Scenographic objects, during performance, might become more important in the hierarchy of the signified as they become the focus for the audience and signify momentum of action.

20   In a production of spoken drama, the presence of the actor is absolutely necessary to any communication, and consequently he takes on abnormal

importance, as the visual requirements we have mentioned prove. But for the author of word-tone drama, the actor is not the sole or even the most important interpreter of the poet's intention, he is rather but one medium, neither more nor less important than the others, at the poet's disposal. Once the actor ceases to be the dominant element in production, having no longer to 'make a speech', he recedes into the background to take his place among his co-workers, the various other poetic-musical devices, ready to follow the convolutions resulting from the momentary importance of any one of them as they are brought into play. He thus becomes part of an organism and must submit himself to the laws of balance regulating this organism. As we have seen, his facial expressions and gestures are prescribed by the music. Furthermore, we see that these are no longer isolated on the stage, for the actor has *become the intermediary* between the music and the inanimate elements of the production.

Adolphe Appia in Barnard Hewitt (ed.), *Adolphe Appia's Music and the Art of the Theatre*, pp. 20–1

Jindřich Honzl focuses on ways in which visual and acoustical signs can swap place and refers to this as 'changeability' of signs: 'For example, the meaning of heard dialogue may push the spectator's perception of dramatic gestures, dramatic appearance, scenery, lighting, and so on, into the background, or conversely it may happen that witnessed dramatic action nullifies acoustical perceptions (words, music, murmuring, and so forth).'[11] Elam uses the example of objects on stage to further clarify the relationship between them and the objects they represent:

> The process of semiotization is clearest, perhaps, in the case of the elements of the set. A table employed in dramatic representation will not usually differ in any material or structural fashion from the item of furniture that the members of the audience eat at, and yet it is in some sense transformed: it acquires, as it were, a set of quotation marks. It is tempting to see the stage table as bearing a direct relationship to its dramatic equivalent – the fictional object that it represents – but this is not strictly the case; the material stage object becomes, rather, a semiotic unit standing not directly for another (imaginary) table but for the intermediary signified 'table', i.e. for the *class of objects* of which it is a member. The metaphorical quotation marks placed around the stage object mark its primary condition as representative of its class, so that the audience is able to infer from it the presence of another member of the same class of objects in the represented dramatic world (a table which may or may not be structurally identical with the stage object).[12]

Elam draws attention to the relationship between the object and the concept that it signifies. This concern has been important in the development of scenography, where pioneers have been motivated to explore the potential of real objects and materials on stage while at the same time acknowledging their relationship to stage realism. The meaning of real objects used by Kantor was transformed when they were removed from real life and placed on stage. Caspar Neher recognised that the meaning of Helene Weigel's costume in *The Mother* was discovered through the process of crafting a blouse which primarily signified the circumstances of her life and not its authenticity.

Elam's clarification helps to explain how an object's potential for significa-tion on stage is related to but not confined by what an object signifies in everyday life. As he points out, in the theatre a real table is, at the same time, an imaginary table and might just as easily be represented by a painting of a table or an actor on all fours.[13]

21   The lower the rank of the object, the greater its chance of revealing its objectness.
   The process of lifting it from the regions of derision and contempt is
   the act of pure
   poetry in art ...
   ... In theatre,
   one must do everything possible to discard eternal justifications and total expression
   and to allow the audience to experience the sphere of i m a g i n a t i o n ...
   It is in imagination that the highest values, being, death, love ...
   exist somewhere in a poor corner,
   a parcel, a stick, a bicycle wheel ...
   bereft of pathos or illusion.
      Tadeusz Kantor, *A Journey through Other Spaces: Essays and Manifestos,*
      1944–1990, p. 30

Understanding of the relationship between space and objects in everyday life is, of course, crucial to the way scenographic material can be interpreted on stage. Erika Fischer-Lichte uses the example of a fur coat. In everyday life a fur coat denotes the utilitarian function of making oneself warm and it might also show wealth or social status. On stage, these meanings may be extended to furnish a depiction of another fictional person. The spectator's understanding of what a fur coat might signify in real life is transferred to the fictional character or the fictional space. Furthermore, clothing on stage can produce additional signs to those that operate in social life. An object appears on stage both as the object itself and as a sign of the dramatic situation or fictional space. What is understood about the object in real life informs understanding of the fictional stage image. At the same time, stage depiction goes beyond everyday life by isolating or distilling aspects of our culture and reflecting them back: 'Theater, in other words, reflects the reality of the culture in which it originates in a double sense of the word: it depicts that reality and presents it in such a depiction for reflective thought.'[14] Clothing has a significant role in the construction of social meaning and personal identity in everyday life.[15]

Clothes might signal a whole array of things about the person wearing them, such as age, gender, nationality or religion, historical period, social status, occupation or membership of a social group. Playwrights exploit such signification in defining individual characters. For instance, in *A Streetcar named Desire* Stanley Kowalski is 'roughly dressed in blue denim work clothes' whilst Blanche is 'daintily dressed in a white suit with a fluffy bodice, necklace and ear-rings of pearl, white gloves and hat, looking as if she were arriving at a summer tea or cocktail party in the garden district'.[16] Another example may be seen in King Lear's descent as reflected by the loss of his regal attire and his nakedness on the heath.

Relative importance of sign functions of different kinds of costumes is governed by particular theatrical codes of a given period.[17] The period from the end of the nineteenth to the early twentieth century demonstrated the operation of several different codes. Realism, such as the kind endorsed by the Meiningen Theatre Company,[18] used costume to signify social aspects of character and aimed for historical accuracy and authenticity, whereas expressionistic costumes, such as Jessner's designs for *Richard III*, used costumes as signs which attempted to make visible the internal workings of characters. A photograph from the production shows that Fritz Kortner, as Richard, wore a stiff and bulky black robe and, in contrast, the actor playing Buckingham wore a kind of pale straitjacket,[19] making it possible for the costumes to express something of their characters and the relationship between them.

Interaction between signs

It is important to remember that scenographic sign systems operate in relation to other sign systems such as setting, lighting and sound or sign systems related to the actors' physicality, movement or signing functions encompassed by text. Meaning may be transferred between these systems. For example, the meaning conveyed by a costume might include not simply its appearance but also the way it is worn and used. Typically, costume has been used to enhance and support the actor's presentation of a character. Designer Christopher Oram and actor Kenneth Branagh worked together to develop a corset-like doublet which literally shaped Branagh's physical interpretation of *Richard III* (2002).[20] On the other hand, signs of costume might deliberately work against the signs of performers' actions. Pina Bausch's dancers in Tanztheater

Wuppertal are often presented in immaculate and elegant gowns and high heels whilst the choreography suggests effort, pain and struggle. The juxtaposition provides a further layer of meaning.

> 22   This difficult, complex poetry assumes many guises; first of all it assumes those expressive means usable on stage such as music, dance, plastic art, mimicry, mime, gesture, voice inflexion, architecture, lighting and décor.
>   Each of these means has its own specific poetry as well as a kind of ironic poetry arising from the way it combines with other expressive means. It is easy to see the result of these combinations, their interaction and mutual subversion.
>   Antonin Artaud, *The Theatre and its Double*, p. 28

Light is a particularly interactive element when it comes to creating meaning. For Appia and Svoboda, light sculpted space and could augment or replace architectonic elements. Light is also intimately associated with the body of the performer in the way that it reveals or hides sculptural form or isolates a character in a spotlight. The potential, during performance, for manipulation of light through intensity, colour, distribution and movement also means that it is possible to mould and shift meaning by highlighting physical action or by exposing dramatic structure.

> 23   Light is the most important part of theatre. It brings everything together, and everything depends on it. From the beginning I was concerned with light, how it reveals objects, how objects change when light changes, how light creates space, how space changes when light changes. Light determines what you see … I paint, I build, I compose with light.
>   Robert Wilson in Arthur Holmberg, *The Theatre of Robert Wilson*, p. 121

Sound, too, operates in conjunction with other elements on the stage to enrich the sign network. Soundscapes may be made to create acoustical scenery, shaping the perception of space that is visually evident on the stage.

'Proxemic' signs, that is, those that are produced in the interaction between characters and their stage environment, show how the performers' occupation of stage space is also important to interpretation of setting and spatial aspects of scenography. On stage, particular spatial arrangements may signal relationships between people and between people and their environment. Such arrangements may point to relationships between power and submission, intimacy and distance or freedom and constraint.[21] Settings often condition spatial relationships which affect various groupings and dynamics between performers. Spatial arrangements of objects and people can also be interpreted through suggested dramatic action:

A decoration which is supposed to signify a ditch, a wall, or something similar points to the difficulties which the characters who are positioned on various sides of these objects will have to overcome in order to come together. Chairs or other objects signifying 'seating opportunities' that are arranged in a circle indicate a form of symmetrical group interaction, whereas a throne standing on an elevation or stairs refers to a certain form of asymmetrical interaction, etc. In other words, the decoration can be interpreted not only in relation to the characters' movements, but also in relation to the patterns and forms of interaction which may be applied by them.[22]

Categories of signs

In addition to the work of Saussure, Charles Sanders Peirce (1839–1914), an American logician and philosopher, investigated the nature of inquiry and interpretation and developed a theory of semiotics which attempted to account for all communication – not just language. His theories are complex but aspects of them, such as those concerning formulation of sign classes, have been adopted generally for the purpose of theatre analysis.[23]

Peirce identified three ways in which signs refer to objects: as 'icons', 'indices' and 'symbols'.[24] In Peirce's terminology, 'icons' work through their resemblance to the things to which they refer, such as a photograph of the thing or its graphic representation. On stage the set can represent a real place and costume can depict an historical character or an occupation. Equally, a part of the whole might suffice as a sign – a crown might signify a king. Or, the likeness might be expressed through metaphor as, for example, in the prison-like forest in Serroni's design for *Salvation Path*. By 'indices' he refers to work through connection with, or cause and effect of, the thing to which reference is made. For instance, the arrangement of stage space can direct the viewer; spotlights can draw attention to particular objects and actions; costume can indicate the status or state of mind of the fictional character; and objects can point to the social milieu of characters.

For Peirce, 'symbols' are signs which work through agreed conventions. No similarity or connection exists between the sign and the thing to which it refers. This corresponds to Saussure's formulation of language, where the relationship between the signifier and the signified is arbitrary and the meaning produced has to be learned. Particular genres and traditions of theatre produce codes which can only be appreciated after some initiation. For example, the styles of make-up in Kabuki performance denote the status and intent of a character.

Iconic signs are particularly important in the theatre. Peirce subdivided iconic operation into 'image', 'diagram' and 'metaphor' as three different kinds of likeness.[25] Images have the appearance of the things to which they refer. Diagrams that indicate structural characteristics have a schematic likeness to the things to which they refer, whereas metaphors create or suggest likeness between themselves and the things to which they refer. Such likeness relies on essences and ideas rather than outward appearance. This is helpful as a means of establishing that analysis of scenography need not be restricted to degrees of similitude. Image icons might operate in this manner and 'encourage the spectator to perceive the performance as a direct image of the dramatic world'.[26] Diagrammatic and metaphoric portrayals suggest other ways of being like the referent. Diagrammatic icons work through rational relation rather than appearance. The 2004 Kneehigh Theatre Company's production of *The Wooden Frock* used flapping umbrellas to signify a flock of geese.[27] Metaphoric icons, already noted earlier in this work, have been important in establishing the potential of scenography as performance. They operate by proposing conceptual rather than physical similarities between things.

Importantly, the functions of signs as symbols, indices or icons or subdivisions of those functions are not fixed. A costume might operate as an icon through depiction of a character from a particular period and at the same time as an index of the character's wealth. An iconic sign might be simultaneously seen as an image, such as a set showing the castle of Elsinore, and as a metaphor for the Danish court or Hamlet's state of mind. Doors on stage might be both iconic and symbolic. In naturalistic performance it might be agreed that they denote the existence of other rooms, although this is not likely to be the physical case. Ultimately, all signs in theatrical performance might be thought of as symbolic in the sense that 'it is only through convention that the spectator takes stage events as standing for something other than themselves'.[28]

24   I have come to regard the *mise en scène* not as something which works directly on the spectator but rather as a series of 'passes', each intended to evoke some association or other in the spectator (some premeditated, others outside my control). Your imagination is activated, your fantasy stimulated, and a whole chorus of associations is set off. A multitude of accumulated associations gives birth to new worlds – whole films which have never got beyond the cutting room. You can no longer distinguish between what the director is responsible for and what is inspired by the associations which have invaded your imagination.
   Vsevolod Meyerhold in Edward Braun (ed.), *Meyerhold on Theatre*, pp. 318–19

Aston and Savona offer another way to think about the functions of scenographic signs. They identify four levels of operation of the stage picture:

'functionalistic', 'sociometric', 'atmospheric' and 'symbolic'.[29] 'Functionalistic' operation usually comes about in response to the needs of the text and the demands of the action or narrative. The mode of operation labelled 'socio-metric' refers to the way scenographic means can provide an 'index of rank and gender'. 'Atmospheric' operation conveys the particular experiential qualities of the fictional place being depicted. Finally, the 'symbolic' operation of the stage picture refers to meaning which can be inferred so that 'the stage picture stands as a metaphorical condensation of the text's ideological preoccupa-tions'.[30] Once applied to a particular example, it can be seen how these four levels of operation inform each other. Aston and Savona use Arthur Miller's stage directions for *Death of a Salesman* (which, as noted earlier, follow Jo Mielziner's design for the original production) as an example. Mielziner's design was functional in the sense that the skeletal house and the use of gauze allowed various rooms in the house to be seen simultaneously. This arrangement provided a practical solution to the shifts between reality and dream states and between past and present. It was also sociometric in the sense that it depicted a small, vulnerable house surrounded by apartment blocks, reflecting Willy Loman's status. Atmosphere was conveyed through the fra-gility of the house and the lyrical quality of the lighting used for scenes of the past. This became a symbolic expression when compared to the towering, glowering nature of the surrounding city in the present. Willy's house stood as a metaphor for his fading dreams and this was reinforced by the brutal nature of modern life which threatened it. 'Old-fashioned' individual aspirations were set against contemporary corporate values. Like all symbols, the impact of this relies on shared cultural sensibilities and potent images held in common by the creators of the production and their audience.

The limits of semiotics

Aston and Savona consider semiotics as a means not only of analysing 'the stage picture' but also of determining the staging of a play. They propose four distinct phases: the dramatist encodes the text; the director decodes the text; the designer re-encodes the text and finally the spectator decodes the produc-tion.[31] Although this model provides a welcome focus on the visual, it also presents some problems for scenographic consideration. Aston and Savona's linear model is driven by notions about language which firstly emanates from the playwright. This suggests that the creation of scenography and its analysis relies on translation from the linguistic to the visual and then back again. This, of course, is problematic.

Much of the scepticism regarding the use of semiotics as a tool to analyse non-verbal material arises from the tendency for semiotic theories to be applied too mechanistically. The suggestion here is that non-linguistic signs are translated into linguistic 'signifieds' in order to give them currency. As Pavis points out, 'nothing obliges (nor allows, for that matter) spectators to translate into words the experience of contemplating a light, gestures, or music in order for that experience then to be integrated into the global meaning of the stage'.[32] Nor does emphasis on language help in the analysis of postdramatic performance which prioritises the scenographic. Colin Counsell's semiotic analysis of Robert Wilson's scenography leads to his claim that Wilson's images are hollow and 'semically gratuitous':[33]

> Wilson's stage abounds with what appear to be signifiers, material, manufactured phenomena – startling images, patterned word sequences, crafted and synchronised movements and rituals – which advertise their own purposefulness and significance, demand to be scanned for meaning. But such meanings, such conceptual signifieds are not only absent, their absence itself is, paradoxically, signified.[34]

Stephen Di Benedetto, on the other hand, suggests that Wilson's work can be more effectively accounted for if it is thought of as visual form or 'an abstracted language'. Di Benedetto concentrates on the formal qualities of Wilson's composition to trace its effects:

> In Wilson's theatre, the visible elements act as an organizational spine, thereby carrying the weight of the narrative content … Where other playwrights provide a verbal narrative, Wilson uses the abstracted language of visual form to present a ballet of shape and space. Changing shapes, spaces and images flow by the spectators asking them to accept a visible journey filled with visual stimuli to goad their interest. The position of visible elements often is taken for granted, and so deserves scrutiny.[35]

Scenographic material has particular qualities which are set apart from other aspects of the stage and has much in common with painting and sculpture. So, one way to analyse scenography is to draw on formalist strategies that have been used to analyse the aesthetic effect of fine art. Di Benedetto adopts such a strategy here in analysing Wilson's 1989 production of *Orlando*:

> Wilson places Orlando recumbent on stage in a narrow horizontal band of blue light. The height of the frame is only several feet. The weight of the blackness pushes down on the narrow band of space … The colored planes are the forms that convey the expression of the images … the space becomes endowed with a sense of weight and pressure upon the characters … the movement through space offers a visual narrative of changing spatial relationships.[36] (Figure 27.)

27. Robert Wilson, *Orlando* (from the novel by Virginia Woolf). Director
Robert Wilson with Ann-Christin Rommen, Schaubühne am Lehniner
Platz, Berlin, 1989

Application of analytical and interpretive techniques used in art can be
helpful towards analysis of scenography. In particular, formalist approaches
can be useful in that they deal with elements which are unique to scenographic
aspects of performance. These include moments such as those observed by
Veltruský when a live human performer is absorbed into the scene. Colour,
shape, space and line of objects, the use of light and darkness and the compositional relation between objects are some of the means by which scenography
promotes meaning. Spatial relationships are conveyed through height, depth,
distance and scale. Compositional principles include contrast, juxtaposition,
harmony, balance, proportion and rhythm that act to engage the viewer's
attention. Isolation of these formal elements permits an acknowledgement
that scenography amounts to a visual language which is capable of operating
independently from those of the textual, verbal and gestural.

In an attempt to systematise the way visual images communicate meaning,
Gunther Kress and Theo van Leeuwen consider a wide range of examples of
visual design which include paintings, advertisements and diagrams. Using a

broadly semiotic approach, they identify compositional structures and analyse how these produce meaning. They stress that 'visual language is not transparent and universally understood; it is culturally specific'.[37] For example, divisions of space in visual composition reflect wider social practices in order to communicate meaning. Organisational principles in composition include working from left to right where established or 'given' information is placed on the left and structure or development is achieved by placing 'new' ideas on the right. This reflects the way text is read in Western cultures.[38] In Western theatre, there are conventional uses of 'left' and 'right' associated with different traditions of performance. For example, in Roman comedies foreign characters, arriving from the country or the harbour, are thought to have entered from the right side of the stage (as viewed by the audience), whereas the left side is thought to have led to the locality, the city and the forum.[39] But it is not always clear whether those practices reflect the logic of old to new as suggested by Kress and van Leeuwen. Besides, confusion is sometimes created in accounts of staging practices and conventions where it is not clear whose perspective 'right' and 'left' relate to. Is it to the actors or the audience? Richard H. Palmer's observation on lighting design is that 'the flow of light left to right in our visual field stimulates a greater sense of harmony than the opposite'.[40]

Meaning derived from examples of vertical organisation of scenographic space is more easily traced on the Western stage. It is noticeable in many instances of scenography that organisation of stage space works from 'top' to 'bottom'. Ralph Koltai's 1967 futuristic Forest of Arden design created from metal and perspex for *As You Like It* was suspended above the stage.[41] Kress and van Leeuwen refer to this relationship as 'Ideal-Real' where the 'Real' is earthbound, at the bottom of the composition, and the 'Ideal' reaches up into the realm of the metaphysical or supernatural.[42]

This sort of orientation helps to isolate the particular contribution of scenographic elements to the overall theatre experience. However, Anne Ubersfeld points out that 'we must resist the temptation to think of the perception of theatrical space as we would a painting'.[43] Even where theatre architecture attempts to focus spectators' attention by framing the performance within the proscenium arch, the position of each seat can afford a very different view. It is possible that these distinctions between stage and theatre space reflect socio-cultural space. Typically, seating arrangements and viewing positions reinforce social structure, as may be seen in examples from Italian Renaissance theatre where 'the sponsoring prince could look down upon his assembled subjects as well as provide a visual anchor for the stage perspective'.[44] From this elevated position in the centre of the auditorium, the perspective scene had its full effect.

At the same time the spatial arrangement offered a representation of the social hierarchy and privilege of the time. Ubersfeld suggests that 'spatial structures reproduced in the theatre define not so much a concrete world, but rather the image people have of spatial relationships and the conflicts underlying those relationships in the society in which they live'.[45]

Analysis of paintings, or for that matter, sculptures, is rarely concerned with spatial relationships between spectator and art object or the spatial context in which objects are viewed. However, scenographic space is contiguous with the space of performance, whether it be in a theatre or elsewhere. The concept of Svoboda's set for *Oedipus* was reinforced by the common arrangement often found in Western theatres which features the 'pit' below the level of the stage and the 'gods' at the very top of the auditorium.

Formal analyses of visual composition do not fully account for the operation of scenography because they are not concerned with the socio-spatial dimension. Additionally, there are other considerations to be taken into account in relation to the nature of the visual which are helpful in the analysis of scenography. Images are polysemiotic in nature and what follows from this is that images can slide between significations and thus offer a more poetic experience for viewers.

Levels of meaning

The poetic or 'obtuse' nature of images is revealed where semiotic discourse has been applied specifically in consideration of the visual. In his discussion of photographs and film imagery, Roland Barthes uses a semiotic approach to identify three kinds of meaning: 'informational', 'symbolic' and 'a third meaning' which is more obtuse and 'obstinate' than the first two categories, but which offers the possibility of a more penetrating meaning, a more 'poetic' insight.[46] In comparison to language, the image is seen to be weak or rudimentary because it is polysemous, potentially offering multiple meanings or signifiers which imply a 'floating chain' of signifieds.[47] On the other hand, it may be that signification 'cannot exhaust the image's ineffable richness'.[48] Visual elements appear to be less stable in terms of signification than words, but this opens up ways in which images may be experienced and interpreted. Barthes stresses the role of the individual as interpreter. There are potentially as many meanings as there are viewers. In respect of the informational and symbolic meanings of images, these readings are not anarchic because they are dependent on shared practical, national, cultural, aesthetic knowledge which is invested in the image.[49] The third, obtuse meaning is locatable, in that its impact can be registered, but it is not easily translated into words.[50]

Barthes uses a still from Eisenstein's film *Ivan the Terrible* to illustrate these three levels of meaning. The image shows a scene from Ivan's coronation where gold coins are being tipped over his head by two courtiers. Costumes are important in determining informational meaning and the relative status of personnel and situation. The coins offer more symbolic meaning via general references to baptism and wealth but also to something more specific in relation to the narrative of the film. The gold, for example, obscures or disfigures the Czar's face.

Barthes further describes aspects of the image that hold his attention but which do not yield any obvious meaning. This is the 'third' meaning. He identifies signifiers, for example 'a certain compactness of the courtiers' make-up, thick and insistent for the one, smooth and distinguished for the other',[51] but cannot say exactly what is being signified. In contrast, the informational and symbolic meanings that Barthes can grasp might be said to be 'obvious' or complete. This third kind of meaning is 'persistent and fleeting, smooth and elusive' and cannot be absorbed intellectually. It is 'obtuse' in the sense that it is difficult to explain, but this difficulty does not lessen its impact for the viewer. The 'obtuse meaning is outside (articulated) language while nevertheless within interlocution'.[52] Barthes describes this third meaning as penetrating and disturbing more obvious meanings.

This obtuse nature of images, and therefore of scenography, is hard to accommodate within a semiotic approach, which tends to break down the whole into units and has limited use for the analysis of scenography or of theatre performance in general. 'The division of stage materials into signifying systems is arbitrary and the legacy of a critical tradition; it impedes theoretical reflection by requiring us to think in terms of fixed categories.'[53] Although concentration on details and elements that make up performance might be seen to have helped in bringing scenographic elements, such as set, light, props and costume, to the attention of analysts, there is a risk of isolating them from the performance as a whole if there is a failure to address the complex way in which scenographic signs operate in relation to other signifying aspects of the whole performance. Any idea that semiotics will provide a means of translating scenography into an exhaustive catalogue of units of meaning seems both unachievable and inappropriate.

Furthermore, Aston and Savona's account of the stage picture as a sequence of encoding and decoding operations downplays the subjective nature of the interpretation of images. The more penetrating 'third' meaning is a matter of the way an image works on an individual, regardless of the intentions that the creator of the image might have had. Audiences have an active role in viewing scenography and their interpretation of it may exceed that originally envisaged by the designer.

The important point about semiotics, Pavis claims, is that it shows that 'meaning is a construction of signification' and not 'the communication of a signification already existing in the world'.[54] In any case, much of the time and experience of scenography is about impressions, suggestions, implications and inferences and not clear-cut messages and signals. Pavis draws on psycho-analytical perspectives to describe the experience of contemporary perform-ance, where 'spectators are analysts confronted with enigmatic mechanisms comparable to dreams and phantasms, mechanisms whose latent content they have to decipher (rather than decode)'.[55]

Pavis' own proposal is a theory of 'vectors', which permits a mapping operation of different aspects of the stage in relation to each other in ways which have more in common with graphical communication than with language. Vectors describe trajectories in space as well as in time, as in the example of a costume blowing in the wind and 'inscribing the trajectory of its train in space, thus making the flow of time apparent'.[56] 'Vectorisation is the dynamic momentum created in a narrative or chronology between the various parts of a stage work; the itinerary of meaning through the labyrinth of signs, the ordering of the performance.'[57] Pavis is here moving towards an analytical approach which embraces the per-spective of the audience and the subjective experience of the spectator:

> What is important, therefore, is not to enumerate signifiers exhaustively, but rather to perceive their dynamics using all five of our senses: their emergence, the ways in which they are linked as sequences and memorized, their ability to occupy the foreground or the background and to establish correlations and alliances … The experience of the senses – *aesthesis* – is also the emotional participation of the spectator, the very fact of being there and allowing oneself to be transported for a moment.[58]

In recognition of the sensory and emotional participation of the spectator, Pavis reflects the influence of phenomenology which, in offering an opposing perspective to semiotics, has been seen to provide a corrective or complement when it comes to analysing performance and, as may be seen from what follows, has some advantages in accounting for the way scenography works.

Phenomenological perspectives

Phenomenology has its roots in philosophy, particularly through the work of Edmund Husserl (1859–1938) and his follower Martin Heidegger (1889–1976). Both were concerned to account for consciousness in human beings not from a scientific, abstract point of view but from a first-person perspective.

In other words, they were concerned with what it is to be a conscious being in the world, or how the world and the things in it might be perceived. Writing on phenomenology that has particularly interested scholars of theatre and performance is that of Maurice Merleau-Ponty (1908–61). For Merleau-Ponty phenomenology is concerned with attempts to capture experience, in direct and 'primitive' essence and at a stage before intellectual analysis begins to sort, edit and render it as an artificial 'reconstruction'.[59] He emphasises how encounters with the world are made up from multiple perspectives in terms of what is seen, heard, felt, sensed, imagined, anticipated and remembered. These various perspectives inform one another. Perception is considered to be a synaesthetic process in which the senses communicate with each other:

> The form of objects is not their geometrical shape: it stands in a certain relation to their specific nature, and appeals to all our other senses as well as sight. The form of a fold in linen or cotton shows us the resilience or dryness of the fibre, the coldness or warmth of the material … One sees the weight of a block of cast iron which sinks in the sand, the fluidity of water and the viscosity of syrup. In the same way, I hear the hardness and unevenness of cobbles in the rattle of a carriage, and we speak appropriately of a 'soft', 'dull' or 'sharp' sound.[60]

Actually, Veltruský had anticipated some of this in his essay, 'Some Aspects of the Pictorial Sign'. Not only does he point out that the formal qualities of art are as important as thematic content in carrying meaning, he identifies these formal qualities as multi-sensory. In painting, for example, colours can be warm and cold and give the impression of advancing or receding. Line, shape and composition within the picture field, together with texture and scale, can arouse affective or 'psychophysical' responses in viewers:

> The capacity to convey meanings independently of any referential function, just through the psychophysical effects of the material itself, is a feature that the pictorial sign has in common not only with sculpture, architecture, gestures, theater, and dance but also with music. I am referring neither to tone painting nor to musical quotation but to the semiotic potential of such phenomena as what might broadly be called synesthesia, various qualities of the tone which arouse 'affective responses', the impact the rhythm may have on the beating of the heart, the ability of music to bring about 'physiognomic perception', and so on.[61]

Bert O. States pursues the idea of phenomenology as a means of addressing 'the perceptual impression that theatre makes on the spectator'. He advocates phenomenology as an approach which can be used to counter or balance semiotic analysis:

> It has become evident to me … that semiotics and phenomenology are best seen as complementary perspectives on the world and on art … If we think of semiotics and phenomenology as modes of seeing, we might say that they constitute a kind of binocular vision: one eye enables us to see the world phenomenally; the other eye enables us to see it significatively.[62]

In terms of scenography, States is particularly interested in the way the senses communicate with each other in the perception of scenery. Senses intermingle so that 'the ear sees scenery and the eye hears it'.[63] An illuminated scene can communicate through vision alone. Lines of text may initially intrude upon the individual's contemplation of the scene but over time focus may shift to the speaking characters as perception of the scenery fades. But the scene and the speech may penetrate one another. In States' words, 'the speeches become a kind of metaphysical light cast on the setting, while the illuminated setting encompasses the speech and gives it a kind of environmental meaning' in a 'reciprocal exchange'.[64] Here, States goes beyond Honzl's account of the 'changeability' of signs outlined earlier in this chapter. Whereas Honzl concentrates on the way attention shifts from visual signs to aural signs and back again during the course of a performance, States emphasises the effect that interpenetration of sight and hearing may have on the way audience members perceive scenography.

Consideration of the qualities of sound as a performative medium also moves beyond the rhythms and structures of external material to address inner processes and phenomenological experiences of sound. Drawing on his extensive experience as a sound composer, Ross Brown interrogates jazz producer and writer Joachim-Ernst Berendt's concepts of 'ear-thinking' and 'eye-thinking' as modes of perception and understanding. Ear-thinking is a primary process where:

> First we hear and configure the universe in an analogue space/time map (hearing tends to reconcile space and time as pitch and melody far more elegantly and beautifully than space/time can be modelled diagrammatically on the page). Then, if necessary – if noise in the map demands our attention – we instigate secondary *eye-processes*. Then we look. Then we analyze. Then we seek logically to explain.[65]

Berendt's model suggests that 'ear-thinking' is a phenomenological experience which may later be modified by more conscious and cognitive processes of interpretation which he terms 'eye-thinking'. Brown proposes new approaches to sound design by considering the 'phenomenal potency' of theatre sound and advocates acceptance of all noise as part of that phenomenal field.[66]

Perception and embodiment

Merleau-Ponty's assertion that 'there is an immediate equivalence between the orientation of the visual field and the awareness of one's own body as the potentiality of that field'[67] further extends considerations of how sense is made of scenography. First of all, Merleau-Ponty says that our bodily, lived experience informs our perception of the world: 'Experience discloses beneath objective space, in which the body eventually finds its place, a primitive spatiality of which experience is merely the outer covering and which merges with the body's very being. To be a body, is to be tied to a certain world ... our body is not primarily *in* space: it is of it.'[68] This has important implications for scenography because it suggests that audiences can appreciate what they see on stage in ways which are embodied and precognitive.

Stanton B. Garner has applied this idea of bodily understanding to examining the relationship between performing bodies and spectators. Garner claims that whereas the presence of performers will set in train a phenomenological appreciation on the part of the audience, the scenic space is an objectified and detached spectacle.[69]

Garner, like States, acknowledges a duality in our experience of the stage. Whereas States proposes a binocular approach moving between semiotic (objectified, intellectual understanding of signs) and phenomenological (the total effect of all that the individual spectator apprehends or experiences), Garner distinguishes between the 'scenic space' where the spectator views the scene with 'visual objectification' and detachment and the 'environmental space' where spectators connect with performers through 'phenomenal embodiment'.[70] He claims that these two fields of perception are 'rival' ones and looking at a scene is like looking at a painting or a sculpture until the actors appear.[71] Where States reflects Veltruský's ideas about the interchangeability of subject and object on stage, Garner insists that scenic elements can only be pulled into the phenomenological field through the actor, who is 'a site of agency within a world of things'.[72] But Merleau-Ponty's account of the phenomenological aspects of art and paintings makes it clear that we might relate to all material on a bodily level. His reflection on the experience of colour is informed by sensations as well as observations:

> as I fix my eyes on an object or allow them to wander, or else wholly
> submit myself to the event, the same colour appears to me as superficial
> (*Oberflächenfarbe*) – being in a definite location in space, and extending
> over an object – or else it becomes an atmospheric colour *(Raumfarbe)*
> and diffuses itself all around the object. Or I may feel it in my eye as a

> vibration of my gaze; or finally it may pass on to my body a similar
> manner of being, fully pervading me, so that it is no longer entitled to be
> called a colour.[73]

Di Benedetto has explored methods of investigating sensorial stimulation in
contemporary performance, particularly that which is scenographically driven.
His first-person descriptions (see chapter 4 on Space) attempt to chart the way
scenography works on his whole body because, he says, 'before interpreting,
one needs to have a vocabulary to understand the ways in which an object or
experience exists in space'.[74] A phenomenological approach to analysing
scenography is particularly useful when it comes to looking at work such as
Oskar Schlemmer's which emphasises the 'phenomenal reality and experienced physicality of the stage'.[75] Trimingham describes how in his work at the
Dessau Bauhaus in the 1920s, Schlemmer used low levels of light to draw in
spectators in order to play with their sense of perception of space 'before giving
them a powerful physical sensation of it'.[76] Schlemmer's purpose was to create
complex and dynamic images which 'through pure form and bodily engagement' would lead to transcendental experience.[77]

Merleau-Ponty's account of perception of an object is not simply that of
viewing a flat surface as in a picture, but is informed by our experiential
knowledge of how the object appears from different viewpoints or perspectives
and by our appreciation of the action of time and memory on that object. These
varied perspectives come together to inform the totality of our perception:

> My field of perception is constantly filled with a play of colours, noises
> and fleeting tactile sensations which I cannot relate precisely to the
> context of my clearly perceived world, yet which I nevertheless
> immediately 'place' in the world, without ever confusing them with my
> daydreams. Equally constantly I weave dreams round things. I imagine
> people and things whose presence is not incompatible with the context,
> yet who are not in fact involved with it: they are ahead of reality, in the
> realm of the imaginary.[78]

So, the viewing of an object is not just what is given through the provision of
one fixed viewpoint. Even when a theatre spectator is seated to watch a
performance, this individual's perception of seen objects is informed by his
or her bodily experience. Perceptual capabilities come about by way of understanding of the world as developed through the physical body in its entirety.
Seeing something on stage is inevitably linked with embodied understanding
or memories of actual bodily experience, so the appearance of a long velvet coat
might also evoke an understanding of what it feels like to touch it or how it feels
to wear it and move in it.

Chapter 7

Reception of scenography

The previous chapter moved from consideration of the analysis of scenography as an object to a concern with the scenographic event. This chapter concentrates on the experience and reception of scenography. This, of necessity, involves consideration of the audience as an active agent.

Analyses of performances, or the ways in which the mise-en-scène works, are governed by the person(s) conducting the analysis, who 'have neither the apparent objectivity of empirical observation, nor the absolute universality of abstract theory; they negotiate a space between detailed yet fragmentary description and general unverifiable theory, between formless signifiers and polysemic signifieds'.[1] The richness of the theatrical experience and its reception means that performance varies from one spectator to another. The idea of the spectator as 'reader' has some interesting implications in terms of the way theatre, and scenography in particular, as a form of communication is conceptualised.

As noted in relation to semiotics, theatre theorists have found useful models in the fields of linguistics and literature which can be applied to 'reading' the theatre event. Susan Bennett gives a very clear account of how reception theory and reader-response criticism might be used to think about the 'emancipation' of audiences and the diversity of roles that they can take on in the variety of forms which make up contemporary theatre and performance practice. Furthermore, ideas that arise from semiotics and post-structuralist thinking also inform ideas about the active role of audiences at 'the nexus of production and reception'.[2]

'Reading' the image – the role of the spectator

In literary criticism of the 1960s and 1970s, responsibility for the resolution and communication of meaning in a text was seen by some to shift from author to reader. Barthes' essay went so far as to claim 'The Death of the Author'. He disputed that the meaning of a literary text could be determined by the author's intentions or that there could be a single meaning to be deciphered. Instead, he argued that the reader disentangles multiple possible meanings so that 'a text's unity lies not in its origin but in its destination'.[3]

It is already clear that an approach to the analysis of scenography which concentrates solely on the aims of the designer or the production denies the important nature of the theatre event, which occurs at the point of reception. Although reader-response and theories of reception were developed primarily as theories of the way literature communicates to its readers, they contain some useful formulations which have been applied to theatre audiences and which can be applied more specifically to viewing scenography.

Wolfgang Iser's theories about the nature of reading were influenced by phenomenology and focused on the 'act of reading'[4] and on the experience of reading and the way readers relate and respond to a particular text. It is an interactive model of communication between the text and the reader, rather than a linear transmission from text to reader. Of particular interest in consideration of the reception of scenography is Iser's notion of the 'wandering viewpoint'.[5] This describes how 'the whole text can never be perceived at any one time' and how a reader actively evaluates material against past experience and expectations of future events in a continuous process of interpretation and reinterpretation as reading progresses: 'There is a moving viewpoint which travels along inside that which it has to apprehend.'[6]

Although Iser says that this process is unique to literature, the spectator's experience of the theatre event might be said to be informed in several ways by wandering viewpoints. During the flow of performance, spectators may register moments which stand out against their expectations and cause them to re-evaluate what they have already witnessed and adjust their interpretation accordingly. Moreover, members of an audience are free to focus their attention on any part of the stage or auditorium. Although theatre architecture and various traditions of theatre production have attempted to direct attention towards a single viewpoint, spectators are able to choose that which they concentrate upon. In comparison to the experience of watching film, where the audience sees the product of controlled filming and editing, the experience of theatre is much more open and invites more active responses. Anne Ubersfeld expresses this in terms of negotiation of the signs of performance:

> It is the spectators, much more than the director, who create the spectacle: they must reconstruct the totality of the performance, along both the vertical axis and the horizontal axis. Spectators are obliged not only to follow a story, a fabula (horizontal axis), but also to constantly reconstruct the total figure of all the signs engaged concurrently in the performance. They are at one and the same time required to engage themselves in the spectacle (identification) and to back off from it (distancing).[7]

A wandering viewpoint is required to make sense of the unfolding drama in terms of the particular way it is presented in performance. Significance of the scenography is seen to evolve in the light of dramatic action and vice versa. Ubersfeld's description of engagement and distance chimes with States' idea of the binocular vision that theatre seems to require; a surrender to the whole event whilst simultaneously registering and interpreting significant details.

Iser also suggests that the key to an interactive readership consists of the indeterminate features of the text. These arise through what is written and what is unwritten or through the way literature refers to external reality at the same time as creating its own reality. The 'blanks' that arise from this indeterminacy structure the readers' participation and propel the process of creating meaning in such a way as to require the readers to fill in the blanks or make their own connections in order to make sense of the whole.[8] This formulation has resonances with some of the pioneering scenography already identified. Often, a deliberate strategy of gaps and omissions is detectable in scenography. Caspar Neher's scenography made use of the gaps between what was being said and what was being shown, between the reality of the stage and the social reality to which it referred. Half-curtains and placards demanded an engagement and re-evaluation of stage presentation from the audience. Tadeusz Kantor's 'poor' objects such as old rotten planks or discarded wheels were transformed, despite or because of their abject nature, into objects of contemplation and, potentially, transcendence for the spectators. Svoboda's spare and elegant spaces contained blank walls and reflective surfaces which invited spectators to contribute to the imaginative process.

Aesthetic perception

Hans Robert Jauss distinguishes between understanding and interpretation through reading. The initial response from the reader is built on the aesthetic dimension. Reflective interpretation follows on from the 'immediate' understanding that is found 'within aesthetic perception'.[9] Interpretation, which in the case of the poetic text can be reductive, is allowed to 'remain suspended' within aesthetic perception so that the reader can experience the full significance of the text.[10] Scenography plays an important role in the aesthetic perception of theatre, and the suspension of interpretation may be a valuable viewing strategy, especially in work that might be described as image-based or postdramatic. Viewing strategies, rather than the work itself, might determine 'the shape of what is read'.[11] Stanley Fish's theory of 'interpretive communities' states that strategies for interpreting texts and assigning meaning are shared within communities of readers and are developed through culturally and socially formed expectations and understandings. Application of this formulation to scenography needs to stress the extent to which particular viewing strategies are adopted and shaped by culture and the way meaning is determined through such viewpoints and not through the intentions of the scenographer or director. Robert Wilson's work invites spectators to make their own sense of it with little or no guidance within the work itself. The viewing strategy that Wilson encourages is one where spectators make their own serendipitous choices in selecting that to which they pay attention and their created associations. This approach suggests a way of viewing his work which reflects the way he himself develops it. This appears to hand over the process of creating meaning to the viewer. Thus, the viewer, shaped by membership of an interpretive community, brings individual expectations and strategies to the event which may or may not coincide with those of Wilson.

Anthony Howell describes a state of stillness which enables a spectator to read performance:

> Stillness enables a reading of the performance piece which is more akin to the way we read a painting than the way we read a conventional play. When a still tableau is presented, the audience is not required to 'follow' the action. They read the scene at their own pace, and the eye travels as it wills, upwards, downwards, across in either direction. When we follow a drama, on the other hand, we are given little time to develop our own thoughts. Instead, we are the receivers of the piece. Our thoughts about it occur in its intervals or after the final curtain. In front of a painting, we develop our own thoughts, and this is an active form of contemplation which the canvas stimulates.[12]

The means by which the 'canvas' of a performance (the scenography) stimulates contemplation is through composition. Wilson's audiences are encouraged to let their eyes wander and develop their own thoughts, but the stage is nonetheless carefully controlled and arranged; the spectator's attention is drawn and held through the way the stage space is moulded and shaped. As noted earlier, much of this is achieved by a carefully orchestrated interaction of space, objects, human figures and light. The spectator's eye 'travels at will' but it is guided towards the 'apprehension of significant structural patterns'.[13] Palmer develops this approach in his consideration of the aesthetics of stage lighting. He points out that even when stage lighting is being used to signify natural light, principles of composition are at work:

> Discussions of composition involve a considerable degree of abstraction. We will analyze what the audience sees in such terms as line, balance,

focus, and tonal value, even though the audience member thinks of the scene as a living room or a clearing in the woods. This abstract analysis of composition seems more natural when the production itself uses an abstract approach. We easily conceive of light, like music, in abstract terms without reference to realistic, natural sources. However, even when the context is realistic and the audience thinks of the lighting as coming from the sun or clearly motivated sources, the composition, as an abstract form, creates an impression, albeit subconsciously.[14]

Scenographers might be guided in their composition by principles of line, focus, balance and pattern. Spectators are subsequently influenced by these compositional choices as they respond to the stage, but audience members are not passive receivers. The capacity to seek out and recognise overall patterns is an active and creative one for the audience: 'All perceiving is also thinking, all reasoning is also intuition, all observation is also invention.'[15] Rudolf Arnheim attempted to locate the 'perceptual mechanisms' that account for what is understood through vision by investigating the principles of composition at work in art and the way meaning is generated through images.[16] Influenced by Gestalt psychology, he concentrated on the human tendency towards holistic apprehension where the seeing eye seeks out form. Gestalt psychologists showed that while clues are taken from constituent parts of an image, simultaneous clues may be seen in relation to the whole picture for forms and figures, even when the components of an image only provide partial information.

Perception rather than reception

Although Jauss acknowledges the role of aesthetics, it is the role of the reader and the received message which tend to be emphasised by reception theories and reader-response criticism. Application of these sorts of theories to scenography offers accounts of possible relationships between scenography and spectators in terms of end results but not in terms of the way in which meanings and messages are transferred or exchanged. A book can be picked up and put down at the will of the individual reader, whereas a performance happens at a given time and place for a group of people. As such, the experience of being there, the emotional and sensory engagement that occurs in the immediacy of the performance is crucial. Willmar Sauter says the 'theatre event' should be understood in terms of perception, not reception. Reception implies the analysis of 'social values and mental worlds' whereas perception implies phenomenological experience. Perception happens at the time of the performance; reception happens afterwards. The creation of a performance and experience of it are simultaneous at such a live event.[17] This implies that 'the meaning of a performance is created by the performers and the spectators together, in a joint act of understanding'.[18] Sauter also claims that semiotics is not helpful in empirical research into how audiences perceive theatre because it has 'no way of accounting for the pleasure and the enjoyment which spectators experience'.[19] He prefers a model which takes account of the phenomenological dimension of perception and structures an account of perception of the theatre event which moves from the sensory to the symbolic.

For Sauter, theatrical communication happens at three levels 'distinguishable by their nature but dynamically interconnected' and, crucially, the changes of meaning that are communicated over time.[20] At the sensory level the spectator perceives the physical and mental presence of the actor, while the actor senses audience response and mood. The artistic level is a recognition of the event as a separation from everyday life, as a particular presentation or interpretation of everyday life. At the third level, the symbolic aspect is 'a consequence of the artistic otherness of the event: meaning can be attributed to the artistic actions'. Ultimately 'nothing is symbolic in itself unless it is perceived as such by the observer'.[21]

The senses which are called on in the reception of theatre are reflected in terms used to describe the perceivers of theatre. These terms also carry with them implications about the nature of reception. 'Audience' implies hearing and it also implies a homogeneous group. Susan Bennett favours this term for considering cultural conditions that inform the production and reception of theatre.[22] Anne Ubersfeld tends to prefer the term 'spectator', with its stress upon 'seeing' and its tendency to suggest a group of individuals. 'Spectator' also suggests a more active role than 'viewer' and offers a sense of being part of the spectacle. McAuley agrees that spectators are not passive, even when they are sitting in a darkened auditorium. There is interaction between stage and auditorium even through 'weak signs' that indicate audience attentiveness or restlessness. According to McAuley, spectators sort and choose that upon which to focus and that with which to engage. This gives individuals in the audience an 'independence of vision'[23] which resists a model of communication between the stage and the auditorium as one of transmission:

> Spectators in the theatre have so many calls on their attention, conditions of visibility and audibility vary considerably from different points in the auditorium of even the most democratically designed theatre, there are so many things one can look at in the presentational space and in the performance space more generally, that it is not surprising that a moment when everyone present seems to be focusing on the same thing is relatively rare.[24]

Spatial and bodily dimensions of perception

A group of spectators is not homogeneous in its response. The 'multiplicity of spectators who react to each other'[25] allows the signals that pass between stage and auditorium to be refracted among other spectators in a complex exchange. This complex network of communication and exchange reverberates in and around the performance space. McAuley points out that this exchange is a spatial and phenomenological experience rather than a purely visual one:

> The stress on looking and seeing, the insistence on the visual, are problematic insofar as they may encourage a misleading elision between theatre and film spectatorship. Even when sight lines and lighting techniques are good, spectators sitting or standing in a theatre experience the space with all their senses, and it would be more appropriate in the circumstances to speak of a spatial than a visual experience.[26]

Carlson and Ubersfeld demonstrate that theatre space has semiotic significance, but McAuley shows that it can also be thought of as a defining aspect in the perception of theatre. Perception in the theatre, as elsewhere, is related to the act of seeing the rest of the world in respect of oneself. Being a spectator, being part of an audience, is a spatial experience in that one is conscious of one's own reactions and responses in relation to other spectators and performers on stage. In scenographic terms, specifically, this includes sensing distance, movement, weight and scale in relation to one's own body.

Di Benedetto has proposed the term 'attendant' (one who has a role in a ceremony) as one which promotes thinking about the experience of a viewer as an active and creative agent in the theatre event:

> With this in mind we can encounter the theatrical event in a more active manner as we would an experience of a building or a sculpture, by processing a range of stimuli to get a picture of the whole. To be *attendant* to a theatrical experience – rather than to be a spectator or part of an audience – transfers the focus of reception away from the material object to our proprioceptors, our own experience of the stimuli presented during the event.[27]

This concept of the audience emphasises spatial and sensory dimensions of scenographic reception. Arnold Aronson claims that 'we are spatial creatures; we respond instinctively to space'. The stage, he says, creates the impression of a 'boundless space beyond' and although its effect may be subliminal 'it is the apprehension of space that may be the most profound and powerful experience of live theatre'.[28]

He also suggests that the plasticity of the stage links with the theatre's ability to engage audience imagination. It seems that in the theatre, imaginations are unlocked by the tangible and actual nature of stage space which is inhabited by real performers and defined within a specific frame of time that is located in a particular place. Instinctive responses to space are inflected by individual and embodied experience of the world.

Although Cartesian divisions between the body and the mind have been influential in the past and may account, in part, for the suspicion about scenographic appeals to the senses, it is becoming clear that our intellect and emotions are informed directly by changes sensed in the body. Neurophysiologist Antonio Damasio has described how 'the brain is truly the body's captive audience'[29] with regard to the way higher levels of consciousness and creativity arise from the basic level of 'life regulation' and 'sensory patterns signaling pain, pleasure and emotion'.[30] The sensory modalities are 'visual, auditory, olfactory, gustatory and somatosensory'. This last term refers to sensory systems inherent in the body and includes the sensing of changes in 'the chemical environment' of cells through the operation of the nervous system and the visceral dimension of our internal organs. These are influenced by flows of blood which might be registered as feelings of calm or agitation, flushing skin or sweating palms. The musculoskeletal functions are those which allow the possibility of muscular empathy and they also account for the vestibular system which 'maps the coordinates of the body in space'.[31] The somatosensory also includes touch and the sensors in the skin which inform us about texture, form and weight.

25   Every show will contain physical, objective elements perceptible to all. Shouts, groans, apparitions, surprise, dramatic moments of all kinds, the magic beauty of the costumes modelled on certain ritualistic patterns, brilliant lighting, vocal, incantational beauty, attractive harmonies, rare musical notes, object colours, the physical rhythm of the moves whose build and fall will be wedded to the beat of moves familiar to all, the tangible appearance of new, surprising objects, masks, puppets many feet high, abrupt lighting changes, the physical action of lighting stimulating heat and cold, and so on ...
   Antonin Artaud, *The Theatre and its Double*, p. 72

Much scenography, experienced from a seat in the auditorium and apprehended principally through eyes and ears, creates understanding of the world previously obtained through other senses which in turn informs and extends visual and aural information. Understanding of space is developed through somatosensory means as well as visual and auditory ones. The appearance of a performer on stage provokes automatic reactions in the audience, who spontaneously recognise the mood and mental presence of a fellow human being.[32] This is not just a matter of identification, but one of recognition and response that is registered in the body of the spectator through 'muscular empathy'.[33] Watching actions on stage triggers a physical reaction which may manifest itself in tension or relaxation in the spectator's body. The audience member may hardly be aware of this bodily response. Even so, it has an impact on reception. Bernard Beckerman claims that 'Perception includes subception, bodily response to stimuli before we are focally aware of the stimuli. In theatre, this means that our bodies are already reacting to the texture and structure of action before we recognize that they are doing so.'[34] Beckerman suggests that spectators' bodies respond to all that occurs on stage. Understanding of what is happening and what this means works through successive impressions of a presentation, suggesting that 'we absorb the segmental pattern of presentation kinaesthetically rather than perceive it focally, that is, we absorb it through our muscles as well as our minds'.[35]

This idea is developed from philosopher Michael Polanyi who investigated the bodily roots of perception and thought. Polanyi describes how the whole body is involved in viewing objects. Although individuals may not be conscious of it, they bring to bear bodily experience of things when focused on external objects. Individuals attend to internal processes (which cannot be felt in themselves) and to the qualities of the outside object, transposing bodily experience into the perception of objects. In viewing an object, individuals incorporate 'it in our body – or extend our body to include it – so that we come to dwell in it'.[36] This tacit and embodied understanding that people have of the world is an important condition in the perception of scenography.

Appeals to the senses

Perception of colour in the theatre can be a powerful experience. Scientific accounts of how colour is registered in the brain do not account for the psychological and emotional impact that colour can have in the context of a performance.

Kandinsky's composition for stage, *The Yellow Sound* (1912), is an abstract piece based on the exploration of spiritual connections between movement, colour and sound.[37] The colour is particularly important and may almost be considered a character in itself. There is no plot, as such, but the shape of the piece is guided by an 'invasion' of giant yellow figures into the blue environment of the stage space. Gösta Bergman gives a detailed account of the piece

as described in Kandinsky's directions[38] which shows how Kandinsky imagined the interaction of coloured light with three-dimensional forms and music
to create symbolic meaning. Coloured light, especially, was intended to be
used to change intensity and 'character' of the scenes. Kandinsky's descriptions are not easy to understand; his writing is poetic and mystical and 'a
matter of scenic expressionism in a visionary dream-play'. The piece draws on
Kandinsky's interpretation of colour as a vehicle of spiritual significance and
was intended to connect to the 'inner sounds' of art and the 'inner vibrations'
of the audience. Kandinsky writes: 'Yellow is the typically earthly colour ... It
can never have profound meaning. An intermixture of blue makes it a sickly
colour. It may be paralleled in human nature, with madness, not with
melancholy or hypochondriacal mania, but rather with violent raving
lunacy.'[39] Kandinsky's account of the meaning of colour is, of course, a highly
subjective one. Attempts to categorise the effect of colour in the abstract are
limited and cannot account for the impact that colour has on the individual
viewer in a particular context. Although physiological responses to colour
have been recorded, these responses vary according to the personality of the
viewer. For example, coloured light has been shown to influence blood
pressure, heart beat, respiration, perspiration, eye movement and muscular
tension, but there is no clear agreement about specific responses to particular
colours and there is no agreement either about emotional responses.[40]
Clearly, the perception of colour is influenced by many factors. Some of
these are physical: light levels, the surface of the object on which the colour
appears and the capacity of the eye to register colour. Some are culturally
informed: colours have symbolic significance shaped by cultural traditions
and trends which can be read and understood by anyone familiar with a
given culture. But, as Arnheim points out, 'the effect of colour is much
too direct and spontaneous to be only the product of an interpretation
attached to the percept by learning'.[41] An individual's experience of
colour in a theatrical context is an immediate and affective encounter.
The combination of coloured light and pigment on stage can provide an
intense experience of colour which is part of the aesthetic perception of
theatre.

   Arnheim points to light as the initial cause of visual perception. It is an
'animating power' and without it there can be no perception of shape, colour
and space.[42] Baugh links the development of lighting design and the realisation
of theatre 'as a distinctive phenomenon of perception', an event in its own right
and not simply the staging of dramatic literature.[43] As with colour, light seems
to have a physical and emotional effect and this is reflected in the vocabulary
used to describe light. Low levels of light are often perceived as 'gloomy'

whereas 'brightness' refers to the relative amount of light as well as its effect on mood.[44] Levels of light and changes in them can also be sensed in the body. A stage flooding with warm light might induce a shift in the muscular tension of the viewing body.

David Belasco, an American actor-manager and playwright working at the beginning of the twentieth century, is also considered to have been a pioneer of lighting design. He undertook painstaking experiments with lighting in order to achieve atmospheric colour which spectators would be able to experience 'not with their intellects, but with their senses'. Belasco believed that light affected actors in such a way as to subconsciously stimulate their imaginations. As such, the performers' response to light was sensed by the audience. This, in turn, heightened atmosphere and emotion which affected audience perception of performance.[45]

Sound, too, can be felt as much as heard. Socìetas Raffaello Sanzio uses sound to stir and unnerve the audience (Figures 28 and 29). Here is Nicholas Ridout's account of the Berlin episode (B.#0) *Tragedia Endogonidia* (2003):

> Each episode of *Tragedia Endogonidia* opens with a kind of breathing, as though there were a membrane between the stage and the auditorium through which, once we begin, breath may pass, that deep breath we take before we take the plunge. Scott Gibbons and Chiara Guidi process human breath into a sound that spreads through the space like a smoke, creeping into all the cavities and passageways of the stage and auditorium, opening them up to their own vibrations ... it starts as a distant rumble, the long-since-accomplished aftershock of an exploding star reaching us through galactic time, perhaps, prefiguring the appearance of something that died long before human memory was born; or signalling, at least, that something of magnitude has occurred, something that we were not there to see.[46]

The effect of sound like this is intimate and visceral, touching the audience 'intimately, somatically, each of us in our own blood'.[47]

Dixon claims that much of the work that juxtaposes live performance and projected media seeks to 'excite visceral, subjective, or subconscious audience responses'.[48] Although more traditional technologies of the stage are capable of doing just that, the suggestion is that the sheer speed and scale of the transformations that video editing and computer-generated images permit amount to a 'bombardment of images from different times and spaces quite impossible in live performance within three-dimensional theatrical space'.[49]

28. Socìetas Raffaello Sanzio, Bn. 05, *Tragedia Endogonidia*, Bergen International Festival, Norway, 2003

Subjective and psychoanalytical perspectives

Although some tendencies may be emphasised in the way that people respond to scenographic elements such as space, colour and light, it must also be recognised that any attempts to codify these into general responses and describe their effects in language is limited. Although much of what is experienced in a performance is met with a degree of common understanding, the phenomenological impact of scenography, the multi-sensory and synaesthesic nature of its perception, emphasises the importance of the response of the individual spectator and the subjective nature of perception. Pavis recalls his own response to Brith Gof's production of *Camlann* when he states that 'the

29. Socìetas Raffaello Sanzio, L. 09, *Tragedia Endogonidia*, London International Festival of Theatre, 2004

multiple stimuli that act on corporeal memory include the noise of empty oil drums, the disturbing darkness of the factory space, the acrid smell of smoke'.[50] It is important to note how the real and 'material action' of the scenography registered directly and drew upon multiple sensory perceptions of touch, smell, sense of space, movement, sight and sound.

Multi-sensory aspects of scenography offer a phenomenological encounter for the audience that stimulates embodied understandings of the physical and material world. Light fading to black on stage can evoke feelings in the pit of one's stomach while the throwing of confetti or the swish of a skirt may induce other musculatory responses. These sensations are often registered through impressions and fragments rather than fully formed images, and although they are hard to grasp in conscious thought, this does not mean that they do not have significant impact on individual spectators.

Barthes' notions of 'studium' and 'punctum', as applied to the viewing or experiencing of photographs, distinguish between a polite or cursory interest in and attention to an image (studium) and a more immediate and more idiosyncratic response (punctum). The concept of 'punctum' as 'that accident which pricks me' highlights the visceral potential of an image[51] and helps to develop the idea of unstable but potent scenographic material. The initial level of polite interest (studium) involves a kind of contract or an agreement to behave; it is educated and in harmony with the artist's intentions and can be disrupted by the experience of an image which cuts through or punctures the more obvious meaning. McAuley identifies the capability of objects on stage to work in a similar way to Barthes' theory of 'punctum'. She calls them 'arbitrary' objects. They are like Artaud's 'objects of unknown form and purpose' which induce a 'rupture' with the real world. It is 'the realization that the object can be neither understood nor controlled that gives such surrealistic objects their power'.[52]

26   I want you to learn how the reactions of an audience differ from the reactions of every individual in that audience. I want to repeat that. I want you to learn how the reactions of an audience differ from the reactions of every individual in that audience. I want you to know that audiences have capacities for feeling that no dramatist has ever touched.
    Robert Edmond Jones in Delbert Unruh (ed.), *Towards a New Theatre: The Lectures of Robert Edmond Jones*, p. 50

The subjective nature of the reception of theatre has led many to consider the psychoanalytical dimension of the experience. This perspective foregrounds the individual spectator in relation to the body and the sense of self. It helps to draw both conscious and unconscious reactions into the understanding of responses to scenography. Psychoanalysis as applied to theatre reception is particularly useful with regard to ideas about self-identity and the role of the unconscious. Building on Sigmund Freud's theories of child development, Jacques Lacan identified the 'mirror stage' as the point at which young children begin to understand themselves as separate beings and start to develop a sense of themselves; consequently, Lacan's theories of the 'gaze' emphasise how seeing always means being seen and that 'we are beings who are looked at, in the spectacle of the world'.[53]

However, the illusion of consciousness and objectivity and the image of ourselves as complete and coherent entities that appear to stare back at us from the mirror is, in itself, illusory: 'The gaze I encounter … is not a seen gaze, but a gaze imagined by me in the field of the Other.'[54] The 'gaze' is the 'underside of consciousness' and disrupts, questions or threatens the fragile sense of self.

James Elkins has written an accessible account of Lacan's ideas in his study of the nature of 'seeing'. Elkins discusses the reciprocal process of 'seeing' and 'being seen' as fundamental processes of understanding who we are: 'I see myself in the other person's gaze, and so I see myself being seen.'[55] Vision is a 'cat's cradle of crossing lines of sight' or an intersection of gazes in which we can be caught. This idea is not difficult to grasp when we think about the gaze of ourselves in the mirror or the gaze of other people, but it can be applied to objects, which might also be said to 'send back our sight'.[56] Elkins states that 'Objects look incomplete or inviting; they seem to be waiting for us to notice them.'[57] But these exchanges of gaze are fraught and the field of vision is 'clotted with sexuality, desire, convention, anxiety, and boredom'.[58]

According to Lacan, the fragile sense of completeness of the subject is forever undermined by unconscious desire for the time, before the mirror stage, of 'pure plenitude', where child and mother exist in a 'hermetically sealed circuit of need and satisfaction'.[59] The gaze, 'pulsatile, dazzling and spread out',[60] operates to reveal this lack of completeness and threatens to dismantle illusions of selfhood. But cultural objects and artworks are used as a way of mediating the threat. The concept of the 'gaze' has been discussed particularly with regard to its application to cinema.[61] Hal Foster claims that picture-making and viewing are the means by which we can tame, pacify, 'manipulate and moderate the gaze'. A picture is a screen (or a mask) between the subject and the gaze and allows the subject to view the object without being 'blinded by the gaze'.[62]

The scenographic image also provides a kind of 'screen' which presents a tamed view of the world. The 'screen' of scenography can be an object of contemplation and also a means of speculation about the world and the fears and desires which lie beyond the performance. In Lacan's terms, the spectator is 'mapped' in the image and 'isolates the function of the screen and plays with it', knowing that what lies beyond is the gaze.[63]

Michal Kobialka uses psychoanalytic terms to frame investigation of Kantor's development as a theatre artist. He sees Kantor's work as a journey of discovery of the self and of the 'quest for the other'. Kantor's early work amounted to a series of explorations in capturing the individual artist's response to the world and to contemporary events, leading to theatre which produced 'its own space within the space of the world'.[64] From 1975 (the year of the first production of *The Dead Class*), Kantor began to investigate the presentation of memory and multiple reflections of past events from his own life and childhood.

> 27   That is why I can include among my works of art the following objects: a lumber room, a cloakroom like a slaughterhouse, people hanging in a wardrobe, an academic discourse on a heap of coal, a mad woman with teaspoons, a woman with a plank, a woman in a henhouse, a fully dressed woman who was thrown into a bathtub, bags, parcels, school desks, wrecks, facades, umbrellas, an apocalyptic death machine made of folding chairs.
>   Tadeusz Kantor, *A Journey through Other Spaces: Essays and Manifestos, 1944–1990*, p. 30

The figure of Kantor as the instigator of the work was clarified through his presence on stage where he observed and sometimes intervened in the action. Using fragments of action drawn from his own experience and memory, Kantor required his performers to repeat sequences until the effect produced was an impression or intricate collage of memory. In *Wielopole, Wielopole*, images and events from his childhood were presented and re-presented in 'an attempt to visualize memory in a three-dimensional theatrical space. Kantor as the holder of the discourse/memory, watched the process of materialization of the most intimate aspects of the Self in the form of the Other(s).'[65] The stage space, a simple room, became the site of an irresolvable attempt to reconcile the here and now with the past and to investigate the illusion of the self through representations of images of the other. Kantor refers to the performance space as 'the Room of Memory' and it is the place where characters and events from the past meet.[66] Images assembled, disassembled and reassembled on the stage are attempts to grasp at the ungraspable and that which lies beyond everyday reality.

Attention and distraction

Shifts of attention and moments of distraction form a key part of the meaning-making process in theatre. Determination of the spectator's view has been an important aspect of the development of theatre architecture and scenography. The viewers' attention can easily be manipulated by use of scenography but individuals are also capable of making their own choices concerning focus.

Disruption and surprise in the scenographic composition help to instigate critical distance. At the same time, distraction that results from prolonged attention might induce a productive reverie where individual spectators are open to associations which are significant to them alone.

Jonathan Crary's 'genealogy of attention' shows how modernity has shaped concepts of attention and human subjectivity[67] and attempted to regulate the effect of the image: 'attention is the means by which an individual observer can transcend those subjective limitations and make perception *its own*, and attention is at the same time a means by which a perceiver becomes open to control and annexation by external agencies'.[68] 'Attention' enables individual viewers to focus on what they choose. Such choices continue to shape the perceptions of individuals but they can also induce docility, passive acceptance, absorption or manageable patterns of consumption and loss of self. Richard Wagner's theatre at Bayreuth was shaped by 'his belief in the transformative effects of the *collective* experience of music drama'. Wagner distinguished between higher forms of art (such as his own) which required a deeply attentive audience and the more popular and 'distracted modes of cultural consumption'.[69] The design of the Bayreuth auditorium reduced the tendency to make audience members aware of each other as had been encouraged, perhaps unintentionally, by the layout of earlier theatres. By sinking the orchestra pit and making the stage far more brightly illuminated than the auditorium he helped to remove the spectator's consciousness of the construction of the event in a 'systematic concealing and mystification of the processes of production'.[70] This resulted in a state of attentiveness that was hypnotic and produced a dreamlike condition of perception. The autonomy of the audience was subordinated to Wagner's own vision.

Distraction, the apparent opposite of attention, has been associated with deviancy, lack of control and social disintegration. But it may come about when attention reaches a threshold and disintegrates leading to 'distraction, reverie, dissociation and trance': 'Attention always contained within itself the conditions for its own disintegration, it was haunted by the possibility of its own excess – which we all know so well whenever we try to look at or listen to any one thing for too long.'[71] Attention and distraction, then, exist on a continuum: 'the two ceaselessly flow into one another, as part of a social field in which the same imperatives and forces incite one and the other'.[72] In contemporary scenography, distraction is as much an organising principle as attention was in the modernist period.

Returning to psychoanalysis, Julia Kristeva identifies 'the semiotic' and 'the symbolic' as two modalities of the same signifying process.[73] The symbolic is tied to language, communication and the regulating function of theory, order and identity.[74] Kristeva's notion of the semiotic refers particularly to non-verbal signs which, although they cannot be grasped by conceptual thought, are nonetheless an essential part of our understanding of the world. As infants, our world is informed by semiotic understanding that precedes and transcends language, focused by the 'chora', a mobile, provisional articulation and the precondition for attaining a signifying position. The '*chora* precedes and under-lies figuration' and is analogous to 'vocal or kinetic rhythm'.[75] Scenographic distraction seems to provide a chora-like state which is an important part of the whole signifying process. Rich and distracting material – colours, patterns, shapes, movement and rhythm – are brought into focus through spectators' attempts to identify representations of the symbolic. A psychological account of the artwork, as articulated by Lacan and Foster, enables an understanding of the intensely subjective motivation behind the creation and viewing of images. From this perspective, the scenographic image might be seen to have a role in structuring the individual's self-consciousness. Motivation for making and viewing images is part of a human need to 'develop a healthy reciprocity between the embodied subject and its world' so that the subject might find 'its own sense of self defined and realized'.[76]

Chapter 8

Completion and exchange of the image

It is important not to consider experience of scenography separately from the total experience of performance. However, consideration of scenographic aspects of performance serves to highlight particular qualities and characteristics of the theatrical event. A scenographic perspective also emphasises the extent to which individual audience members determine the success and significance of performance. This concluding chapter considers what audiences might take from engagement with scenography and how the role of the audience is reshaped through scenographic practice and understanding.

Theatre images

Alan Read has claimed that images are the essence of theatre and that theatre images are 'part of an economy of symbolic exchange'.[1] The images he describes are not limited to the visual. The kinds of images that theatre produces are informed by space and time and by visual, auditory, and other sensory stimuli. They are not created entirely by the production itself, but come about as a result of the production being able to activate the spectator's imagination:

> a woman reaching for a man, a balloon ascending, sand descending, the reverberation of a forest – like others [they] add up to more than the sum of their parts, they have physical depth and imaginative height. They are not solely literary, visual, or poetic images but potentially theatre images, and as such are produced by the relationship between bodies in place, made space, and the presence of more than a seeing eye; they are regarded by a perceiving audience.[2]

This concept of a perceiving audience that does more than just see recalls Meyerhold's claim that 'the crucial revision of a production is that which is made by the spectator.'[3]

Meyerhold investigated the way his productions affected audiences through consideration of their behaviour. He studied audience laughter, applause, whistling, hisses, fidgeting, sighing, throwing things and people walking out.[4] This rather crude quantitative approach allowed Meyerhold's company to compare one performance to another but it was not appropriate in uncovering the significance of theatre images and the workings of audience imagination. What is needed, says Read, is an understanding of the mechanics of images and how they work: 'how they are received and appropriated by the precondition of their creation, the audience'.[5] The spatial dimension of theatre reception provides a different way of thinking about the creation and effect of theatre images. Recent research into the way audiences respond to scenography has drawn on notions of spatial thinking to help model the working of images as an exchange between scenography and spectators.[6]

Spatial thinking

Henri Lefebvre conceived of space as a medium of cultural expression. He identified three ways in which space operates. 'Perceived space' refers to concrete spatial practices in which every society produces its own space that reflects its ideology and reproduces its dominance. For Lefebvre, writing in the 1970s, these practices could be traced through such examples as 'the daily life of a tenant in a government subsidized high-rise housing project' or the operation of the motorway system and the politics of air transport.[7] An important formulation which might apply directly to scenography is the notion that 'activity in space is restricted by that space'. Lefebvre elaborates by saying 'space commands bodies, prescribing or proscribing gestures, routes and distances to be covered'.[8] 'Conceived space' concerns codes and representations of space, the intellectual, theoretical concepts of space which are made use of by experts: 'scientists, planners, urbanists, technocratic subdividers and social engineers'.[9] Finally, 'lived space' is space as directly and subjectively experienced by individuals. Lefebvre links this to the 'clandestine or underground side of social life'[10] and to art. The everyday reality of space can be transcended via the imagination, which makes use of non-verbal symbols and signs: 'This is the dominated – and hence passively experienced – space which the imagination seeks to change and appropriate. It overlays physical space, making symbolic use of its objects.'[11]

All these categories might be applied to an understanding of scenography. Perceived space might be considered in relation to the dominant modes of experience and consumption of theatre, while conceived space might refer to various attempts to describe and theorise principles and practices of scenography. Arnold Aronson has suggested that 'traditional theatrical scenography is a form of conceived space, which is based on perceived space'.[12] However, it is the third category of 'lived space' in which there is scope for productive consideration of the operation of scenography – now and in the future. Transcendence of the everyday and release of the imagination (in any artistic form) allows individuals to think about how things really are and, perhaps, how they might be otherwise.

Another valuable concept offered by Lefebvre concerns the 'dual nature' of space. On the one hand, for each of us, one 'relates oneself to space, situates oneself in space. One confronts both an immediacy and an objectivity of one's own. One places oneself at the centre, designates oneself, measures oneself, and uses oneself as a measure.'[13] On the other hand, 'space serves an intermediary or mediating role: beyond each plane surface, beyond each opaque form, "one" seeks to apprehend something else. This tends to turn social space into a transparent medium occupied solely by light, by "presences" and influences'.[14]

Thus, space is a simultaneously concrete and conceptual medium; a tangible and measurable entity as well as a medium of imagination. Architects and artists have made use of this in developing new work and proposing new ideas; working with materials allows ideas to literally take shape whilst concepts are modified and developed in the light of practical experiments. This sort of process has also been described as 'projection'. Art can be considered to be based on 'a series of projective relations in a game of reflections, each of which permits the representation of the object, but alone can never succeed in exhausting its content'. Each projection, each reflection, allows the object to assume 'new connotations and interpretive openings'.[15] For the theatre, too, projection has both physical and conceptual purchase. The work of scenographers clearly involves selection of objects and images and their translation and transformation into moments of significance. But members of the audience, too, are invited to project, through their imagination, their own thoughts and feelings as part of the process of engaging with performance. The concrete-and-conceptual nature of theatre images, the way they oscillate between what Read terms the 'the material and the metaphysical',[16] can be compared to what Paul Crowther has to say about the nature of art and aesthetic experience. In the visual arts, literature and the applied arts, what is created is 'a symbolically significant sensuous manifold'. Artworks are physical artefacts which exist in and take up space. At the same time they are conceptualisations, that is, 'a concrete particular which is charged with semantic and conceptual energy'. This dual nature of the artwork is what determines the way it can be fully understood. It is 'a mode of understanding which is half-way between the concrete particularity of material phenomena, and the abstract generality of pure thought'.[17] The physical manifestation of scenography; the construction and nature of materials; the quality and nature of the sound; the movement and texture of a costume; the atmosphere induced by the light; the manipulation of the stage space – all these conditions resonate with possible meanings. Embodied modes of understanding are as important here as clear-cut perceptions and concepts. 'Colour, shape, sound, mass, and weight are not just the means to the meaning generated. They are an essential dimension in its full definition.'[18]

Immersion, participation and exchange

Even in forms of presentation where the audience is seated, the mode of engagement with scenography tends to be an active if not a fully participatory one. The polysemous and fluid nature of images means that the role of the spectator is often cast to invite active interpretation. And the nature of the theatrical event places considerable emphasis on the spectator as the final arbiter of the event where no two audience members are guaranteed the same experience.

Contemporary scenographic practice now includes events that are situated outside traditional theatre venues and where scenography effectively provides the dramaturgical through-line. In newer forms the role of the audience is seen to be a participatory or even an interactive one. Theatre which aims at audience participation is not new.[19] But in some cases it may also be observed that scenographic strategies facilitate participation and invite more fully interactive events than hitherto. Several of the examples of scenography produced in response to specific sites (see Chapter 3) offered a sensory immersion for the audience which activated engagement through simultaneous appeal to the material and the metaphorical.

Punchdrunk, a UK-based company, aims to fuse live performance and installation through creation of a theatrical environment in which masked audience members are free to move around and make connections and associations as they move through evocative spaces and encounter performative episodes. The company describes its work as follows: 'What we do differently is to focus as much attention on the audience and space as we give to the performers and the text. A team of designers takes over deserted spaces and applies a cinematic level of detail to immerse the audience in the world of the play.'[20] The masks are intended to liberate spectators from a self-consciousness which might otherwise limit their engagement with the event. The responses to the performance are revealing, not only of the performance itself, but the nature of this kind of event and the post-performance life that it can take on. Susannah Clapp's review of *The Masque of the Red Death* (2007–8), which took its inspiration from the writing of Edgar Allan Poe and the Victorian origins of the venue, conveys the sense of excitement and anticipation engendered by the evocative mix of scenographic elements:

> Camphor and TCP; cloves and oranges; incense and dust. At Battersea Arts Centre the smells alone set you off on a trail. So do the noises – the striking of a clock; the scream behind a locked door; the low hiss in an empty room, like a record that has reached the end of its song. You can trace a tale through this maze of dusky Victorian corridors by following a hurtling figure – that harlequin, that veiled bride, that distraught dandy. You can bump into mystery and melodrama by moving from what was once a hall and is now a forest of dead trees, to the fragrant cushioned chamber of an opium den … You can stay still, absorbing the give-away detail in a 19th-century drawing-room – the volume of Scott, the suitor's letter to an aunt – and let the stories steal up on you. Whichever route you take, you will end up, after dark passages, swept into an English carnival, a gaudy, golden-lit celebration in a ballroom, the giddiest of pleasures, stalked by the figure of death.[21]

Active attempts to engage the audience are not always successful. Individuals vary in their eagerness to participate in this way, and also the balance between the immediate excitement of joining in and the opportunity to reflect on what the experience amounts to can be difficult to achieve. The critic from *The Sunday Times*, Christopher Hart, felt bullied and herded and, ultimately, irritated: 'Far from engaging with the audience or putting it at the centre of the action, a performance like this leaves you feeling merely hemmed in, ticked off and herded around.' For him, Poe had been stripped of mysticism and 'crudely reduced to the gory and macabre'.[22] Others, though, were intrigued by being both the watcher and the watched: 'The fascinating thing about this immersive theatre experience is its duality – something in the way it works allows you to be both spectator and participant simultaneously. It's like those wonderful moments between waking and sleeping, when you feel as if you have some control over your dreams, but they still veer off in wild directions.'[23] Ultimately, the quality of participation in the Punchdrunk production was determined by individual audience members who made choices about the way they viewed the performance. Where the original material, design and organisation of the experience proved to be sufficiently engaging and stimulating, there was scope for individuals to create their own meaning. Other productions have sought to discover a more extensive and contemplative interaction between audience and scenography. In U-Man Zoo's *The Water Banquet* (2003) eighteen audience members were seated around a large table whose surface was dark water of uncertain depth. Waiters were on hand to prepare and serve. Each actuation of the production was determined by these 'guests' and the choices they made from a menu of 'dishes' and 'courses'. Downing describes the way the performance worked. He expresses something of the open-ended and reciprocal nature of the encounter:

> For example, you order the Kinder Piñata (beginnings). By a great and circuitous route and within a mesh of juxtaposed activity, a young girl, finally, delivers you a duck egg which, cracked into a silver-rimmed glass, produces a cascade of blue liquid and a tiny photograph of an elderly man summoning courage before the camera. On the reverse is written, 'I first picked up the violin when I was five … ' What will you *make* of it? I couldn't say. Nor, when, thirty minutes later (middles), you see an elderly gentleman playing a violin at the table's head whilst a waitress meticulously plants 116 forks into the table in a steady downpour of rain. I can only guess at what it is you see.[24]

In this performance the audience is central to its success and meaning. The frame of the meal and the medium of strange and delicate images allows audience members to be treated as privileged guests, rather than spectators: 'With The Water Banquet we referred not to the *spectator*, but to the *guest* – this has much to do with the necessity of co-presence, but even more to do with recognition of another's imagination as the real site of completion.'[25] In this particular production the audience role was elevated to one of co-creation.

Research carried out by Joslin McKinney proposed the notion of 'the scenographic exchange'. Scenographic performances were used to investigate the nature of communication between scenography and audience. In *Homesick*, audience members were asked to respond by making images of their own which reflected, elaborated and reinterpreted the scenography and demonstrated how the original images of the performance multiplied and mutated. Here, scenography could be seen to be capable of working as an agent of exchange. The audience, stimulated by scenographic constructions, imagined or remembered their own images. The performance and the reflection on it was a construction of multiple refractions and perspectives.[26] Following this line of thinking, audience members can be thought of as co-creators of scenography in so far as it is they who find potential stimulation or agreement in or with an image and complete it for themselves through projection and appropriation.

These last three examples have exploited the possibilities that emerge with movement away from traditional dramatic structures and also from traditional theatre venues. However, this does not necessarily mean that the extent of audience engagement that these examples suggest is limited to forms where audiences are physically engaged. The multi-sensory dimension of scenography is present even when audience members are confined to seats in a theatre auditorium. The nature of produced images always allows for the possibility of an active sensory and intellectual engagement on the part of the audience.

Self-consciousness and the ethics of the image

Crowther and Read share the outlook that the potential of an aesthetic experience is linked to the way it finds agreement with the individual spectator. The extent to which spectators' imaginations are engaged and activated depends on the capacity for the artwork to connect meaningfully with their view of the world. Where this potential is realised, it triggers a process of imaginative development on the part of the spectator.[27] This function of art speaks to the human need to 'see our inner life reflected in, and acknowledged by, the realm of Otherness'[28] and is therefore one of the ways that we achieve self-consciousness.

The 'economy of symbolic exchange' which operates in theatre implies that images are taken up and developed when they are seen to have currency which connects us not only to our own sense of self but to a wider, ethical concern for the individual's position in society.

> Both ethics and theatre are concerned with possibility. On the contrary representation is the reflection of an 'existing' proposition as though it were fact, and this is never what theatre achieves. The theatre image unlike any other is always a possibility without closure, like the ethical relation which awaits creation.[29]

Proposals about the relationships between individuals and the larger community, between human beings and the world, are put forward in the 'disconcerting and unpredictable' images of theatre which oscillate between 'the material and the metaphysical'.[30]

William Kentridge's work with the Handspring Puppet Company in South Africa demonstrates the way a scenographic approach can find a way to stage harrowing and volatile material and ask difficult questions. *Ubu and the Truth Commission* (1997) used material from witness testimonials presented to the Truth and Reconciliation Commission, set up after apartheid was dismantled, as a way of trying to deal with 'the legacies of hatred and violence undergirding the apartheid system'.[31] This process was fraught with difficulties and the play, written by Jane Taylor, deals with the 'painful compromises' which the TRC engendered. Kentridge used two actors (Ma and Pa Ubu) along with puppets and projections of Kentridge's hand-drawn images and animations.[32] This multi-media approach enabled some distance from the actual events. The aim was 'to make sense of the memory rather than be the memory'.[33] Rather than becoming the actual witnesses, the puppets became 'a medium through which the testimony could be heard'. Kentridge describes working with the puppets and the human actors and discovering the different meanings that could be generated. In different positions, Ubu's body was a landscape for the puppet, or the puppet could seem like a figment of Ubu's imagination. When they tried touching Ubu's hip with the 'wooden hand' of the puppet, the image became 'an act of absolution'. Kentridge says 'it is only on the stage, in the moment, that one can judge how the material is given its weight. This changes both from performance to performance and from audience to audience.'[34]

New scenographic forms and practices

Further possibilities are now beginning to emerge regarding the scope of scenographic practice and understanding. It is already clear that the capabilities offered by computer technology are leading to new forms in scenography and also new forms of performance and spectatorship:

> The presentation and performance of self through the creation and 'uploading' into the virtual theatre of a personal website, and the interaction of a performance website, have created significant alternatives to existing narrative modes, forms of representation, dramaturgies and physical places of performance. Within new dramaturgies and within these architectures of performance, the virtual actor, the avatar, may be brought into existence and may walk upon an entirely new space and within a completely re-visioned scenography of performance.[35]

Computers and the Internet clearly open up new possibilities for reconfiguring or redefining traditional relationships between audiences, performers and scenography. Games which permit the creation of virtual selves and virtual spaces allow their users, potentially, to become performers and scenographers.

Additionally, scenographic interventions are currently helping to shape and define new areas of scenographic consideration. Dorita Hannah and Olav Harsløf have used the term 'Performance Design' to examine how scenography, for far too long confined to the 'exclusive and hermetically sealed realm of the stage', might be considered in conjunction with other artists and designers who work to 'transform the public domain with fleeting, time-based interventions that comment on our contemporary condition'.[36] They identify examples of work which include the disciplines of architecture, video art, drawing, software design, lighting, gastronomy and fashion as well as scenography. This work, often collaborative, is establishing new possibilities for scenography. For example, Kathleen Irwin uses scenography to activate new modes of spectatorship. Site-specific performance evokes images and events that call on and reveal the spectator's complex relationship to environments. The scenography that Irwin makes is aimed at revealing the relationship between spectators and the environment rather than making independent visual statements. Scenography is a strategy to gather audiences and provide 'a rich experiential event that engages the senses and both confirms and disturbs a preordained perception of a given place'. She sees this as 'a way of giving back places to people and restoring, however temporarily, a sense of the reciprocal relationship between who we are and where we are'.[37]

The *Weyburn Project* (2002) was based in a disused mental hospital and used scenography and performance to recover the stories of former patients, workers and the wider community. Irwin is interested in how physical surroundings affect mood and behaviour and how particular sites resonate with 'a dense and contested past'[38] revealed through their physical presence. The *Bus Project* (2004) used specially designed interactive computer games and customised bus seats to enable journeys between Regina and Saskatoon in Canada to involve passengers as spectator–participants. The games revealed stories of women's experiences of departure, immigration and displacement, encouraging the spectators to see 'their immediate surroundings in a global context'.[39] Rather than create a scenic construction from scratch, as is usual on the stage, scenographic strategies were employed to reveal the qualities and meanings inherent in a particular space and 'confirm and unsettle the complex and ongoing relationship between our physical environment and ourselves'.[40]

Notes

Chapter 1

1. *OED* 'scenography' 1. The representation of a building or other object in perspective; a perspective elevation. 2. Scene painting (in ancient Greece); 'scenographer' A scene painter; one who draws buildings, etc. in perspective; ADDITIONS SERIES 1993. 2. A designer of theatrical scenery. See also Hannah and Harsløf (eds.), *Performance Design*, p. 11; Rewa, *Scenography in Canada*, p. 119, n1.
2. Rewa, *Scenography in Canada*, p. 120.
3. Ribeiro, *Arquitecturas em Palco*, p. 109.
4. Burian, *The Scenography of Josef Svoboda*, p. 15.
5. Howard, *What Is Scenography?* p. 130.
6. *Ibid.*, p. 33.
7. Shepherd and Wallis, *Drama/Theatre/Performance*, p. 237.
8. Pavis, *Analyzing Performance*, p. 8.
9. *Ibid.*, p. 204.
10. Ingham, *From Page to Stage*; Thorne, *Stage Design*; Parker et al., *Scene Design and Stage Lighting*.
11. Burian, *The Scenography of Josef Svoboda*, p. 18.
12. *Ibid.*, p. 20.
13. Baugh, 'Brecht and Stage Design', p. 241.
14. Ribeiro, *Arquitecturas em Palco*, p. 109.
15. Christopher Baugh points out that through the twentieth century, the development of theatre technology has meant 'an enlargement and a gradual fragmentation of the scenographic team' from the work of one or two artists at the beginning of the twentieth century to the large teams of people responsible for scenography in contemporary mainstream theatre. See Baugh, *Theatre, Performance and Technology*, p. 214.
16. Lehmann, *Postdramatic Theatre*, p. 93.
17. *Ibid.*
18. Pavis, *Analyzing Performance*, p. 178.
19. Howard, *What Is Scenography?* p. xv.
20. Braun (ed.), *Meyerhold on Theatre*, p. 256.
21. Auslander, *Liveness*, p. 19.
22. Phelan, *Unmarked*, p. 146.

23. In *Liveness*, Auslander argues that distinctions between the live and the mediatised are beginning to become blurred across a wide range of performance practices including rock music and sport. Although he wants to question the dominant status of live performance he does acknowledge that 'live performance engages the senses *differently* than mediatized representations' (p. 55).

24. The largest and most influential of these is the Prague Quadrennial, a four-yearly exhibition of international theatre design and architecture which aims to represent the best of contemporary work. Over the forty-year period of its existence, the influence of scenographic perspectives has been notable; lighting and sound design are now given more attention and attempts have been made to move beyond static models and drawings and include interactive audio-visual material and performance to demonstrate the work.

25. Davis, *Stage Design*, p. 10.

26. Aronson, *Looking into the Abyss*, p. 6.

27. Baugh, *Theatre, Performance and Technology*.

Chapter 2

1. Beacham (ed.), *Adolphe Appia: Essays, Scenarios, and Designs*, p. 101. See also Beacham, *Adolphe Appia: Theatre Artist*, pp. 2–5; Beacham (ed.), *Adolphe Appia: Texts on Theatre*, p. 3.

2. Beacham, *Adolphe Appia: Theatre Artist*, p. 40.

3. Hewitt (ed.), *Adolphe Appia's Music and the Art of the Theatre*, p. 2. See also Beacham (ed.), *Adolphe Appia: Texts on Theatre*, pp. 2–3; Beacham, *Adolphe Appia: Theatre Artist*, p. 11.

4. Hewitt (ed.), *Adolphe Appia's Music*, p. 2; Bablet and Bablet (eds.), *Adolphe Appia*, p. 12.

5. Hewitt (ed.), *Adolphe Appia's Music*, p. 26.

6. *Ibid.*

7. Beacham (ed.), *Adolphe Appia: Essays, Scenarios, and Designs*, p. 106. See also Beacham (ed.), *Adolphe Appia: Texts on Theatre*, pp. 62–3.

8. Hewitt (ed.), *Adolphe Appia's Music*, p. 3. See also Bablet and Bablet (eds.), *Adolphe Appia*, p. 12.

9. Hewitt (ed.), *Adolphe Appia's Music*, p. 4.

10. Beacham, *Adolphe Appia: Theatre Artist*, pp. 49–53.

11. *Ibid.*, p. 57.

12. Beacham (ed.), *Adolphe Appia: Texts on Theatre*, p. 8.

13. Hewitt (ed.), *Adolphe Appia's Music*, p. 72. See also Beacham (ed.), *Adolphe Appia: Texts on Theatre*, p. 5.

14. Beacham, *Adolphe Appia: Theatre Artist*, p. 64.

15. *Ibid.*, p. 27. Hewitt, p. 76, translates the term as 'living light'. Bergman translates the term as 'creative light' rather than 'formative light' in *Lighting in the Theatre*, p. 324.

16. Beacham, *Adolphe Appia: Theatre Artist*, p. 27.
17. Hewitt (ed.), *Adolphe Appia's Music*, p. 75.
18. Beacham, *Adolphe Appia: Theatre Artist*, p. 27.
19. Hewitt (ed.), *Adolphe Appia's Music*, p. 74. See also Beacham (ed.), *Adolphe Appia: Texts on Theatre*, p. 5.
20. Hewitt (ed.), *Adolphe Appia's Music*, p. 75.
21. *Ibid.*, p. 6.
22. Beacham (ed.), *Adolphe Appia: Texts on Theatre*, pp. 167–78. Excerpts are taken from Appia's 1919 article 'The Work of Living Art'.
23. Craig, *On the Art of the Theatre*, p. vii, n1.
24. Some examples of his work as actor, designer and/or director are: *Hamlet*, and *Romeo and Juliet*, William Shakespeare, Parkhurst Theatre, London, 1896; *Dido and Aeneas*, Henry Purcell, Hampstead Conservatoire, London, 1900; *The Vikings*, Henrik Ibsen, Imperial Theatre, London, 1903; *Much Ado About Nothing*, William Shakespeare, Imperial Theatre, London, 1903; *Rosmersholm*, Henrik Ibsen, Pergola Theatre, Florence, 1906; *The Deliverer*, Lady Gregory and *The Hour Glass*, W. B. Yeats, Abbey Theatre, Dublin, 1911; *Hamlet*, William Shakespeare, Moscow Arts Theatre, 1912. His principal publications to 1914 are: *A Portfolio of Etchings* (Florence: 1908); editions of the periodical, *The Mask*, begun in 1908 and continued through to 1929; *On the Art of the Theatre* (1911); *Towards a New Theatre* (1913). The most complete bibliography on Craig's published works is Fletcher and Rood (eds.), *Edward Gordon Craig*.
25. Appia, *La Mise en Scène du Drame Wagnérien*, and *Die Musik und die Inscenierung*.
26. Bablet, *The Theatre of Edward Gordon Craig*, pp. 175–6.
27. *Ibid.*, p. 177.
28. Craig, *On The Art Of The Theatre*, pp. 55–6.
29. *Ibid.*, p. 61.
30. *Ibid.*, p. 81.
31. *Ibid.*, p. 87.
32. *Ibid.*, p. 84.
33. Innes, *Edward Gordon Craig*, p. 142.
34. *Ibid.*, p. 143.
35. Baugh et al., 'Gordon Craig and Improvements in Stage Scenery, 1910: Edward Gordon Craig and Patent 1771'.
36. Innes, *Edward Gordon Craig*, p. 141.
37. Bablet, *The Theatre of Edward Gordon Craig*, pp. 127–8.
38. *Ibid.*, p. 145.
39. Senelick, *Gordon Craig's Moscow Hamlet*, p. 152.
40. *Ibid.*, pp. 156–7.
41. *Ibid.*, p. 175.
42. Bablet, *The Theatre of Edward Gordon Craig*, p. 155.
43. *Ibid.*, pp. 125–6.

44. See Serlio, *The second Booke of Architecture*.
45. Bablet, *The Theatre of Edward Gordon Craig*, pp. 122–3.
46. Innes, *Edward Gordon Craig*, p. 180.
47. Schlemmer (ed.), *The Letters and Diaries*, p. 32.
48. González et al. (eds.), *Oskar Schlemmer*, p. 185.
49. On the 'Apollonian' and 'Dionysian', see Nietzsche, *The Birth of Tragedy*, introduction and *passim*.
50. Schlemmer (ed.), *The Letters and Diaries*, pp. 30–1.
51. *Ibid.*, p. 129.
52. *Ibid.*, pp. 127–8.
53. *Ibid.*, p. 128.
54. *Ibid.*, p. 128.
55. Gropius (ed.), *The Theater of the Bauhaus*, p. 34.
56. Schlemmer (ed.), *The Letters and Diaries*, pp. 128–9.
57. Gropius (ed.), *The Theater of the Bauhaus*, p. 85.
58. Trimingham, 'Oskar Schlemmer's Research Practice', p. 129.
59. Gropius (ed.), *The Theater of the Bauhaus*, p. 95.
60. *Ibid.*, p. 95.
61. *Ibid.*, p. 97.
62. *Ibid.*, pp. 97–100.
63. Schlemmer (ed.), *The Letters and Diaries*, p. 203.
64. *Ibid.*, p. 205.
65. Gropius (ed.), *The Theater of the Bauhaus*, p. 91.
66. Artaud, *The Theatre and its Double*, p. 70.
67. Schumacher (ed.), *Artaud on Theatre*, p. 67.
68. *Ibid.*, pp. 74–5.
69. Artaud, *The Theatre and its Double*, p. 72.
70. *Ibid.*, p. 72.
71. Schumacher (ed.), *Artaud on Theatre*, p. 93.
72. Artaud, *The Theatre and its Double*, p. 38.
73. Savarese, 'Antonin Artaud Sees Balinese Theatre', pp. 51–77.
74. Artaud, *The Theatre and its Double*, p. 37.
75. *Ibid.*, p. 41.
76. *Ibid.*, p. 46.
77. Savarese, 'Antonin Artaud Sees Balinese Theatre', p. 68.
78. Artaud, *The Theatre and its Double*, pp. 42–3.
79. *Ibid.*, p. 26.
80. *Ibid.*
81. *Ibid.*, p. 34.
82. *Ibid.*, p. 76.
83. *Ibid.*, p. 74.
84. Innes, *Avant Garde Theatre*, p. 87.
85. Artaud, *The Theatre and its Double*, p. 74.

86. *Ibid.*, p. 75.
87. *Ibid.*, p. 86.
88. Schumacher (ed.), *Artaud on Theatre*, p. 82.
89. Innes, *Avant Garde Theatre*, p. 91.
90. Knapp, *Antonin Artaud*, p. 113.
91. Schumacher (ed.), *Artaud on Theatre*, p. 147.
92. *Ibid.*, p. 147.
93. Knapp, *Antonin Artaud*, p. 114.
94. Innes, *Avant Garde Theatre*, p. 76.
95. Knapp, *Antonin Artaud*, pp. 114–24.
96. Innes, *Avant Garde Theatre*, p. 76.
97. *Ibid.*, pp. 76–7.
98. Schumacher (ed.), *Artaud on Theatre*, p. 147.
99. Innes, *Avant Garde Theatre*, p. 88.
100. Hoover, *Meyerhold and his Set Designers*.
101. Rudnitsky, *Russian and Soviet Theatre*, pp. 191–2.
102. Braun (ed.), *Meyerhold on Theatre*, p. 142.
103. Benedetti, *Stanislavsky*, p. 70.
104. Senelick, *The Chekhov Theatre*, p. 61.
105. Worrall, *The Moscow Art Theatre*, pp. 121–2.
106. Benedetti, *Stanislavsky*, p. 103.
107. Braun, *Meyerhold: A Revolution in Theatre*, p. 13.
108. *Ibid.*, p. 30.
109. *Ibid.*, p. 31.
110. Braun (ed.), *Meyerhold on Theatre*, p. 56.
111. Braun, *Meyerhold: A Revolution in Theatre*, p. 36.
112. *Ibid.*, p. 53.
113. Braun (ed.), *Meyerhold on Theatre*, p. 256.
114. *Ibid.*
115. Braun, *Meyerhold: A Revolution in Theatre*, pp. 62–3.
116. Leach, *Vsevolod Meyerhold*, p. 40.
117. Baugh, *Theatre, Performance and Technology*, p. 67.
118. *Ibid.*, p. 69.
119. Leach, *Vsevolod Meyerhold*, p. 85.
120. Braun, *Meyerhold: A Revolution in Theatre*, p. 67.
121. *Ibid.*, p. 63.
122. *Ibid.*, p. 67; Leach, *Vsevolod Meyerhold*, p. 85.
123. Braun, *Meyerhold: A Revolution in Theatre*, p. 68. See also Braun (ed.), *Meyerhold on Theatre*, pp. 137–9.
124. Braun (ed.), *Meyerhold on Theatre*, p. 141.
125. Braun, *Meyerhold: A Revolution in Theatre*, p. 106; Butterworth, 'Book Carriers', p. 27.
126. Braun, *Meyerhold: A Revolution in Theatre*, p. 106; Braun (ed.), *Meyerhold on Theatre*, pp. 102–3.

127. Leach, *Vsevolod Meyerhold*, pp. 90–1.
128. Leach, *Revolutionary Theatre*, p. 22.
129. Rudnitsky, *Russian and Soviet Theatre*; Braun, *Meyerhold: A Revolution in Theatre*, p. 157.
130. Worrall, 'Meyerhold's Production of the Magnanimous Cuckold', pp. 14–34; Law, 'Meyerhold's The Magnanimous Cuckold', pp. 61–86.
131. Rudnitsky, *Russian and Soviet Theatre*, p. 121; Pitches, *Vsevolod Meyerhold*, pp. 67–76.
132. Baugh, 'Brecht and Stage Design', p. 235.
133. Willett, *Caspar Neher*, p. 14.
134. Baugh, 'Brecht and Stage Design', p. 242.
135. Willett, *Caspar Neher*, p. 106.
136. *Ibid.*, pp. 230–2.
137. Baugh, *Theatre, Performance and Technology*, pp. 77–8.
138. Willett, *Caspar Neher*, p. 109.
139. *Ibid.*, p. 30.
140. *Ibid.*, p. 109.
141. *Ibid.*, p. 113.
142. Willett (ed.), *Brecht on Theatre*, p. 233.
143. Willett, *Caspar Neher*, p. 76.
144. *Ibid.*, p. 75.
145. *Ibid.*, pp. 68–9.
146. *Ibid.*, p. 112.
147. Baugh, 'Brecht and Stage Design', p. 236.
148. Willett, *Caspar Neher*, p. 101.
149. *Ibid.*, p. 101.
150. Willett (ed.), *Brecht on Theatre*, pp. 37–8.
151. Shepherd and Wallis, *Drama/Theatre/Performance*, p. 185.
152. Willett (ed.), *Brecht on Theatre*, p. 37.
153. *Ibid.*, p. 38.
154. Baugh, *Theatre, Performance and Technology*, p. 75.
155. Bablet, *The Revolutions of Stage Design*, p. 243.
156. Larson, *Scene Design in the American Theatre*, p. 42.
157. Jones, *The Dramatic Imagination*, p. 7.
158. *Ibid.*, pp. 13–14.
159. *Ibid.*, pp. 16–17, 77.
160. Dixon, *Digital Performance*, p. 82.
161. Jones, *The Dramatic Imagination*, p. 20.
162. *Ibid.*, pp. 21–2.
163. *Ibid.*, pp. 35–6.
164. Mielziner, *Designing for the Theatre*, pp. 87–8.
165. Henderson, *Mielziner*, p. 87.
166. *Ibid.*, p. 142.

167. Doona, 'Hope, Hopelessness/Presence, Absence', p. 61.
168. Henderson, *Mielziner*, pp. 161–2.
169. Kolin, *Williams*, p. 12.
170. Mielziner, *Designing for the Theatre*, p. 141.
171. Roudané, 'Death of a salesman', p. 64.
172. Doona, 'Hope, Hopelessness/Presence, Absence', p. 64.
173. Dukore, *Death of a Salesman and The Crucible*, pp. 74–7.
174. Roudané, 'Death of a salesman', p. 65.
175. Mielziner, *Designing for the Theatre*, p. 12.
176. Kantor, *A Journey through Other Spaces*, pp. 3–14.
177. *Ibid.*, p. 180.
178. *Ibid.*, p. 135.
179. *Ibid.*
180. Pleśniarowicz, *The Dead Memory Machine*, p. 40.
181. Klossowicz, 'Tadeusz Kantor's Journey', p. 98.
182. Kantor, *A Journey through Other Spaces*, p. 178.
183. *Ibid.*, p. 271.
184. *Ibid.*, p. 211.
185. *Ibid.*, p. 147.
186. Klossowicz, 'Tadeusz Kantor's Journey', p. 100.
187. *Ibid.*, p. 124.
188. *Ibid.*, pp. 121–2.
189. *Ibid.*, p. 343.
190. *Ibid.*, p. 102.
191. Pleśniarowicz, *The Dead Memory Machine*, pp. 181–2.
192. Kantor, *A Journey through Other Spaces*, p. 325.
193. *Ibid.*, p. 64.
194. *Ibid.*, p. 290.
195. Klossowicz, 'Tadeusz Kantor's Journey', p. 103.
196. Kantor, *A Journey through Other Spaces*, p. 286.
197. *Ibid.*, p. 287.
198. *Ibid.*, p. 217.
199. Burian, *The Scenography of Josef Svoboda*, pp. 32–6.
200. *Ibid.*, p. 16.
201. *Ibid.*, p. 16.
202. *Ibid.*, p. 19.
203. *Ibid.*, p. 93.
204. *Ibid.*, p. 63.
205. *Ibid.*, p. 24.
206. *Ibid.*; Burian (ed.), *The Secret of Theatrical Space*, p. 58.
207. Burian, *The Scenography of Josef Svoboda*, p. 65.
208. *Ibid.*, p. 114.

209. *Ibid.*, p. 117.

210. *Ibid.*, p. 115.

211. Burian (ed.), *The Secret of Theatrical Space*, p. 105.

212. *Ibid.*, p. 106.

213. Burian, *The Scenography of Josef Svoboda*, p. 93.

214. *Ibid.*, pp. 93–4.

215. Baugh, *Theatre, Performance and Technology*, p. 83.

216. Burian (ed.), *The Secret of Theatrical Space*, pp. 66–7.

217. Burian, *The Scenography of Josef Svoboda*, p. 57.

218. Uršič (ed.), *Josef Svoboda*, p. 30.

219. *Ibid.*, pp. 64–7.

220. Burian, *The Scenography of Josef Svoboda*, p. 30.

221. *Ibid.*, p. 31.

222. *Ibid.*, p. 19.

223. *Ibid.*, p. 19.

224. *Ibid.*, p. 20.

225. Uršič (ed.), *Josef Svoboda*, p. 54.

226. *Ibid.*, p. 9.

227. *Ibid.*, p. 9.

228. Lehmann, *Postdramatic Theatre*, pp. 77–8.

229. Holmberg, *The Theatre of Robert Wilson*, p. 53.

230. Shyer, *Wilson and his Collaborators*, p. 76.

231. Holmberg, *The Theatre of Robert Wilson*, p. 3.

232. Lehmann, *Postdramatic Theatre*, p. 78.

233. Holmberg, *The Theatre of Robert Wilson*, p. 45.

234. *Ibid.*, p. 77; Bly (ed.), *The Production Notebooks*, pp. 63–124.

235. Holmberg, *The Theatre of Robert Wilson*, p. 84.

236. Aronson, *American Avant-Garde Theatre*, p. 124.

237. Shyer, *Wilson and his Collaborators*, p. 30.

238. Aronson, *American Avant-Garde Theatre*, p. 130.

239. Holmberg, *The Theatre of Robert Wilson*, p. 11.

240. *Ibid.*, p. 18.

241. Aronson, *American Avant-Garde Theatre*, p. 126.

242. Holmberg, *The Theatre of Robert Wilson*, p. 85.

243. *Ibid.*, p. 121.

244. Shyer, *Wilson and his Collaborators*, p. 193.

245. Di Benedetto, 'Concepts in Spatial Dynamics', p. 65.

246. Holmberg, *The Theatre of Robert Wilson*, p. 167.

247. *Ibid.*, p. 146.

248. Di Benedetto, 'Concepts in Spatial Dynamics', p. 67.

249. Holmberg, *The Theatre of Robert Wilson*, p. 176.

250. *Ibid.*, p. 177.

251. *Ibid.*, pp. 177–8.
252. *Ibid.*, p. 179.
253. *Ibid.*, p. 176.

Chapter 3

1. Kennedy, *Looking at Shakespeare*, pp. 5–7.
2. Aristotle, *Poetics*, p. 13.
3. See Kennedy, *Looking at Shakespeare*, p. 5.
4. McKinney, 'The Role of Theatre Design'.
5. Baugh, *Theatre, Performance and Technology*, p. 7.
6. Lindley (ed.), *The Court Masque*, p. 164.
7. Gordon, *The Renaissance Imagination*, pp. 77–101.
8. Leacroft and Leacroft, *Theatre and Playhouse*, pp. 103–6.
9. Styan, *Modern Drama in Theory and Practice*, pp. 11–15; Kennedy, *Looking at Shakespeare*, p. 32.
10. Baugh, *Theatre, Performance and Technology*, p. 25; Bergman, *Lighting in the Theatre*, pp. 286–300.
11. Kennedy, *Looking at Shakespeare*, pp. 29–32; Baugh, *Theatre, Performance and Technology*, p. 96; Bergman, *Lighting in the Theatre*, p. 302.
12. Kennedy, *Looking at Shakespeare*, p. 30.
13. Wallis and Shepherd, *Studying Plays*, p. 3.
14. Shepard, *Seven Plays*, p. 3.
15. Chaudhuri 'Different Hats', pp. 132–4.
16. McMillan and Fehsenfeld, *Beckett in the Theatre*.
17. Beckett, *The Complete Dramatic Works*, p. 92.
18. *Ibid.*, p. 138.
19. *Ibid.*, p. 11.
20. Worth, *Waiting for Godot and Happy Days*, p. 14.
21. McMillan and Fehsenfeld, *Beckett in the Theatre*, p. 82.
22. Worth, *Waiting for Godot and Happy Days*, p. 87.
23. Williams, *Drama from Ibsen to Brecht*, p. 125.
24. Styan, *Modern Drama in Theory and Practice*, p. 10.
25. Strindberg, *Plays One*, p. 101.
26. Williams, *Drama from Ibsen to Brecht*, p. 387.
27. Gottlieb, *Anton Chekhov at the Moscow Art Theatre*, pp. 28–31.
28. Mitter, *Systems of Rehearsal*, p. 9.
29. Gottlieb, *Anton Chekhov at the Moscow Art Theatre*, p. 23.
30. *Ibid.*, p. 24.
31. Williams, *Drama from Ibsen to Brecht*, p. 140.
32. Strindberg, *Plays One*, p. 101.
33. Bablet, *The Revolutions of Stage Design*, p. 83.

34. *Ibid.*, p. 85.
35. *Ibid.*, pp. 87–9.
36. See Kennedy, *Looking at Shakespeare*, p. 90.
37. *Ibid.*
38. *Ibid.*, p. 141.
39. States, *Great Reckonings in Little Rooms*, p. 84.
40. Williams, *Drama from Ibsen to Brecht*, pp. 395–6.
41. States, *Great Reckonings in Little Rooms*, p. 88.
42. Kennedy, *Looking at Shakespeare*, p. 13.
43. Burian, *The Scenography of Josef Svoboda*, pp. 54–6.
44. Davis, *Stage Design*, p. 164.
45. *Ibid.*, p. 106.
46. Howard, *What Is Scenography?* p. 39.
47. *Ibid.*, pp. 40–1.
48. *Ibid.*, p. 17.
49. *Ibid.*, p. 23.
50. Accounts of other contemporary scenographers talking about their work can be found in Davis, *Stage Design*.
51. See Beacham (ed.), *Adolphe Appia: Texts on Theatre*, pp. 77–9.
52. Bablet, *The Theatre of Edward Gordon Craig*, p. 119.
53. Shklovsky, 'Art as Technique', p. 17.
54. Willett, *Caspar Neher*, pp. 70–1.
55. Willett (ed.), *Brecht on Theatre*, p. 232.
56. *Ibid.*, p. 231.
57. www.forcedentertainment.com/projects
58. First performed at the Schaubühne am Lehniner Platz, Berlin.
59. Performed at St. Ann's Warehouse, Brooklyn, New York.
60. www.maboumines.org/
61. Fuchs, Elinor, 'Mabou Mines Dollhouse', pp. 498–500.
62. Kennedy, *Looking at Shakespeare*, pp. 9, 310.
63. See Hodges, *The Globe Restored*; Hodges, *Shakespeare's Second Globe*; Kennedy, *Looking at Shakespeare*, p. 25; Leacroft, *Theatre and Playhouse*, pp. 53–8.
64. For a comprehensive list of 'discovery' requirements in explicit stage directions, see Dessen and Thomson (eds.), *A Dictionary of Stage Directions in English Drama*, pp. 69–70.
65. *Henry V*, Prologue, ll. 17–22 in Evans and Tobin (eds.), *The Riverside Shakespeare*.
66. Kennedy, *Looking at Shakespeare*, is a unique resource in this regard and uncovers various ways in which scenography has been employed to re-examine these texts.
67. Craig, *On the Art of the Theatre*, pp. 21–2.
68. *Ibid.*, p. 23.
69. *Ibid.*, p. 29.
70. See Kennedy, *Looking at Shakespeare*, p. 51.
71. *Ibid.*, pp. 148–51.

72. Kott, *Shakespeare Our Contemporary*.
73. Kennedy, *Looking at Shakespeare*, p. 219. See also Hirst, *Giorgio Strehler*, pp. 77–82.
74. Castellucci, 'The Universal', p. 16.
75. *Ibid.*, p. 21.
76. Kennedy, *Looking at Shakespeare*, p. 354.

Chapter 4

1. McAuley, *Space in Performance*, p. 177.
2. See McAuley, *Space in Performance*, pp. 24–35 for her 'taxonomy of spatial function' and more detailed discussion of how these and other terms have been used.
3. *Ibid.*, p. 31.
4. Carlson, *Places of Performance*, p. 129.
5. *Ibid.*, p. 130.
6. McAuley, *Space in Performance*, p. 55.
7. Leacroft and Leacroft, *Theatre and Playhouse*, pp. 1–26; Wiles, *Greek Theatre Performance*, pp. 118–20.
8. *Ibid.*
9. Wiles, *Greek Theatre Performance*, p. 118; Wiles, *A Short History of Western Performance Space*, p. 120.
10. Carlson, *Places of Performance*, p. 135.
11. Serlio, *The second Booke*, fols. 25^r–26^v.
12. *Ibid.*
13. Nicoll, *The Garrick Stage*, p. 82.
14. Leacroft, *The Development of the English Playhouse*, pp. 43–5, 48–9, 60–1.
15. Baugh, *Garrick and Loutherbourg*.
16. Nicoll, *The Garrick Stage*, p. 88.
17. Leacroft and Leacroft, *Theatre and Playhouse*, p. 104.
18. *Ibid.*, p. 113.
19. Baugh, *Theatre, Performance and Technology*, p. 21.
20. McAuley, *Space in Performance*, pp. 255–70.
21. *Ibid.*, p. 259.
22. *Ibid.*, p. 263.
23. Mackintosh, *Architecture, Actor and Audience*, p. 172.
24. *Ibid.*, p. 162.
25. *Ibid.*, pp. 135–6.
26. *Ibid.*, p. 161.
27. Bablet, *The Theatre of Edward Gordon Craig*, p. 123; Baugh, *Theatre, Performance and Technology*, pp. 52, 225, n9.
28. Bablet, *The Theatre of Edward Gordon Craig*, p. 83.
29. Burian (ed.), *The Secret of Theatrical Space*, pp. 59–60.
30. *Ibid.*, p. 61.

31. Baugh, *Theatre, Performance and Technology*, pp. 88–9.
32. Bablet, *The Theatre of Edward Gordon Craig*, pp. 125–6.
33. Burian, *The Scenography of Josef Svoboda*, pp. 108–11.
34. *Ibid.*, p. 31.
35. *Ibid.*, pp. 124–7.
36. *Ibid.*, p. 127.
37. *Ibid.*, p. 44.
38. Bablet, *The Theatre of Edward Gordon Craig*, p. 169.
39. Baugh, *Theatre, Performance and Technology*, p. 152.
40. A good source of further information is Aronson, *The History and Theory of Environmental Scenography*, pp. 29–46.
41. Burian (ed.), *The Secret of Theatrical Space*, p. 20.
42. Leach, *Revolutionary Theatre*, p. 175.
43. *Ibid.*, p. 180.
44. *Ibid.*, p. 182.
45. Bablet, *The Revolutions of Stage Design*, p. 357.
46. *Ibid.*, p. 359; Aronson, *The History and Theory of Environmental Scenography*, p. 187.
47. Aronson, *The History and Theory of Environmental Scenography*, p. 188.
48. Bablet, *The Revolutions of Stage Design*, p. 359.
49. Miller, *Ariane Mnouchkine*, p. 46.
50. *Ibid.*, p. 47.
51. *Ibid.*, pp. 71–2.
52. Di Benedetto, 'Sensing Bodies', pp. 104–5.
53. *Ibid.*, p. 105.
54. Howard, 'Using the Space', p. 198.
55. Patterson, *Peter Stein*, p. 134.
56. *Ibid.*, pp. 137–8.
57. *Lulu*, by Frank Wedekind, director Jonathan Kent, designer Rob Howell, Almeida Theatre, London, 2001.
58. Lubbock, 'Beyond, Caverns Beckon'.
59. Meller, 'Have We Started Yet?' p. 17.
60. McLucas, 'Ten Feet and Three Quarters of an Inch Theatre', p. 134.
61. *Ibid.*, p. 128.
62. Pavis, *Analyzing Performance*, p. 152.
63. Goldberg, *Performance*, pp. 67–8.
64. Pavis, *Analyzing Performance*, p. 152.
65. Holmberg, *The Theatre of Robert Wilson*, p. 148.
66. Pavis, *Analyzing Performance*, p. 152.
67. Hall, *The Hidden Dimension*.
68. Trimingham, 'Oskar Schlemmer's Research Practice', p. 135.
69. Kantor, *A Journey through Other Spaces*, p. 217.
70. *Ibid.*, pp. 338–9.

71. *Ibid.*, p. 142.
72. *Ibid.*, p. 329.
73. *Ibid.*, p. 339.

Chapter 5

1. See Butterworth, 'Hellfire', pp. 67–101; Butterworth, *Theatre of Fire*, pp. 21–36.
2. Llorens et al. (eds.), *La Festa D'Elx*; King, 'La Festa D'Elx', pp. 21–50; King, 'Elche Again', pp. 4–33; King, 'La Festa D'Elx Revisited', pp. 138–40.
3. Hilleström, *Drottningholmsteatern förr och nu*; Hidemark et al. (eds.), *The Drottningholm Court Theatre*; Bergman, *Lighting in the Theatre*, pp. 241–51.
4. See Baugh, *Theatre, Performance and Technology*, pp. 94–118.
5. Giesekam, *Staging the Screen*, p. 10.
6. *Ibid.*, p. 9.
7. *Ibid.*, p. 10.
8. Programme notes from the 1998 production of *Monsters of Grace* at the Barbican Theatre, London.
9. Williams, *Drama from Ibsen to Brecht*, p. 387.
10. *Ibid.*, pp. 9–10.
11. Dixon, *Digital Performance*, p. 3.
12. Braun, *The Director and the Stage*, p. 154.
13. Willett, *The Theatre of Erwin Piscator*, p. 60.
14. *Ibid.*, p. 124.
15. Patterson, *The Revolution in German Theatre*, pp. 146–7.
16. Braun, *The Director and the Stage*, p. 151.
17. Willett, *Caspar Neher*, p. 111.
18. Dixon, *Digital Performance*, p. 348.
19. *Ibid.*, p. 347.
20. *Ibid.*, p. 348.
21. Burian, *The Scenography of Josef Svoboda*, p. 83.
22. www.laterna.cz/en/repertory/wonderful-circus/.
23. Burian, *The Scenography of Josef Svoboda*, p. 26.
24. Innes, 'Puppets and Machines of the Mind', p. 124.
25. Lepage is also a film director. See Robert Lepage, *Connecting Flights*, pp. 124–8.
26. Innes, 'Puppets and Machines of the Mind', p. 128.
27. *Ibid.*, p. 129.
28. Lepage, Interview with John Tusa.
29. Innes, 'Puppets and Machines of the Mind', p. 128; Dixon, *Digital Performance*, pp. 352–5.
30. Innes, 'Puppets and Machines of the Mind', p. 128.
31. *Ibid.*, p. 131.
32. Lodder, *Russian Constructivism*, p. 84.
33. Fer, Batchelor and Wood (eds.), *Realism, Rationalism, Surrealism*, p. 100.

34. Rudnitsky, *Russian and Soviet Theatre*, p. 90.

35. *Ibid.*, pp. 89, 90–1.

36. Conrad, *Modern Times, Modern Places*, p. 239.

37. Braun, *Meyerhold*, p. 177.

38. *Ibid.*, p. 182.

39. Rudnitsky, *Russian and Soviet Theatre*, p. 92.

40. Lodder, *Russian Constructivism*, p. 173.

41. Rudnitsky, *Russian and Soviet Theatre*, p. 94.

42. Conrad, *Modern Times, Modern Places*, pp. 239–40.

43. Styan, *The Shakespeare Revolution*, p. 224.

44. *Ibid.*, p. 225.

45. *Ibid.*, p. 229; Kennedy, *Looking at Shakespeare*, pp. 182–7.

46. More information on Merce Cunningham's composition techniques can be found in Copeland, *Merce Cunningham*, pp. 14–15.

47. www.troikaranch.org/

48. www.palindrome.de/

49. Gitelman and Martin (eds.), *The Returns of Alwyn Nikolais*, pp. 70–1, 111–12.

50. *Ibid.*, pp. 203–4.

51. Travers, 'Adelaide Festival'.

52. Innes, 'Puppets and Machines of the Mind', p. 135.

53. Berghaus, *Theatre, Performance*, p. 99.

54. Berghaus, *Italian Futurist Theatre*, p. 51.

55. *Ibid.*, p. 177.

56. *Ibid.*, p. 255.

57. *Ibid.*, p. 256.

58. Kirby, *Futurist Performance*, p. 206.

59. Bergman, *Lighting in the Theatre*, pp. 280, 296, 315.

60. Lucchino, 'Futurist Stage Design', pp. 456–7.

61. Berghaus, *Italian Futurist Theatre*, p. 259.

62. *Ibid.*

63. Crisafulli, 'Light as Action', p. 93.

64. *Ibid.*, p. 94.

65. *Ibid.*, p. 94.

66. Baugh, *Theatre, Performance and Technology*, pp. 203–19; Dixon, *Digital Performance*, pp. 3–5.

67. Baugh, *Theatre, Performance and Technology*, p. 219.

68. Lehmann, *Postdramatic Theatre*, p. 93.

69. *Ibid.*, p. 94.

70. *Ibid.*, p. 86.

71. Kaye, *Multi-Media*, p. 163.

72. *Ibid.*, p. 163.

73. Aronson, *Looking into the Abyss*, p. 172.

74. Quick, *The Wooster Group Workbook*, p. 272.

75. Kaye, *Multi-Media*, p. 164.
76. Quick, *The Wooster Group Workbook*, pp. 270–1.
77. *Ibid.*, p. 14.
78. Lehmann, *Postdramatic Theatre*, p. 104.
79. www.blasttheory.co.uk/bt/work_desertrain.html
80. Baugh, *Theatre, Performance and Technology*, p. 215.

Chapter 6

1. Elam, *The Semiotics of Theatre and Drama*, pp. 193–221.
2. Aston and Savona, *Theatre as Sign System*, p. 141.
3. Barnard, *Approaches to Understanding Visual Culture*, p. 146.
4. Elam, *The Semiotics of Theatre and Drama*, p. 1.
5. Matejka and Titunik (eds.), *Semiotics of Art*; Garvin (ed.), *A Prague School Reader*; Elam, *The Semiotics of Theatre and Drama*, pp. 4–17.
6. Elam, *The Semiotics of Theatre and Drama*, p. 4.
7. *Ibid.*
8. Veltruský, 'Man and Object in the Theatre', p. 84.
9. *Ibid.*, p. 84.
10. *Ibid.*, pp. 88–90.
11. Honzl, 'Dynamics of the Sign in the Theater' in Matejka and Titunik (eds.), *Semiotics of Art*, p. 90.
12. Elam, *The Semiotics of Theatre and Drama*, p. 7.
13. *Ibid.*, p. 7.
14. Fischer-Lichte, *The Semiotics of Theater*, pp. 9–10.
15. Goffman, *The Presentation of Self in Everyday Life*, pp. 19–21.
16. Williams, *A Streetcar Named Desire*, p. 117.
17. Fischer-Lichte, *The Semiotics of Theater*, p. 90.
18. Styan, *Modern Drama in Theory and Practice*, pp. 11–15.
19. See Kennedy, *Looking At Shakespeare*, p. 88.
20. *Richard III*, by William Shakespeare, Crucible Theatre, Sheffield, England (2002), designer Christopher Oram, director Michael Grandage.
21. Elam, *The Semiotics of Theatre and Drama*, p. 50; Fischer-Lichte, *The Semiotics of Theater*, p. 104.
22. Fischer-Lichte, *The Semiotics of Theater*, p. 104.
23. For further reading on Peirce's theories, see Chandler, *Semiotics*; Eco, *A Theory of Semiotics*; Elam, *The Semiotics of Theatre and Drama*, pp. 18–22.
24. Elam, *The Semiotics of Theatre and Drama*, p. 18.
25. *Ibid.*, p. 21.
26. *Ibid.*
27. The same idea was used earlier in the National Theatre's *Noah* in *The Mysteries* to signify the returning dove and, additionally, to shelter from the rain.

28. Elam, *The Semiotics of Theatre and Drama*, p. 24.
29. Aston and Savona, *Theatre as Sign System*, pp. 146–7.
30. *Ibid.*, p. 148. Aston and Savona use a broader definition of symbolic operation than that used by Peirce.
31. *Ibid.*, p. 142.
32. Pavis, *Analyzing Performance*, p. 14.
33. Counsell, *Signs of Performance*, p. 206.
34. *Ibid.*, pp. 200–1.
35. Di Benedetto, 'Concepts in Spatial Dynamics', p. 70.
36. *Ibid.*, p. 65.
37. See Gunther Kress and Theo van Leeuwen, *Reading Images*, p. 3.
38. *Ibid.*, pp. 181–92.
39. Marshall, *The Stagecraft and Performance of Roman Comedy*, p. 50. It is frequently asserted that in traditional British pantomime there is an association between 'right' as 'good' and 'left' as 'evil', so that the good fairy is required to enter from stage right and the villain from stage left. 'Stage left' refers to the actors' 'left' as they face the audience. Thus the audience witnesses the appearance of the villain on its right.
40. Palmer, *The Lighting Art*, p. 117.
41. Backemeyer (ed.), *Ralph Koltai*, pp. 13–16.
42. Kress and van Leeuwen, *Reading Images*, pp. 193–202.
43. Ubersfeld, *Reading Theatre*, pp. 112–13.
44. Carlson, *Places of Performance*, p. 137.
45. Ubersfeld, *Reading Theatre*, p. 97.
46. Barthes, *Image Music Text*, pp. 52–68.
47. *Ibid.*, p. 39.
48. *Ibid.*, p. 32.
49. *Ibid.*, p. 46.
50. *Ibid.*, p. 60.
51. *Ibid.*, p. 53.
52. *Ibid.*, p. 61.
53. Pavis, *Analyzing Performance*, p. 173.
54. *Ibid.*, p. 14.
55. *Ibid.*, p. 244.
56. *Ibid.*, pp. 165–6.
57. *Ibid.*, p. 126.
58. *Ibid.*, p. 197.
59. Merleau-Ponty, *Phenomenology of Perception*, pp. vii–ix.
60. *Ibid.*, pp. 229–30.
61. Veltruský, 'Some Aspects of the Pictorial Sign', p. 246.
62. States, *Great Reckonings in Little Rooms*, p. 8.
63. *Ibid.*, p. 53.
64. *Ibid.*, p. 52.

65. Brown, 'The Theatre Soundscape and the End of Noise', p. 111.
66. *Ibid.*, p. 119.
67. Merleau-Ponty, *Phenomenology of Perception*, p. 206.
68. *Ibid.*, p. 34.
69. Garner, *Bodied Spaces*, p. 3.
70. *Ibid.*, p. 4.
71. *Ibid.*, p. 46.
72. *Ibid.*, p. 88.
73. Merleau-Ponty, *Phenomenology of Perception*, p. 227.
74. Di Benedetto, 'Concepts in Spatial Dynamics', p. 62.
75. Trimingham, 'Oskar Schlemmer's Research Practice', p. 132.
76. *Ibid.*, p. 138.
77. *Ibid.*
78. Merleau-Ponty, *Phenomenology of Perception*, p. x.

Chapter 7

1. Pavis, *Analyzing Performance*, p. 9.
2. Bennett, *Theatre Audiences*, p. vii.
3. Barthes, *Image Music Text*, p. 148.
4. Iser, *The Act of Reading*.
5. *Ibid.*, pp. 108–18.
6. *Ibid.*, p. 109.
7. Ubersfeld, *Reading Theatre*, p. 23.
8. Iser, *The Act of Reading*, pp. 180–231.
9. Jauss, *Towards an Aesthetic of Reception*, p. 141.
10. *Ibid.*, p. 142.
11. See Bennett, *Theatre Audiences*, p. 40.
12. Howell, *The Analysis of Performance Art*, pp. 9–10.
13. Arnheim, *Art and Visual Perception*, p. 6.
14. Palmer, *The Lighting Art*, p. 125.
15. Arnheim, *Art and Visual Perception*, p. 5.
16. *Ibid.*, pp. 4–6.
17. Sauter, *The Theatrical Event*, p. 5.
18. *Ibid.*, p. 2.
19. *Ibid.*, p. 3.
20. *Ibid.*, p. 31.
21. *Ibid.*, p. 7.
22. Bennett, *Theatre Audiences*, p. vii.
23. McAuley, *Space in Performance*, p. 271.
24. *Ibid.*, p. 271.

25. Ubersfeld, *Reading Theatre*, p. 23.
26. McAuley, *Space in Performance*, p. 256.
27. Di Benedetto, 'Sensing Bodies', p. 102.
28. Aronson, *Looking into the Abyss*, p. 1.
29. Damasio, *The Feeling of What Happens*, p. 150.
30. *Ibid.*, p. 55.
31. Shepherd, *Theatre, Body, Pleasure*, p. 74; Damasio, *The Feeling of What Happens*, p. 153.
32. Sauter, *The Theatrical Event*, p. 7.
33. Shepherd, *Theatre, Body, Pleasure*, p. 74.
34. Beckerman, quoted *ibid.*, p. 75.
35. Beckerman, *Dynamics of Drama*, p. 43.
36. Michael Polanyi, *The Tacit Dimension*, p. 16.
37. Listengarten, 'Kandinsky's Stage Composition as a Total Work of Art'.
38. Bergman, *Lighting in the Theatre*, pp. 320–1.
39. Kandinsky, *Concerning the Spiritual in Art*, p. 38.
40. Palmer, *The Lighting Art*, p. 100.
41. Arnheim, *Art and Visual Perception*, p. 368.
42. *Ibid.*, p. 303.
43. Baugh, *Theatre, Performance and Technology*, p. 95.
44. Palmer, *The Lighting Art*, pp. 79–80.
45. Bergman, *Lighting in the Theatre*, pp. 306–7.
46. Castellucci et al. (eds.), *The Theatre of Societas Raffaello Sanzio*, p. 84.
47. *Ibid.*, p. 45.
48. Dixon, *Digital Performance*, p. 337.
49. *Ibid.*, p. 336.
50. Pavis, *Analyzing Performance*, p. 230.
51. Barthes, *Camera Lucida*, p. 27.
52. McAuley, *Space in Performance*, p. 199.
53. Lacan, *The Four Fundamental Concepts*, p. 75. See also Grosz, *Jacques Lacan*, p. 79.
54. Lacan, *The Four Fundamental Concepts*, p. 84.
55. Elkins, *The Object Stares Back*, p. 71.
56. *Ibid.*, p. 71.
57. *Ibid.*, p. 72.
58. *Ibid.*, p. 95.
59. Grosz, *Jacques Lacan*, pp. 34–5.
60. Lacan, *The Four Fundamental Concepts*, p. 89.
61. Laura Mulvey used it to dissect the way that the female figure was represented by Hollywood. See Mulvey, 'Visual Pleasure and Narrative Cinema', pp. 6–18.
62. Foster, *The Return of the Real*, p. 140.
63. Lacan, *The Four Fundamental Concepts*, p. 107.
64. Kobialka, 'The Quest for the Self/Other', p. 310.
65. *Ibid.*, pp. 331–2.

66. *Ibid.*, p. 341.
67. Crary, *Suspensions of Perception*, p. 2.
68. *Ibid.*, p. 5.
69. *Ibid.*, p. 248.
70. *Ibid.*, p. 251.
71. *Ibid.*, p. 47.
72. *Ibid.*, p. 51.
73. Kristeva, *Revolution in Poetic Language*, pp. 21–4. Kristeva's definition of the semiotic is quite different from the way that the term was used in chapter 6; see pp. 3–4 in the same volume.
74. Lechte, *Julia Kristeva*, p. 130.
75. Kristeva, *Revolution in Poetic Language*, p. 26.
76. Crowther, *Art and Embodiment*, p. 5.

Chapter 8

1. Read, *Theatre and Everyday Life*, p. 63.
2. *Ibid.*, p. 101.
3. Braun (ed.), *Meyerhold on Theatre*, p. 256.
4. Leach, *Vsevolod Meyerhold*, p. 44.
5. Read, *Theatre and Everyday Life*, p. 92.
6. McKinney, 'The Nature of Communication', pp. 64–8.
7. Lefebvre, *The Production of Space*, pp. 38–41.
8. *Ibid.*, p. 143.
9. *Ibid.*, p. 38.
10. *Ibid.*, p. 33.
11. *Ibid.*, p. 39.
12. Aronson, 'The Power of Space in a Virtual World', p. 32.
13. Lefebvre, *The Production of Space*, p. 182.
14. *Ibid.*, p. 183.
15. Puglisi, *Hyper Architecture*.
16. Read, *Theatre and Everyday Life*, p. 58.
17. Crowther, *Art and Embodiment*, p. 5.
18. *Ibid.*, p. 172.
19. For further examples, see Shank, *American Alternative Theatre*, and Aronson, *The History and Theory of Environmental Scenography*.
20. This company explains its aims and methods at www.punchdrunk.org.uk/about.htm
21. Clapp, 'Into the Velvet Darkness …'.
22. Hart, 'Punchdrunk'.
23. Gardner, 'The Masque of the Red Death'.
24. Downing, 'The Water Banquet', p. 316.

25. *Ibid.*, p. 317.
26. McKinney, 'Homesick', pp. 306–314; McKinney, 'Projection and Transaction', pp. 128–37.
27. Crowther, *Art and Embodiment*, pp. 173–4.
28. *Ibid.*, p. 6.
29. Read, *Theatre and Everyday Life*, p. 90.
30. *Ibid.*, p. 62.
31. Gilbert (ed.), *Postcolonial Plays*, p. 25.
32. William Kentridge is a visual artist and animator as well as a theatre designer and director.
33. William Kentridge, 'Ubu and the Truth Commission'.
34. *Ibid.*
35. Baugh, *Theatre, Performance and Technology*, p. 219.
36. Hannah and Harsløf (eds.), *Performance Design*, p. 12.
37. Irwin, 'The Ambit of Performativity', p. 54.
38. *Ibid.*
39. Irwin, 'Arrivals and Departures'.
40. Irwin, 'The Ambit of Performativity', p. 55.

Bibliography

Appia, Adolphe, *Die Musik und die Inscenierung* (Munich: F. Bruckmann, 1899)
    La Mise en Scène du Drame Wagnérien (Paris: Léon Challey, 1895)
Aristotle, *Poetics*, trans. Malcolm Heath (London: Penguin, 1969)
Arnheim, Rudolf, *Art and Visual Perception: A Psychology of the Creative Eye*
    (Berkeley; London: University of California Press, 2004)
Aronson, Arnold, *American Avant-Garde Theatre: A History* (London: Routledge,
    2000)
    The History and Theory of Environmental Scenography (Ann Arbor: University
    of Michigan Research Press, 1981)
    Looking into the Abyss: Essays on Scenography (Ann Arbor: University of
    Michigan Press, 2005)
    'The Power of Space in a Virtual World' in Hannah and Harsløf (eds.),
    Performance Design, 23–37
Artaud, Antonin, *The Theatre and its Double*, trans. Victor Corti (London: Calder
    and Boyars, 1970)
Aston, Elaine and George Savona, *Theatre as Sign System: A Semiotics of Text and
    Performance* (London; New York: Routledge, 1991)
Auslander, Philip, *Liveness* (London: Routledge, 1999)
Bablet, Denis, *The Revolutions of Stage Design in the 20th Century* (Paris; New
    York: L. Amiel, 1977)
    The Theatre of Edward Gordon Craig (London: Eyre Methuen, 1966)
Bablet, Denis and Marie-Louise Bablet (eds.), *Adolphe Appia 1862–1928 Actor –
    Space – Light*, trans. Burton Melnick (London; New York: John Calder;
    Riverrun Press, 1982)
Backemeyer, Sylvia (ed.), *Ralph Koltai: Designer for the Stage* (London: Nick Hern,
    2002)
Barnard, Malcolm, *Approaches to Understanding Visual Culture* (Basingstoke:
    Palgrave, 2001)
Barthes, Roland, *Camera Lucida: Reflections on Photography*, trans.
    Richard Howard (London: Vintage, 1993)
    Image Music Text, trans. Stephen Heath (London: Fontana Press, 1977)
Baugh, Christopher, 'Brecht and Stage Design: The *Bühnenbildner* and
    Bühnenbauer' in Peter Thomson and Glendyr Sacks (eds.), *The
    Cambridge Companion to Brecht* (Cambridge University Press, 1994),
    235–53

Garrick and Loutherbourg (Cambridge: Chadwyck-Healey in association with The Consortium for Drama and Media in Higher Education, 1990)

Theatre, Performance and Technology: The Development of Scenography in the Twentieth Century (Basingstoke: Palgrave Macmillan, 2005)

Baugh, Christopher, Gavin Carver and Cat Fergusson, 'Gordon Craig and Improvements in Stage Scenery, 1910: Edward Gordon Craig and Patent 1771', *Scenography International*, 1 (no date), www.scenography-international.com/journal/issue1/gordoncraig.pdf

Beacham, Richard C., *Adolphe Appia: Theatre Artist* (Cambridge University Press, 1987)

Beacham, Richard C. (ed.), *Adolphe Appia: Essays, Scenarios, and Designs*, trans. Walther R. Volbach (Ann Arbor; London: UMI Research Press, 1989)

Adolphe Appia: Texts on Theatre (London; New York: Routledge, 1993)

Beckerman, Bernard, *Dynamics of Drama: Theory and Method of Analysis* (New York: Drama Book Specialists, 1979)

Beckett, Samuel, *The Complete Dramatic Works* (London: Faber and Faber, 1986)

Benedetti, Jean, *Stanislavsky: A Biography* (London: Methuen, 1988)

Bennett, Susan, *Theatre Audiences: A Theory of Production and Reception*, 2nd edn (London; New York: Routledge, 1997)

Berghaus, Günter, *Italian Futurist Theatre, 1909–1944* (Oxford: Clarendon Press, 1998)

Theatre, Performance, and the Historical Avant-Garde (New York; Basingstoke: Palgrave Macmillan, 2005)

Bergman, Gösta M., *Lighting in the Theatre* (Stockholm: Almqvist & Wiksell International, 1977)

Bly, Mark (ed.), *The Production Notebooks*, Theatre in Process, 1 (New York: Theatre Communications Group, 1996)

Braun, Edward, *The Director and the Stage: From Naturalism to Grotowski* (London: Methuen, 1982)

Meyerhold: A Revolution in Theatre, 2nd edn (London: Methuen, 1995)

Braun, Edward (ed. and trans.), *Meyerhold on Theatre* (London: Eyre Methuen, 1969)

Brook, Peter, *The Empty Space* (London: MacGibbon and Kee, 1968)

Brown, Ross, 'The Theatre Soundscape and the End of Noise', *Performance Research*, 10:4 (December 2005), 105–19

Burian, Jarka, *The Scenography of Josef Svoboda* (Middletown, CT: Wesleyan University Press, 1971)

Burian, Jarka (ed. and trans.), *The Secret of Theatrical Space: The Memoirs of Josef Svoboda* (New York; Tonbridge, Kent: Applause Theatre Books, 1993)

Butterworth, Philip, 'Book Carriers: Medieval and Tudor Staging Conventions', *Theatre Notebook*, 46:1 (1992), 15–30

'Hellfire: Flame as Special Effect' in Clifford Davidson and Thomas H. Seiler (eds.), *The Iconography of Hell*, Early Drama, Art, and Music Monograph

Series, Medieval Institute Publications, 17 (Kalamazoo: Western Michigan University, 1992), 67–101

Theatre of Fire: Special Effects in Early English and Scottish Theatre (London: The Society For Theatre Research, 1998)

Carlson, Marvin, *Places of Performance: The Semiotics of Theatre Architecture* (Ithaca, NY: Cornell University Press, 1989)

Castellucci, Romeo, 'The Universal: The Simplest Place Possible', Socìetas Raffaello Sanzio interviewed by Valentina Valentini and Bonnie Marranca, trans. Jane House, *Performing Arts Journal*, 77 (2004), 16–25

Castellucci, Claudia, Romeo Castellucci, Chiara Guidi, Joe Kellcher and Nicholas Ridout (eds.), *The Theatre of Socìetas Raffaello Sanzio* (London; New York: Routledge, 2007)

Chandler, Daniel, *Semiotics: The Basics* (London: Routledge, 2002)

Chaudhuri, Una, 'Different Hats', *Theater*, 33:3 (2003), 132–4

Churchill, Caryl, *Far Away* (London: Hern, 2000)

Clapp, Susannah, 'Into the Velvet Darkness …', *The Observer*, 7 October 2007, www.guardian.co.uk/stage/2007/oct/07/theatre

Conrad, Peter, *Modern Times, Modern Places* (London: Thames & Hudson, 1998)

Copeland, Roger, *Merce Cunningham and the Modernizing of Modern Dance* (New York; London: Routledge, 2004)

Counsell, Colin, *Signs of Performance: An Introduction to Twentieth-Century Theatre* (London; New York: Routledge, 1996)

Craig, Edward Gordon, *On the Art of the Theatre* (New York: Theatre Arts Books, 1956)

Towards a New Theatre (London; Toronto: J. M. Dent, 1913)

Crary, Jonathan, *Suspensions of Perception: Attention, Spectacle and Modern Culture* (Cambridge, MA; London: MIT Press, 2001)

Crisafulli, Fabrizio, 'Light as Action' in Hannah and Harsløf (eds.), *Performance Design*, 93–103

Crowther, Paul, *Art and Embodiment: From Aesthetics to Self-Consciousness* (Oxford; New York: Oxford University Press, 1993)

Damasio, Antonio, *The Feeling of What Happens: Body, Emotion and the Making of Consciousness* (London: Vintage, 2000)

Davis, Tony, *Stage Design* (Crans-près-Céligny; Hove: RotoVision, 2001)

Dessen, Alan C. and Leslie Thomson (eds.), *A Dictionary of Stage Directions in English Drama, 1580–1642* (Cambridge University Press, 1999)

Di Benedetto, Stephen, 'Concepts in Spatial Dynamics: Robert Wilson's Dramaturgical Mechanics and the Visible on Stage' in Irene Eynat-Confino and Eva Šormová (eds.), *Space and the Postmodern Stage* (Prague Theatre Institute, 2000), 62–70

'Sensing Bodies: A Phenomenological Approach to the Performance Sensorium', *Performance Research*, 8:2 (2003), 100–8

Dixon, Steve, *Digital Performance: A History of New Media in Theater, Dance, Performance Art, and Installation* (Cambridge, MA; London: MIT Press, 2007)

Doona, Liam, 'Hope, Hopelessness/Presence, Absence: Scenographic Innovation and the Poetic Spaces of Jo Mielziner, Tennessee Williams and Arthur Miller' in Malcolm Griffiths (ed.), *Exploring Scenography* (London: The Society of British Theatre Designers, 2000), 55–64

Downing, Richard, 'The Water Banquet' in Hannah and Harsløf (eds.), *Performance Design*, 317–24

Dukore, Bernard F., *Death of a Salesman and The Crucible: Text and Performance* (Basingstoke; London: Macmillan, 1989)

Eco, Umberto, *A Theory of Semiotics* (Bloomington: Indiana University Press, 1976)

Elam, Keir, *The Semiotics of Theatre and Drama*, 2nd edn (London; New York: Routledge, 2002)

Elkins, James, *The Object Stares Back: On the Nature of Seeing* (San Diego; London: Harcourt Brace, 1997)

Evans, G. Blakemore and J. J. M. Tobin (eds.), *The Riverside Shakespeare: The Complete Works*, 2nd edn (Boston; New York: Houghton Mifflin, 1997)

Fer, Briony, David Batchelor and Paul Wood (eds.), *Realism, Rationalism, Surrealism: Art Between the Wars* (New Haven; London: Yale University Press in association with The Open University, 1994)

Fischer-Lichte, Erika, *The Semiotics of Theater*, trans. Jeremy Gaines and Doris L. Jones (Bloomington; Indianapolis: Indiana University Press, 1992)

Fish, Stanley, *Is There a Text in This Class?* (Cambridge, MA: Harvard University Press, 1980)

Fletcher, Ifan Kyrle and Arnold Rood, *Edward Gordon Craig: A Bibliography* (London: The Society For Theatre Research, 1967)

Foster, Hal, *The Return of the Real: The Avant-Garde at the End of the Century* (Cambridge, MA; London: MIT Press, 1996)

Fuchs, Elinor, 'Mabou Mines Dollhouse', *Theatre Journal*, 56:3 (October 2004), 498–500

Gardner, Lyn, 'The Masque of the Red Death left me Punchdrunk', *The Guardian*, 4 October 2007, www.guardian.co.uk/stage/theatreblog/2007/oct/04/ themasqueofthereddeathle

Garner, Stanton B., *Bodied Spaces: Phenomenology and Performance in Contemporary Drama* (Ithaca; London: Cornell University Press, 1994)

Garvin, Paul L. (ed. and trans.), *A Prague School Reader on Esthetics, Literary Structure, and Style* (Washington: Georgetown University Press, 1964)

Giesekam, Greg, *Staging the Screen: The Use of Film and Video in Theatre* (Basingstoke: Palgrave Macmillan, 2007)

Gilbert, Helen (ed.), *Postcolonial Plays: An Anthology* (London; New York: Routledge, 2001)

Gitelman, Claudia and Randy Martin (eds.), *The Returns of Alwyn Nikolais: Bodies, Boundaries and the Dance Canon* (Middletown, CT: Wesleyan University Press, 2007)

Goffman, Erving, *The Presentation of Self in Everyday Life* (Harmondsworth: Penguin, 1971)

Goldberg, RoseLee, *Performance: Live Art 1909 to the Present* (London: Thames & Hudson, 1979)

González, Ángel, Karin von Maur, Eric Michand and Marga Paz (eds.), *Oskar Schlemmer* (Madrid; Barcelona: Museo Nacional Centro de Arte Reina Sofía; Centre Cultural de la Fundación 'la Caxia', 1997)

Gordon, Donald James, *The Renaissance Imagination; Essays and Lectures*, ed. Stephen Orgel (Berkeley; London: University of California Press, 1975)

Gottlieb, Vera, *Chekhov in Performance in Russia and Soviet Russia* (Cambridge; Teaneck, NJ: Chadwyck-Healey, 1984)

Gottlieb, Vera (ed. and trans.), *Anton Chekhov at the Moscow Art Theatre: Archive Illustrations of the Original Productions from the Original Journal Edited by Nikolai Efros* (London: Routledge, 2005)

Gropius, Walter (ed.), *The Theater of the Bauhaus*, trans. Arthur S. Wensinger (Middletown, CT: Wesleyan University Press, 1961)

Grosz, Elizabeth, *Jacques Lacan: A Feminist Introduction* (London; New York: Routledge, 1990)

Hall, Edward T., *The Hidden Dimension* (Garden City, NY: Doubleday, 1990)

Hannah, Dorita and Olav Harsløf (eds.), *Performance Design* (Copenhagen: Museum Tusculanum Press, 2008)

Hart, Christopher, 'Punchdrunk: The Masque of the Red Death', *The Sunday Times*, 7 October 2007, http://entertainment.timesonline.co.uk/tol/ arts_and_entertainment/stage/theatre/article2582820.ece

Henderson, Mary C., *Mielziner: Master of Modern Stage Design* (New York: Back Stage Books, 2001)

Hewitt, Barnard (ed.), *Adolphe Appia's Music and the Art of the Theatre*, trans. Robert W. Corrigan and Mary Douglas Dirks (Coral Gables, FL: University of Miami Press, 1962)

Hidemark, Ove, Per Edström, Birgitta Schyberg et al. (eds.), *The Drottningholm Court Theatre: Its Advent, Fate and Preservation* (Stockholm: Byggförlaget, 1993)

Hilleström, Gustaf, *Drottningholmsteatern förr och nu: The Drottningholm Theatre – Past and Present* (Stockholm: Bokförlaget Natur Och Kultur, 1956)

Hirst, David L., *Giorgio Strehler* (Cambridge University Press, 1993)

Hodges, C. Walter, *The Globe Restored: A Study of the Elizabethan Theatre* (London: Ernest Benn, 1953)

    Shakespeare's Second Globe: The Missing Monument (London: Oxford University Press, 1973)

Holmberg, Arthur, *The Theatre of Robert Wilson* (Cambridge University Press, 1996)

Honzl, Jindřich, 'Dynamics of the Sign in the Theater' in Matejka and Titunik (eds.), *Semiotics of Art: Prague School Contributions*, 74–93

Hoover, Marjorie, *Meyerhold and his Set Designers* (New York: Peter Lang, 1988)

Howard, Pamela, 'Using the Space' in John Goodwin (ed.), *British Theatre Design: The Modern Age* (London: Weidenfeld & Nicolson in association with the Society of British Theatre Designers, 1989), 198–201

    What Is Scenography? (London; New York: Routledge, 2002)

Howell, Anthony, *The Analysis of Performance Art: A Guide to its Theory and Practice*, Contemporary Theatre Studies, 32 (Amsterdam: Harwood Academic, 1999)

Ingham, Rosemary, *From Page to Stage: How Theatre Designers Make Connections Between Scripts and Images* (Portsmouth, NH: Heinemann, 1998)

Innes, Christopher, *Avant Garde Theatre 1892–1992* (London: Routledge, 1993)
   Edward Gordon Craig (Cambridge University Press, 1983)
   'Puppets and Machines of the Mind: Robert Lepage and the Modernist Heritage', *Theatre Research International*, 30:2 (2005), 24–38

Irwin, Kathleen, 'The Ambit of Performativity: How Site Makes Meaning in Site-Specific Performance' in Hannah and Harsløf (eds.), *Performance Design*, 39–61
   'Arrivals and Departures: How Technology Redefines Site-related Performance', *Scenography International*, 9 (no date), www.scenography-international.com/journal/issue9/issue%209%20irwin.pdf

Iser, Wolfgang, *The Act of Reading: A Theory of Aesthetic Response* (London; Henley: Routledge and Kegan Paul, 1978)

Jauss, Hans Robert, *Towards an Aesthetic of Reception*, trans. Timothy Bahti (Minneapolis: University of Minnesota Press, 1982)

Jones, Robert Edmond, *The Dramatic Imagination: Reflections and Speculations on the Art of the Theatre* (New York; London: Routledge, 2004)

Kandinsky, Wassily, *Concerning the Spiritual in Art* (New York: Dover, 1977)

Kantor, Tadeusz, *A Journey through Other Spaces: Essays and Manifestos, 1944–1990*, ed. and trans. Michal Kobialka (Berkeley; London: University of California Press, 1993)

Kaye, Nick, *Multi-Media: Video – Installation – Performance* (London; New York: Routledge, 2007)

Kennedy, Dennis, *Looking at Shakespeare: A Visual History of Twentieth-Century Performance* (Cambridge University Press, 2001)

Kentridge, William, 'Ubu and the Truth Commission: Director's Note', www.handspringpuppet.co.za/html/frameind.html

King, Pamela, 'Elche Again – The Venida and Semana Santa', *Medieval English Theatre*, 12:1 (1990), 4–20
   'La Festa D'Elx: The Festival of the Assumption of the Virgin, Elche (Alicante)', *Medieval English Theatre*, 8:1 (1986), 21–50
   'La Festa D'Elx Revisited: Elx, August 2003', *Medieval English Theatre*, 24 (2002), 138–40

Kirby, Michael, *Futurist Performance*, trans. Victoria Nes Kirby (New York: Dutton, 1971)

Klossowicz, Jan, 'Tadeusz Kantor's Journey', *The Drama Review*, 30:3 (1986), 176–83

Knapp, Bettina L., *Antonin Artaud: Man of Vision* (Athens, OH: Swallow Press, 1980)

Kobialka, Michal, 'The Quest for the Self/Other: A Critical Study of Tadeusz Kantor's Theatre' in Kantor, *A Journey through Other Spaces*, 269–403

Kolin, Philip C., *Williams: A Streetcar Named Desire* (Cambridge University Press, 2000)

Kott, Jan, *Shakespeare Our Contemporary*, trans. Boleslaw Taborski (London: Methuen, 1965)

Kress, Gunther and Theo van Leeuwen, *Reading Images: The Grammar of Visual Design* (London; New York: Routledge, 1996)

Kristeva, Julia, *Revolution in Poetic Language*, trans. Margaret Waller (New York: Columbia University Press, 1984)

Lacan, Jacques, *The Four Fundamental Concepts of Psycho-Analysis*, trans. Alan Sheridan (London: Penguin, 1977)

Larson, Orville K., *Scene Design in the American Theatre from 1915 to 1960* (Fayetteville; London: University of Arkansas Press, 1989)

Law, Alma, 'Meyerhold's The Magnanimous Cuckold', *The Drama Review*, 26:1 (1982), 61–86

Leach, Robert, *Revolutionary Theatre* (London: Routledge, 1994)
    Vsevolod Meyerhold (Cambridge University Press, 1989)

Leacroft, Richard, *The Development of the English Playhouse* (London: Eyre Methuen, 1973)

Leacroft, Richard and Helen Leacroft, *Theatre and Playhouse: An Illustrated Survey of Theatre Building from Ancient Greece to the Present Day* (London: Methuen, 1984)

Lechte, John, *Julia Kristeva* (London; New York: Routledge, 1990)

Lefebvre, Henri, *The Production of Space* (Oxford: Blackwell, 1991)

Lehmann, Hans-Thies, *Postdramatic Theatre*, trans. Karen Jürs-Munby (London; New York: Routledge, 2006)

Lepage, Robert, *Connecting Flights: Conversation with Rémy Charest*, trans. Wanda Roma Taylor (London: Methuen, 1997)
    Interview with John Tusa, www.bbc.co.uk/radio3/johntusainterview/lepage_ transcript.shtml

Lindley, David (ed.), *The Court Masque* (Manchester University Press, 1984)

Listengarten, Julia, 'Kandinsky's Stage Composition as a Total Work of Art', *Scenography International*, 5 (no date), www.scenography-international. com/journal/issue5/kandinsky.pdf

Llorens, Alfons, Rafael Navarro Mallebrera and Joan Castano Garcia (eds.), *La Festa D'Elx*, trans. Pamela M. King and Ascunción Salvador-Rabaza Ramos (Alicante: Patronato Nacional Del Misterio De Elche, 1990)

Lodder, Christina, *Russian Constructivism* (New Haven; London: Yale University Press, 1983)

Lubbock, Tom, 'Beyond, Caverns Beckon, the Darkness Lit in Pools', *The Independent*, 19 September 1995

Lucchino, Gianfranco, 'Futurist Stage Design' in Günter Berghaus (ed.), *International Futurism in Arts and Literature* (Berlin; New York: Walter de Gruter, 2000), 449–72

Mackintosh, Iain, *Architecture, Actor and Audience* (London; New York: Routledge, 1993)

Marshall, C. W., *The Stagecraft and Performance of Roman Comedy* (Cambridge University Press, 2006)

Matejka, Ladislav and Irwin R. Titunik (eds.), *Semiotics of Art: Prague School Contributions* (Cambridge, MA; London: MIT Press, 1976)

McAuley, Gay, *Space in Performance: Making Meaning in the Theatre* (Ann Arbor: University of Michigan Press, 1999)

McKinney, Joslin, 'Homesick' in Hannah and Harsløf (eds.), *Performance Design*, 306–14

    'The Nature of Communication between Scenography and its Audiences', unpublished PhD thesis, University of Leeds (2008)

    'Projection and Transaction: The Spatial Operation of Scenography', *Performance Research*, 10:4 (2005), 128–37

    'The Role of Theatre Design: Towards a Bibliographic and Practical Accommodation', *Scenography International*, 2 (no date), www. scenography-international.com/journal/issue2/practicalaccommodation.pdf

McLucas, Clifford, 'Ten Feet and Three Quarters of an Inch Theatre' in Nick Kaye (ed.), *Site-Specific Art: Performance, Place, and Documentation* (London; New York: Routledge, 2000), 125–37

McMillan, D. and M. Fehsenfeld, *Beckett in the Theatre: The Author as Practical Playwright and Director*, vol. I (New York: Riverrun Press, 1988)

Meller, Fred, 'Have We Started Yet?' in Kate Burnett (ed.), *Collaborators: UK Design for Performance 2003–2007* (London: The Society of British Theatre Designers, 2007), 14–19

Merleau-Ponty, Maurice, *Phenomenology of Perception*, trans. Colin Smith (London; New York: Routledge, 1962)

Mielziner, Jo, *Designing for the Theatre* (New York: Atheneum, 1965)

Miller, Judith G., *Ariane Mnouchkine* (London; New York: Routledge, 2007)

Mitter, Shomit, *Systems of Rehearsal: Stanislavsky, Brecht, Grotowski and Brook* (London; New York: Routledge, 1992)

Mulvey, Laura, 'Visual Pleasure and Narrative Cinema', *Screen*, 16:3 (1975), 6–18

Nicoll, Allardyce, *The Garrick Stage: Theatres and Audience in the Eighteenth Century*, ed. Sybil Rosenfeld (Manchester University Press, 1980)

Nietzsche, Friedrich, *The Birth of Tragedy*, trans. Shaun Whiteside (London: Penguin, 2003)

Palmer, Richard H., *The Lighting Art: The Aesthetics of Stage Lighting*, 2nd edn (Englewood Cliffs, NJ: Prentice-Hall, 1994)

Parker, W. Oren, R. Craig Wolf and Dick Block, *Scene Design and Stage Lighting*, 8th edn (Belmont, CA: Thomson/Wadsworth, 2003)

Patterson, Michael, *Peter Stein: Germany's Leading Theatre Director* (Cambridge University Press, 1981)

    The Revolution in German Theatre: 1900–1933 (London: Routledge and Kegan Paul, 1981)

Pavis, Patrice, *Analyzing Performance: Theater, Dance, and Film*, trans. David Williams (Ann Arbor: University of Michigan Press, 2003)

Phelan, Peggy, *Unmarked: The Politics of Performance* (London: Routledge, 1993)

Pitches, Jonathan, *Vsevolod Meyerhold* (London; New York: Routledge, 2003)

Pleśniarowicz, Krzysztof, *The Dead Memory Machine: Tadeusz Kantor's Theatre of Death*, trans. William Brand (Aberystwyth: Black Mountain Press, 2004)

Polanyi, Michael, *The Tacit Dimension* (London: Routledge and Kegan Paul, 1967)

Puglisi, Luigi Prestinenza, *Hyper Architecture: Spaces in the Electronic Age* (Basel; Boston; Berlin: Birkhäuser, 1999)

Quick, Andrew, *The Wooster Group Workbook* (New York; London: Routledge, 2007)

Read, Alan, *Theatre and Everyday Life: An Ethics of Performance* (London: Routledge, 1993)

Rewa, Natalie, *Scenography in Canada: Selected Designers* (University of Toronto Press, 2004)

Ribeiro, João Mendes, *Arquitecturas em Palco / Architectures on Stage* (Coimbra: Almedina, 2007)

Roudané, Matthew C., 'Death of a Salesman and the Poetics of Arthur Miller' in Christopher Bigsby (ed.), *The Cambridge Companion to Arthur Miller* (Cambridge University Press, 1997), 60–85

Rudnitsky, Konstantin, *Russian and Soviet Theatre: Tradition and the Avant-Garde* (London: Thames & Hudson, 2000)

Sauter, Willmar, *The Theatrical Event: Dynamics of Performance and Perception* (Iowa City: University of Iowa Press, 2000)

Savarese, Nicola, 'Antonin Artaud Sees Balinese Theatre at the Paris Colonial Exposition', *The Drama Review*, 45:3 (2001), 51–77

Schlemmer, Tut (ed.), *The Letters and Diaries of Oskar Schlemmer*, trans. Krishna Winston (Evanston, IL: Northwestern University Press, 1990)

Schumacher, Claude (ed.), *Artaud on Theatre* (London: Methuen, 1989)

Senelick, Laurence, *The Chekhov Theatre: A Century of the Plays in Performance* (Cambridge University Press, 1999)

Gordon Craig's Moscow Hamlet: A Reconstruction (Westport, CT; London: Greenwood Press, 1982)

Serlio, Sebastiano, *The second Booke of Architecture, made by Sebastian Serly, entreating of Perspective, which is, Inspection, or looking into, by short-ening of light* in *The Five Books of Architecture: An Unabridged Reprint of the English Edition of 1611* (New York: Dover Publications, 1982)

Shank, Theodore, *American Alternative Theatre* (London; Basingstoke: Macmillan, 1982)

Shepard, Sam, *Seven Plays* (London: Faber and Faber, 1985)

Shepherd, Simon, *Theatre, Body and Pleasure* (New York; Abingdon: Routledge, 2006)

Shepherd, Simon and Mick Wallis, *Drama/Theatre/Performance* (London; New York: Routledge, 2004)

Shklovsky, V., 'Art as Technique' in L. T. Lemon and M. Reis (eds.), *Russian Formalist Criticism* (Lincoln: University of Nebraska, 1965), 3–24

Shyer, Laurence, *Wilson and his Collaborators* (New York: Theater Communications Group, 1986)

States, Bert O., *Great Reckonings in Little Rooms: On the Phenomenology of Theatre* (Berkeley; London: University of California Press, 1985)

Strindberg, August, *Plays One: The Father, Miss Julie, The Ghost Sonata*, trans. Michael Meyer (London: Methuen, 1976)

Styan, John Louis, *Modern Drama in Theory and Practice: Realism and Naturalism* (Cambridge University Press, 1981)

    The Shakespeare Revolution: Criticism and Performance in the Twentieth Century (Cambridge University Press, 1977)

Thorne, Gary, *Stage Design: A Practical Guide* (Marlborough: Crowood, 1999)

Travers, Sophie, 'Adelaide Festival: Dancing, Prosthetically', *RealTime Arts Magazine*, 71 (2006), www.realtimearts.net/article/issue71/8014

Trimingham, Melissa, 'Oskar Schlemmer's Research Practice at the Dessau Bauhaus', *Theatre Research International*, 29:2 (2004), 128–42

Ubersfeld, Anne, *Reading Theatre*, trans. Frank Collins (Toronto; Buffalo; London: University of Toronto Press, 1999)

Unruh, Delbert (ed.), *Towards a New Theatre: The Lectures of Robert Edmond Jones* (New York: Limelight, 1992)

Uršič, Giorgio Ursini (ed.), *Josef Svoboda: Scenographer* (Paris: Union of the Theatres of Europe, 1998)

Veltruský, Jiří, 'Man and Object in the Theatre' in Garvin (ed.), *A Prague School Reader*, 83–91

    'Some Aspects of the Pictorial Sign' in Matejka and Titunik (eds.), *Semiotics of Art*, 245–64

Wallis, Mick and Simon Shepherd, *Studying Plays* (London: Arnold, 2002)

Walton, J. Michael (ed.), *Craig on Theatre* (London: Methuen, 1983)

Wiles, David, *Greek Theatre Performance: An Introduction* (Cambridge University Press, 2000)

    A Short History of Western Performance Space (Cambridge University Press, 2003)

Willett, John, *Caspar Neher: Brecht's Designer* (London: Methuen, 1986)

    The Theatre of Erwin Piscator: Half a Century of Politics in the Theatre (London: Eyre Methuen, 1978)

Willett, John (ed.), *Brecht on Theatre* (London: Methuen, 1964)

Williams, Raymond, *Drama from Ibsen to Brecht* (Aylesbury: Pelican Books, 1973)

Williams, Tennessee, *A Streetcar Named Desire* (London: Penguin, 1959)

Worrall, Nick, 'Meyerhold's Production of the Magnanimous Cuckold', *Tulane Drama Review*, 17:1 (1973), 14–34

    The Moscow Art Theatre (London; New York: Routledge, 1996)

Worth, K., *Waiting for Godot and Happy Days: Text and Performance* (Basingstoke; London: Macmillan, 1990)

Index

Cambridge Introductions to . . .

AUTHORS

Jane Austen Janet Todd

Samuel Beckett Ronan McDonald

Walter Benjamin David Ferris

J. M. Coetzee Dominic Head

Joseph Conrad John Peters

Jacques Derrida Leslie Hill

Emily Dickinson Wendy Martin

George Eliot Nancy Henry

T. S. Eliot John Xiros Cooper

William Faulkner Theresa M. Towner

F. Scott Fitzgerald Kirk Curnutt

Michel Foucault Lisa Downing

Robert Frost Robert Faggen

Nathaniel Hawthorne Leland S. Person

Zora Neale Hurston Lovalerie King

James Joyce Eric Bulson

Herman Melville Kevin J. Hayes

Sylvia Plath Jo Gill

Edgar Allan Poe Benjamin F. Fisher

Ezra Pound Ira Nadel

Jean Rhys Elaine Savory

Shakespeare Emma Smith

Shakespeare's Comedies Penny Gay

Shakespeare's History Plays
  Warren Chernaik

Shakespeare's Tragedies Janette Dillon

Harriet Beecher Stowe Sarah Robbins

Mark Twain Peter Messent

Virginia Woolf Jane Goldman

W. B. Yeats David Holdeman

Edith Wharton Pamela Knights

Walt Whitman M. Jimmie Killingsworth

TOPICS

The American Short Story
  Martin Scofield

Comedy Eric Weitz

Creative Writing David Morley

Early English Theatre Janette Dillon

English Theatre, 1660–1900
  Peter Thomson

Francophone Literature Patrick Corcoran

Modern British Theatre Simon Shepherd

Modern Irish Poetry Justin Quinn

Modernism Pericles Lewis

Narrative (second edition)
  H. Porter Abbott

*The Nineteenth-Century American
  Novel* Gregg Crane

Postcolonial Literatures C. L. Innes

Postmodern Fiction Bran Nicol

Russian Literature Caryl Emerson

Scenography Joslin McKinney and
  Philip Butterworth

The Short Story in English
  Adrian Hunter

Theatre Historiography
  Thomas Postlewait

Theatre Studies Christopher Balme

Tragedy Jennifer Wallace